MW00676545

THE FRESHMAN EXPERIENCE: OPTIONS TOWARD SUCCESS

JUNIOR DIVISION
SOUTHERN UNIVERSITY-BATON ROUGE

Pearson
Custom
Publishing

ISBN 0-536-59037-0
BA 97537

PEARSON CUSTOM PUBLISHING
75 Arlington Street, Boston, MA 02116
A Pearson Education Company

Various committees were formed to address each unit and to construct materials that are utilized in the program. They are as following:

I. Improving Speaking Skills .... Lelia Taylor*

II. Improving Reading Skills .... Pearlie Williams

III. Improving Writing Skills .... Josephine Fortune

IV. DEVELOPING SOCIAL SKILLS

.... Betty Johnson*

.... Fannie Dunn

.... Dana Carpenter

.... LaJoyce Wilson

.... Lois Heath

V. IMPROVING STUDY SKILLS

  a. Content Areas .... Marvel Hughes*

  b. Test-Taking .... LaJoyce Wilson

      Dana Carpenter

      Nathaniel Harrison

VI. ENHANCING VOCABULARY SKILLS

  a. Word Components .... Eddye Sue Grey

      1. Root Words

      2. Prefixes

      3. Suffixes

  b. Synonyms and Antonyms .... Charles Bryant*

  c. Analogies

  d. Abused Words and Expressions .... B. J. Johnson

  e. Foreign Words and Phrases

  f. Spelling .... Eddye Sue Grey

VII. IMPROVING TEST-TAKING SKILLS .... Laurita Guillory*

  a. American College Test (ACT) .... Mary Haynes

  b. Nelson-Denny Reading Test .... Gladys Jordan

  c. Medical College Admission Test

  d. National Teacher Examination (NTE)

  e. Graduate Record Examination (GRE)

  f. Graduate Management Admission Test (GMAT)

*Chairperson

Table of Contents

ALMA MATER

"DEAR SOUTHERN"

O Southern, Dear Southern
Thy praises we shall sing
Until all the heavens
And echoes loudly ring.
The winds of the sky as they pass us by
Will adoration bring.

O Southern, Dear Southern
We owe our all to Thee
In downfall or victory
We'll always loyal be.
Thy Sons and Daughters as they work
Will be inspired by Thee.

O Southern, Dear Southern
Thy name will ever be
As mighty as the river
That flows on to the sea.
As pure and true as the Gold and Blue
That stand out bold for Thee.

Acknowledgments

The **Skills Enhancement Program** is the brainchild of Dr. William E. Moore, Vice Chancellor for Academic Affairs at Southern University-Baton Rouge. The Skills Enhancement Program is a component of the Environmental Intervention Model that is described in Dr. Moore's article, **"Changing the Learning Environment at Historically Black Colleges."** pp. 72–74; *College Teaching.* Later he developed units which contained the practical tools necessary for undergraduate and graduate success.

Special thanks to Dr. William E. Moore, author of the Skills Enhancement Program and all persons who assisted in the initial preparation of this module. The writers of this module used Dr. Moore's materials as a basis for its development. We are extremely grateful for his leadership, guidance and technical assistance that enabled the development and construction of materials that focused on the identified needs of students at Southern University-Baton Rouge.

We give a special thanks to Dr. Myrtly Joyner who served as editor and coordinator of this document, the Junior Division faculty and staff for the excellent team effort throughout the development and completion of this document, and Charlotte Henderson of the John B. Cade Library. Thanks to Paulette Barrow and Vallory Hills who typed and prepared an attractive document.

Special recognition is given to Executive Vice Chancellor Juanita B. Robinson, former Dean of the Junior Division, under whose leadership the Freshman General Assembly Series and the Skills Enhancement Program was initiated and, also to C. Norman St. Amant, Jr., Dean of the Junior Division for the confidence he had in giving me the opportunity to serve as coordinator of the Revision Committee.

Again, thanks to the Junior Division faculty and staff for their continuous support and cooperation in making the Freshman Experience a success!

Nathaniel F. Harrison, Jr.
Coordinator
1996 Revision Committee

Historical Statement

The hope for an institution of higher learning for black Louisianians was expressed in the 1879 Louisiana State Constitutional Convention meeting in New Orleans. The movement was sponsored by delegates P.B.S. Pinchback, T.T. Allain, T.B. Stamps and Henry Demas. Their efforts resulted in the establishment in the city of New Orleans of this institution for the education of persons of color. Article 231 of the Constitution authorized the General Assembly to establish the institution that was chartered as Southern University by Legislative Act 87 in April, 1880. This act provided for its incorporation and governance by a twelve member Board of Trustees, and established a faculty of "arts and letters" competent in "every branch of liberal education" that would "graduate students and grant degrees pertaining to arts and letters . . . on persons competent and deserving."

The Board of Trustees was organized on October 19, 1880 with Dr. J.B. Wilkerson as chairperson, Alfred Mercier as president, T.T. Allain as vice president, and Edwin W. Fay as secretary-treasurer. Other members of the first Board were General Zebulon York, Washington Saunders, S.D. Stockman, I.N. Marks, A.R. Gourrier, and George Fayerweather. The Board appointed A.R. Gourrier president of Southern University. He resigned on February 14, 1881 before the university was opened. The Board then named George Fayerweather, an educator and concert performer, interim president. It was during his administration that the university was officially opened in March, 1881 with twelve students. Experiencing financial difficulties, the institution remained open for only a few months, closed briefly, and reopened in October, 1881. It remained a thriving institution in the Crescent City until June, 1913, a period of slightly over thirty-one years. Presidential succession was as follows: 1881–1883, Reverend Dr. Charles H. Thompson, pastor of St. Phillips Protestant Episcopal Church of New Orleans; 1883–1886, Reverend Joshua Harrison, a Vanderbilt University alumnus; 1886–1887, George W. Bothwell, a local school teacher and pastor of Central Congregational Church; 1887–1913, Henry A. Hill, a businessman and an alumnus of Washington and Lee University.

Initially the Board members had to place a security bond upon themselves in order to establish a university treasury. The first building and site was the Hebrew Girls' School, formerly the Israel Sinai Temple Synagogue on Caliope Street between St. Charles and Camp Streets in New Orleans. The first legislative appropriation of $10,000 was made in late 1881 and the Board of Trustees was recognized. Growth was constant and within a decade three new changes occurred. In 1886, an appropriation of $14,000 was made to the Trustees to purchase a new site and erect larger buildings at Magazine and Soniat Streets, and on June 27, 1890, an Agricultural and Mechanical Department was established. The following year, in 1891, Southern University was recognized by the federal government as a Land Grant College, under the Federal Act of 1890, known as the Second Morrill Act.

The twentieth century has witnessed growth and change at the university. In 1912, Legislative Act 118 authorized the closing of Southern University in New Orleans, the sale of its property, and the reestablishment of the University on a new site. This act further authorized the reorganization of the university with a new Board of Trustees to be appointed to four-year terms by the state governor. The Supreme Court, on June 14, 1913, validated the act. In July of 1913 the Board of Trustees elected Joseph Samuel Clark, who was president of Baton Rouge

College and the Louisiana State Colored Teachers Association, to serve as president of the "new" Southern University. After a nine month search, a new location was established and on March 9, 1914, the "new" Southern University opened in Scotlandville, Louisiana.

The Louisiana Constitutional Convention of 1921 authorized the reorganization and expansion of Southern University. Legislative Act 100 of 1922 effectively provided that the university be reorganized under the control of the State Board of Education.

Dr. Joseph Samuel Clark was retired and named president emeritus in 1938. He was succeeded by Dr. Felton Grandison Clark, the dean of the college and director of instruction. Clark served as president for thirty years and retired in 1968. During his tenure, Southern University in New Orleans and Southern University in Shreveport were authorized by Legislative Acts 28 and 42 in 1956 and 1964, respectively. On October 13, 1968, Dr. George Leon Netterville, Jr., who was serving as the Vice President for Business Affairs, was named as the succeeding president. Dr. Jesse N. Stone, Jr., attorney, became president on July 1, 1974 and was inaugurated March 14, 1975. In 1977, the Southern University Board of Supervisors, a management board authorized by the Louisiana Constitution of 1974, was created. Dr. Stone was designated as system president, with office and residence remaining on the Baton Rouge campus. The chief administrative officer on each campus was entitled chancellor. They were: Dr. Roosevelt Steptoe, Baton Rouge campus; Mr. Leonard Barnes, Shreveport campus; and Dr. Emmitt W. Bashful, New Orleans campus. On September 1, 1982, Dr. James J. Prestage became the second chancellor of the Baton Rouge campus.

On September 1, 1985, Dr. Joffre T. Whisenton, educator and officer with the Southern Association of Colleges and Schools, became the fifth president of Southern University. Dr. Wesley Cornelious McClure became the third chancellor of the Baton Rouge campus on August 16, 1985. On June 19, 1985, the A. A. Lenoir Law School was designated the Southern University Law Center, and Dean B. K. Agnihotri was named chancellor on July 1, 1985.

On October 29, 1988, a new era began and history was made when Dr. Dolores Richard Spikes was named unanimously by the Southern University Board of Supervisors president of the Southern University System. As the sixth president, and the first female to be named to this position, Dr. Spikes accepted the challenge to restore both the fiscal stability of the university and the academic credibility consistent with the mission of the university.

With the departure of Chancellor McClure (who became President of Virginia State); the Southern University Board of Supervisors appointed Dr. Spikes as Chancellor of the Baton Rouge Campus. Dr. Spikes served in a dual capacity until June 30, 1991, when Dr. Marvin L. Yates became the fourth Chancellor of the campus.

To the Students

The Skills Enhancement Book has been developed as a requirement for the Freshman Experiences Series which is a two-hour required course offered in two parts, one hour each. This series is designed to develop and maintain a high level of academic motivation among all-freshman students, to provide wide-range cultural and personal-social experience and ultimately to work toward the development of the whole individual. The weekly class meeting will serve only to present and introduce contents in this module. You are encouraged to review and complete all materials at your own pace. In addition, it is the intent of the Junior Division that you will retain this module for use as a supplement to your total studies while you are enrolled at Southern University-Baton Rouge.

The Skills Enhancement Program contains a compilation of practical tools necessary for undergraduate and postgraduate success. Each freshman will be held accountable for mastering basic contents which include the following:

I.   Making The Transition From High School to College

   • Introducing The College Experience

   • Exploring The Value of Higher Education in America

   • College: Your New Frontier—Introducing Your Campus

   • Motivation

   • Exploring Your Personal Attributes and Increasing Your Self-Esteem

II.   Improving Your Academic Skills For Survival

   • Time Management

   • Tips on Improving Study Skills

   • Attending Classes

   • Improving Your Test Taking Skills

   • Enhancing Your Vocabulary Skills Using the Library

   • Improving Your Critical Thinking Skills

III. Enhancing Your Social Skills

   • Developing Social Skills and Managing Social Relationships

   • Becoming Culturally Literate in a Multicultural Society

   • Making Responsible Social Decisions

IV. Looking Ahead

- Improving Your Knowledge of Current Issues

- Improving Your Money Managing Skills

- Becoming Computer Literate

The Skills Enhancement Program is designed to change the learning environment at Southern University-Baton Rouge. It will:

- Promote the development of environments that foster student interaction with students, faculty, and staff.

- Promote the intellectual development of students.

- Provide a learning environment that enhances individual growth and development.

- Provide students with instruction in the development of skills necessary for effective performance in and positive adjustment to the learning environment.

- Assist in the development of skills through interaction among students, faculty and staff in the Mentor Program.

I.
Making the Transition from High School to College

**Introducing the College Experience:
The New Frontier**

**Exploring the Value of Higher Education
in America**

**College: Your New Frontier—Introducing
Your Campus**

Motivation

**Exploring Your Personal Attributes and
Increasing Your Self-Esteem**

Introducing the College Experience: The New Frontier

Going to college is a big change from those high school days. Beginning freshmen will experience a great deal more freedom and less supervision:

1. freedom to go to class or stay in your dormitory,

2. freedom to eat breakfast or stay another hour in bed,

3. freedom to withdraw from school or stay in school.

Beginning freshmen must learn self-discipline and practice it as never before because living apart from family is probably the first true experiment with independence. They must also learn to budget their time and money wisely and meet new responsibilities with determination.

Every beginning freshman has his own preconceptions of what college will be like. Some expect college to have an intensely intellectual atmosphere with tough courses and scary competition for grades. Others think it's going to be sundown-to-sunrise social life, athletic games, dances, fraternity or sorority mixers, and special parties off-campus. These preconceptions of college are often planted by information that comes from college catalogs, high school counselors, friends already in college and parents who remember their own college experience. Considering all this, some of their ideas of college are often erroneous or "half true."

Many freshmen find it expedient to reorganize their visions of college and adapt firmly to the reality of college, meaning that the adjustment depends on their understanding of themselves and how well they learn the techniques of survival. In order to adjust, they may have to tell themselves that some things are not going to be the way they used to be—they have to be ready for change.

Personal and social adjustments are not the only adjustments that students must make. The beginning freshman must also adapt to the academic routine of college. Academic survival in college is, in a real sense, completely up to the student.

Beyond freedom—responsibility—mistakes can be costly, they can hurt—but they rarely kill. Most students survive their mistakes admirably. Responsibility can mean mixing lots of experiences (even mistakes) and opinions (of parents, peers, friends) to form one's own ideas. College just happens to be the time most people take to re-examine their own sense of personal responsibility and come up with a system that fits them.

Exploring the Value of Higher Education in America

American public education has, in spite of its problems and issues, played a vital role in the growth of this country and the development of its democratic ideals. American education is one of the noblest single cultural achievements of our society and mankind.

Some of the purposes of Higher Education include:

1. To foster the intellectual development of students.

2. To assist students in developing life and work-planning careers.

3. To develop personal goals—realistic work-ethics and self actualization.

4. To disseminate new ideas and knowledge.

These purposes are universal concepts and should be adopted and experienced by the beginning freshman. The purposes stated above and rooted in the early seventeenth and eighteenth centuries concept that "every society is concerned about its youth, and that its educational institutions are a reflection of that concern." Educational institutions are also measures of people's hope for the future. Thus the college ideas was planted and the seeds of education sprung up in America like the concept of freedom itself.

The Beginning and Development of Education in the United States

1. Compulsory education laws, of which the famous acts of 1642 and 1647 in Massachusetts as examples, were passed by all New England colonies except Rhode Island.

2. Some of these colonies also passed only laws requiring that parents and masters instruct their children in reading and writing for religious and governmental reasons. Examples were the "Great Law" in Pennsylvania and 1682 the Public Art School in 1732 in New York.

3. Virginia passed legislation in 1642 providing for the education of orphans.

4. Thomas Jefferson offered the most definitive plan for a state school system in 1779. Jefferson and Wythe introduced a bill in the Virginia assembly calling for all free children, girls as well as boys, to attend school for three years without paying tuition and longer at private expense if their parents, guardians, or friends thought proper. Jefferson's plan was too farsighted for the times; the bill did not pass.

5. Early federal legislation pertaining to education had to do chiefly with land grants and the establishment of land grant colleges. In the Ordinance of 1785, Congress declared that in the land of the Northwest Territory, later to become the states of Indiana, Illinois, Michigan, Ohio, Wisconsin, and part of Minnesota, "there shall be reserved the lot No. 16 of every township, for the maintenance of public schools, within said township."

6. Senator Justin Morrill of Vermont introduced a bill in 1857 which granted 20,000 acres of land to each state for each senator and representative in Congress for the purpose of establishing colleges of agriculture. Congress approve the bill, but it was vetoed by President Buchanan. In 1862, however, the Morrill Act passed, and the grant had been increased to 30,000 acres for each senator and representative.

7. Other legislation pertaining to the land grant colleges include the Hatch Act of 1887 which established the experiment stations, the Second Morrill Act of 1890 which established the historical black land grant institutions and the Nelson Amendment of 1907 which allowed the training of teachers.

8. In 1917, influenced to some extent by World War I, Congress passed the Smith-Hughes Act for the support of vocational education.

9. The National Defense Education Act of 1958, Public Law 85-864, provided for loans to college students, fellowships for graduate study centers for research and study of foreign languages, experimental study with television and related media, and improvement of statistical services in state departments of education.

10. The Vocational Education Act of 1963 represented a new emphasis for the federal government in the area of vocational training.

11. The most sweeping extension of federal involvement in education was provided in the Elementary and Secondary Education Act of 1965. The law directed federal attention to local education agencies for the education of children of low-income families (Title I)—an "Impact on Poverty." Also, Title II, Title III, Title IV, and Title V.

12. Other significant acts passed by Congress include in Manpower Development and Training Act of 1962, the Economic Opportunity Act of 1964, the Higher Education Act of 1965, and the Education Professions Development Act of 1967.

Objectives

Upon completion of this module, you will be able to:

1. identify historical events in education that contributed to the development of the "college" concept today.

2. manifest a knowledge of the development of higher education in America and its value to this society.

3. assess the importance of higher education training as it relates to personal development and the pursuit of individual goals.

What we have today is in large part the result of past historical developments in higher education. This has led us to value two forms of education: liberal arts education, and career education is noted in the tradition that students should learn the effective use of language and use of numbers. Based on this concept, the student must learn art, music, logic, and grammar, as well as learning how to compute in arithmetic, geometry, and astronomy. With a liberal arts education, we learn the value of communication and computation to help us understand the fast changing world.

However, the Vocational Education Act of 1963 helped us make sweeping changes in our concepts of higher education. We started valuing career education because it focused on jobs for the future. It gave a new meaning to higher education with the introduction of internships, vocational training, co-ops, practicums, and a reduced emphasis on the arts. Science and technology became the central focus. Undergraduate education became the centerpiece of training youth in computer science, engineering, allied health professions, and others. Thus, our concepts of higher education had crossed into the twenty-first century.

Today's education requires a mix of both the old ideas and concepts with the new. Higher education goes beyond the four walls of the university because society requires us to volunteer our time through programs in "service learning" that can have personal as well as professional value. We value higher education as a place to practice our skills and prepare for multiple careers in our lifetime. Higher education today focuses on the development of the total human being.

Activity

Directions: Write a brief history of higher education in America. Use the following terms in your paper:

a. Colonial America
b. compulsory education
c. religious purposes
d. tuition
e. land grant institutions
f. Morrill Act
g. National Defense Education Act
h. Vocational Education
i. Higher Education Act

Develop an outline listing some personal values and benefits of Higher Education.

College: Your New Frontier— Introducing Your Campus

Objectives

This module will:

1. Encourage you to be aware of your college—its regulations, its activities and the physical plant.

2. Assist you in making an effective adjustment to college life.

3. Help you consider major fields of concentration and some information about course selection.

4. Get you started thinking and preparing you for where you will go after completing college work.

When we speak of "the college campus" we are really talking about a great variety of places where a great variety of objectives are being met. Colleges and universities vary in size. They may be in the downtown section of a large city or in an isolated rural area. They may be operated by a branch of government (city, county or parish, or state), or operated under a private endowment or by a religious group.

The Campus

Colleges today offer a variety of services to their students ranging from on-campus beauty and barbershops; to a variety of eating places (students always complain about the food) to activity centers (student unions or centers).

Becoming Familiar with the Physical Plant

After the first few days on even the largest of campuses, you will have learned how to get to your classrooms, the cafeteria, the bookstore, dormitories, and certain social areas, such as the Student Union. You will also have learned a few short cuts; and, if you drive to school, a bit about where you may find a parking space.

If your campus is large, much still remains that you have not yet located. You may still be uncertain about how to get to the:

1. The Infirmary (campus medical facility)
2. The Business or Comptroller's Office
3. The Faculty Offices
4. The Counseling Areas
5. The Campus Police Office
6. The Vice Chancellor for Student Affairs
7. The Placement Center

Such knowledge can usually be obtained as you need it; but you will save time and confusion later by noticing those buildings you do not enter and finding out what offices they contain.

The University Catalogue

A college or university catalogue is probably the *best single reference* work a student has to guide him through the institution. A vast amount of useful information is contained in it; and, though the arrangement of material varies, most catalogues contain the same basic kinds of information.

Colleges and universities revise their catalogues annually or biannually to reflect changes in procedures, schedules, and personnel. Generally the current college calendar appears near the front, and notes many important items, including *the days of instruction, holidays* and *deadline dates*.

Also the catalogue will list:

1. the last day to enroll and the date to file applications for many different activities
2. the dates to add or drop courses
3. ways to obtain refunds
4. method to make up incomplete examinations
5. early-registration for "upcoming" semesters
6. procedures and requirements for transferring from the Junior Division
7. dates for withdrawal from the University
8. the system of grading and scholarship standards
9. class attendance policies
10. degrees offered

Many consider the heart of the catalogue as the portion on curricula and courses. The program of study and the degrees to which they lead are usually listed before the course offerings and description. Generally they are found at the beginning of each individual department or college course offerings. The requirements fall into several categories:

1. Lower division (Junior Division) requirements and prerequisites to a major.
2. Upper division courses required in the major department.
3. Electives within the major department.
4. Required courses in related departments.

Courses are generally numbered according to difficulty; that is, introductory courses are given the lowest numbers and the more advanced ones are assigned higher numbers. Year-long courses may also be indicated by consecutive numbers (History 104, 105). Many universities number their courses according to the year in college in which a student would normally take them—Freshman courses might have numbers in the 100's, sophomore courses in the 200's, junior courses in the 300's, and senior courses in the 400's. It is important to note if there are any prerequisites for courses listed.

Major Fields of Concentration

Students select major fields for many different reasons. Although most choices are based on vocational goals, some students turn to a particular major because of interests, because of a favorite instructor, or because they think it will be easy. Sometimes the choice is made simply because the student is interested in the field, without a particular goal in mind.

The student who feels confident of his or her vocational goals and who recognizes the relationship between these goals and the college program may choose a major before entering college. *On the other hand, many students do not know which way they are headed vocationally.* These students may be better off postponing their final decision for a short time. In deciding on a major, you may consider these questions:

1. Will this field help me become the sort of person I wish to become?

2. Will it provide the satisfactions I especially desire?

3. Will it be sufficiently challenging to enable me to make the greatest use of my abilities?

4. Will it give me a sense of accomplishment?

5. Will it help me reach my vocational goals?

6. Will it enable me to develop my special talents?

7. Will I be able to learn what I want to learn?

8. Will I enjoy the courses I must take and be able to take the courses I want to take?

For some fields, the undergraduate major is very important. You cannot become a nurse, a teacher, an engineer, or a laboratory technologist without certain educational requirements. Also some fields such as medicine, sociology, psychology and law require graduate work.

Counseling

Large universities have a variety of services, including special counselors for foreign students, returning veterans, study-methods problems, for vocational help, and for personal and emotional disturbances.

SUMMARY OF IMPORTANT IDEAS

1. Colleges offer a great variety of services, and it takes a while to learn where everything is on your campus.

2. Knowing about regulations that govern your academic and nonacademic pursuits is important.

3. Selecting the correct major is an important task and should not be hurried.

4. Selecting courses require attention both to college requirements and to your own needs.

5. Participation in campus activities can add to both enjoyment and to vocational and avocational skills.

Motivation

Objectives

This module is designed:

      1. To show the application of motivation to learning.

      2. To describe simple methods for coping with distractions.

      3. To suggest specific ways to improve motivation.

Goal Setting

Educators are far from certain about exactly how students learn. On one point there is agreement—the number one factor is motivation. Without this factor—the desire to learn—little learning takes place.

      Psychologists have done a vast amount of research on principles of motivation, learning, and memory. *Motivation refers to a condition in which you are activated to move toward a goal.* In a specific sense, motivation is required for you to read a textbook, listen to a lecture, or study for an examination. In a more general sense, motivation is needed in order for you to make the sacrifices that college attendance demands.

      Some people assume that conditions beyond their control prevent them from being good students. They may blame home pressures, bad luck, or other matters they feel they can do nothing about. Other people assume that the power to be successful comes from within themselves. The former attitude is termed external locus of control; the latter internal locus of control. Most evidence points out that students who accept the responsibility for what happens to them do better in their academic work than do those who chalk success and failure up to matters beyond their control. Your success may; to some extent, be limited by external factors, but you will not know how well you can overcome these restrictions unless you assume that you do indeed have the power and control to do so.

      Low academic motivation can be attributed to these reasons:

      1. Some people may not see college as relevant to their important goals.

      2. Not everyone is able to settle down to college.

      3. Some students have selected the wrong college or university.

      4. Some students select the wrong college program (major).

      5. Some people resent education in general.

      6. Personal problems sometimes obscure all other matters.

      7. Some students are frustrated by the amount of time required by education.

      To improve your motivation, you need to have a realistic notion of what is holding you back in the first place. Only then can you develop a reasonable way to overcome it.

      Abraham Maslow identifies basic human needs and arranges them in a hierarchy. He states that the factors that motivate us to act are in an order of importance. We act as a result of the needs we feel. Of highest importance is self-actualization—knowing and accepting yourself and realizing your fullest potential. The hierarchy of basic needs are:

Self-Actualization
Self-Esteem
Love and Belonging
Safety Needs
Physiological Needs

Many of these factors related to learning reflect the importance of motivation. If students see the personal benefit and purpose in the learning situation, they will have the necessary drive to learn.

SUMMARY OF SOME IMPORTANT IDEAS

1. Little if any learning can occur without motivation.

2. Students who assume that conditions outside their control prevented them from being good students are less successful then are those who assume that they themselves are responsible for their performances.

3. Poor academic motivation can be caused by factors such as students *seeing college as irrelevant to their important goals, students being unable to settle down, students having selected the wrong college or wrong major or course of study*, or *students having personal or attitudinal problems.*

4. There are ways to overcome motivational difficulties.

5. People can distract from your studying by making noise or by intruding on your privacy.

6. Personal problems can also reduce study effectiveness.

7. Distractions in the study area include room temperature, location, furniture, and lighting.

8. A number of principles of learning theory can be applied to study effectiveness:
   a. Warm-up
   b. Repetition and Overlearning
   c. Massed versus distributed practice
   d. Whole versus part learning
   e. Transfer of training
   f. Rate versus meaningful learning

Exercise

Write an essay titled "My Own Motivation in Attending College." In the essay, describe how your motivation has helped you in college. You may wish to discuss other motivations that compete with the motivation to succeed in college.

Your instructor will tell you more about how he or she wants this essay to be handled—for example, in regard to length and style.

Exploring Your Personal Attributes
and Increasing Your Self-Esteem

Overview

Knowing yourself—your abilities, skills, limitations, interests, personality, and goals could be termed self-awareness. When you are aware of and can draw some conclusions about these attributes you can approach and develop a realistic college plan and career direction.

Objectives

After studying and practicing skills in the module you will be able:

1. To enhance self-understanding through knowledge of heredity and environment.

2. To differentiate between physiological and psychological needs.

3. To understand that behavior is motivated by human needs and when not satisfied frustration and anxiety enters one's lifestyle.

4. To understand forms of behavior—aggressive behavior—assertive action and defense mechanisms.

5. To understand what constitutes mental and special abilities and how they are significant to the individual.

It is felt that being aware of your attributes is a logical starting point in organizing sequential steps to college experiences and career development. Complete several interest inventories (Strong-Campbell-Holland-Vocational Preferences Inventory, and others) and discussing your interest with a Career Counselor can assist you in knowing yourself better. With this approach, you are an active participant in exercises where you report interests, "feelings," and abilities are tied to broad career fields which can be classified as realistic, artistic, social, investigative, enterprising, and conventional.

In addition, realistically:

1. Identify your positive traits, such as are you a loyal friend? A good listener? Can you say they proper thing or possibility in a difficult situation?

2. Meet fear or failure head-on. Assure yourself that you will not always meet every short-term goal or pass every test—*no one* does. Another way to enhance your self-esteem—confront the fear that affects about 99% of the population—Fear of Failure.

3. Remember your past accomplishments—when you are feeling overwhelmed—remind yourself of other obstacles you mastered or overcome in the past. Many people evaluate themselves merely by their current accomplishments.

4. Give yourself credit—congratulate yourself—no matter how small or insignificant the accomplishment—congratulate yourself for doing well.

5. Do not overestimate the confidence of others. Some persons have "Huge Egos."

Remember

THE ABILITY TO CONTROL ONE'S DESTINY IS THE ABILITY TO START, CHANGE, AND STOP OURSELVES PHYSICALLY, EMOTIONALLY, AND MENTALLY AT WILL. ONE CAN THEN ACT, RATHER THAN REACT.

Bibliography

Bachhuber, Thomas D. and Harwood, Richard. *Directions: A Guide To Career Planning*, Boston, Houghton-Mifflin Company, 1978.

Flemming, Laraine E. and Leet, Judith. *Becoming A Successful Student*, New York, Harper Collins College Publishers, 1994.

Shertzer, Bruce. *Career Planning—Freedom To Choose*. Boston, Houghton-Mifflin Company, 1985.

II.
Improving Your Academic Skills for Survival

Time Management

Tips On Improving Study Skills

Attending Classes

Imroving Test Taking Skills

Enhancing Your Vocabulary Skills

Using the Library

Improving Reasoning and Critical Thinking Skills

Improving Your Academic Skills for Survival

Unit Concepts

The modules in this section are devoted to college level study strategies that assist with academic competencies required in higher education. All students enrolling in college deserve a fair chance to succeed in higher education. In this century, our nation has attempted to expand its efforts and assist in providing access of college to a majority of high school graduates. This expansion includes many persons with inadequate preparation which hinders some and deprive many other students of a fair chance to take advantage of this opportunity.

The development and use of effective learning strategies is fundamental to successful academic achievement.

Time Management

Overview

During the growth and exploration stages, one finds circumstances in which we seem to "run-out-of-time" for endeavors. Time management does not mean sacrificing pleasurable activities for routine and mundane responsibilities; however, it means developing a reasonable schedule and adhering to it—with legitimate exceptions.

Objectives

1. The development of a clear and reasonable schedule.

2. Assist students in establishing priorities both academic and personal.

3. Analyzing and revising your schedule to make it realistic and practical.

Some authors recommend:

1. Apply a principle of divide and conquer to difficult tasks.

2. Develop weekly and monthly long-range schedules. (Master schedule)

3. Identify one's high-energy prime time. (Morning or Evening) (People and Traits)

4. Using a daily "To-Do" list.

5. Breaking the procrastination habit.

The authors Rathus and Rathus advise generally, that schedules should:

1. Constructed Clearly and within reason.

2. Select certain classes and activities for the "Right Time of Day."

3. Schedule time between classes when possible. (This can permit review time before the next class).

4. Schedule sufficient time for study.

5. Plan Ahead—allow time for tests, major examinations and unexpected problems.

6. Be specific and strategic.

7. Be realistic and aware of your limits.

8. Schedule and save the Best for Last.

9. Congratulate and reward yourself for achieving study goals and other academic responsibilities.

10. Be flexible.

In addition, a quotation by poet Kenneth Atchelty, states, "finding time begins with an act of will. You also have to look for time in the right places." Time may be conserved by:

1. Combining two activities (while commuting to the university via bus, etc.)

2. Be prepared to study while you wait (while waiting for appointments).

3. Use the telephone to get information.

4. Organize your desk and have a system to locate important items. (Papers, pens, notebooks, etc.).

5. Don't let a one-hour task take two or more hours.

6. Seriously cut down on television!

7. Practice three R's of behavior modification—(3 R's)
   - Recognize when you are procrastinating.
   - Refuse to procrastinate.
   - Replace that behavior with positive action.

Taking charge or managing time means paying attention and planning how and where you spend time. You must take charge of your time and your life.

How to Manage Time

We are not born knowing how to manage time. We learn how to manage time. Learning how to manage time—and ourselves—is one of the unstated tasks of college life. Unstated, but vital.

Managing time means making a reasonable schedule and then sticking to it, except for . . . the legitimate exceptions. What are legitimate exceptions? Some are obvious, like getting sick or getting so wrapped up in library work that you get to dinner late. We can't list all the legitimate exceptions that will occur, but you'll know them when you see them. Watching *Police Academy 15* for the tenth time is not one of them.

Now let's check your notes about squandering time against the facts. Fill out the following What-Do-You-Do-Now? exercise on "Finding Out How You Spend Your Time." Maybe you'll discover that you were too hard on yourself—that you don't waste as much time as you think. Perhaps you will find that you weren't hard enough on yourself. After we have seen how you actually spend your time, we'll go through the basics of making up a schedule.

What Do You Do Now?

Finding Out How You Spend Your Time

The goal of this chapter is to teach you how to spend your time more efficiently. Psychologists have found that when you're trying to help people change their behavior for the better, the best place for them to start is to find out exactly what they're doing now. Making a record of what you do is called recording a baseline. As a matter of fact, in one study, psychologists increased the amount of time students spent studying merely by having the students keep a record of where and when they studied!

Why does playing detective with yourself have such a remarkable effect? For one thing, if you find that you're squandering your time, coming face to face with the fact may help motivate you to do something about it. For another, the baseline record may suggest ways of marshaling your time. For example, the discovery that you spend 12 hours a week napping and another 12 watching television suggests a couple of "activities" that could be cut down. Then, too, the baseline makes you generally more aware of time. As a result, time becomes less likely to slip through your fingers.

You can create a record of your baseline by using the time chart on page 19. The last months of high school or the first weeks of college are an ideal time to do so. Enter the hours spent in classes, at meals, studying, sleeping, socializing, musing, fantasizing, napping, watching TV, lying by the pool—all of it.

Now do some adding. How much time did you spend:

In classes?	_____	Watching TV?	_____
Studying?	_____	Reading for pleasure?	_____
At work?	_____	On athletics or exercise?	_____
On chores (family, personal?)	_____	On other leisure activities?	_____
Preparing and eating meals?	_____	On transportation	
Sleeping?	_____	(e.g., commuting)?	_____
Socializing (friends, family)?	_____	Other? (_____)	_____
In religious activity?	_____	Other? (_____)	_____
		TOTAL	_____

Now total the hours. There are 168 hours in a week, so if your total exceeds 168, you've overestimated here and there. On the other hand, if your total is less than 168, you've "lost" some time.

We're not going to be your judges. (In college, you're your own boss.) But we'll give you some information, you'll see that normal, healthy students can get by on about six hours of sleep a night, although they prefer to get eight or so. With naps, do you average ten or eleven hours of sleep a day? Are you squandering time?

Now check the table. It shows how much time college students in a national sample report devoting to certain activities. How do your estimates compare? If, for example, you spent 11 or more hours watching television, you belong to the top 14 percent of students. We offer our congratulations or our commiserations—whichever you believe are in order.

So are you spending your time wisely or are you squandering time? How much time slips through your fingers? Are you willing to do something about it? If the answer is yes, keep reading. If not, well, why waste the time?

ACTIVITY	HOURS PER WEEK						
	NONE	1-2	3-4	5-6	7-8	9-10	11 or MORE
Talking informally to other students	3	19	16	13	9	9	31
Watching television	13	22	18	14	11	8	14
Leisure reading	23	35	17	11	6	4	4
Talking to faculty members	26	56	11	4	1	1	1
Studying in the library	27	24	14	9	5	6	15
Attending campus cultural events	46	36	11	4	1	1	1
Participating in organized student activities (other than athletics)	50	26	10	6	3	2	3
Participating in intramural sports	70	16	8	3	1	1	1
Participating in intercollegiate athletics	93	1	*	*	*	1	4

How to Set Up a Schedule: General Advice

Construct a Clear and Reasonable Schedule

You should be able to live with and feel good about your schedule. Give yourself some time for socializing or just for relaxing in a pretty part of campus.

Pick the Right Times of Day

Schedule classes for the time of day when you are most alert. Our bodies have certain built-in rhythms. There are times during the day when functions like attentiveness are at their peak. Some of us ("morning people") are more productive and animated in the morning; others are at their best in the afternoons. Put your classes, especially your toughest classes, in the slots when you're at your sharpest.

Schedule Enough Time for Studying

As a rule of thumb, you should study two hours for every hour of class. That approach works better for some subjects than for others. For example, in an art studio course, you may get all of your work done during class. In a course on the nineteenth-century English novel, you may need to read five hours for every hour spent in class.

The flip side of this advice should be obvious enough: *Don't schedule several courses with heavy reading loads for the same term!* Not unless you're into masochism.

Schedule Time Between Classes

If possible, schedule some time between classes. This will allow you to preview the text and your notes before classes (10-15 minutes) and review your notes after classes (15-20 minutes) Research on memory shows that we forget about *half* of what we have learned *within a half hour.* By studying course notes right after class, we

A Time Chart for Making a Baseline Record of the Ways in Which You Use Your Time.

Days Time	Monday	Tuesday	Wednesday	Thursday	Friday	Saturday	Sunday
7:00							
8:00							
9:00							
10:00							
11:00							
12:00							
1:00							
2:00							
3:00							
4:00							
5:00							
6:00							
7:00							
8:00							
9:00							
10:00							
11:00							

strengthen our learning and remember more. If we wait until a few days before the exam to pull out our notes, we are trying to rebuild a crumbling edifice.

Plan Ahead!

Allow yourself enough time to prepare for examinations. Plan to have assignments completed a day or two ahead of their due dates, so that you have room in your schedule in case a problem causes you to fall behind.

Be Specific

Break big tasks like "work on paper" into concrete, reachable goals. "Work on term paper" doesn't tell you where to begin. Instead, you might break the task down into bits and pieces that you work on, say, twice a week. If you check Chapter 7, you will see that the first few scheduled slots could say something like "Select topic for paper," "Delimit topic," "Check library card catalog for references." Slots scheduled later on could specify "Outline the paper," "Write an introduction, based on the outline," "Work on the body of the paper," and so forth. You could also specify slots for revising, proofreading, and producing the final draft.

Schedule Time for Mundane Chores

Give yourself time to take care of your personal responsibilities. Cleaning and doing laundry take time, so budget time for them in your schedule.

Be Strategic

Study your difficult subjects during times of day when you are alert and when you are least likely to be disturbed or interrupted.

Give Yourself Some Variety

Yes, variety does appear to add some spice to life. We become more alert and motivated when we are presented with novel stimulation or a change of pace. Apply these maxims to your schedule as follows: Don't study physics all day Monday, literature all day Tuesday, and psychology all day Wednesday. Study each one for a while every day so you will avoid boredom and maintain a lively interest in the subject matter.

Save the Best for Last

Consider scheduling your most enjoyable work last. This will give you something to look forward to.

Be Aware of Your Limits

The "In-Your-Own-Write" exercise highlights the fact that we all have different attention spans. Some of us can work for two hours or more without looking up. Others cannot last for more than 15 minutes without needing a break of some kind. After years of high school, you must have a reasonably accurate impression of the extent of your own attention span.

Try not to be unrealistic by scheduling too many hours of studying in a row. For most students, we would not recommend more than three hours of studying without a break. Also, during those three hours, you will probably profit from a number of brief breaks. We recommend taking a ten-minute break each hour. Get up and stretch. Get a sip of water.

If you've been realistic and you've decided that you probably can't keep your nose to the grindstone as long as you need to in college, don't throw up your hands in despair. Many students have been able to gradually lengthen their study periods by adding a few minutes each day. Intersperse those brief breaks and tell yourself what a wonderful job you're doing!

"The Play's the Thing"
Remember that "all work and no play" makes for a miserable and unproductive college career. People who manage to fit some fun into their work tend to be more motivated and creative and more capable of meeting the challenges that lie ahead. Reserve slots for recreational activities. Make sure that you don't study right through them! (Make an occasional exception when you're onto something great, but then reward yourself by having some extra fun later on.)

Pat Yourself on the Back
Reward yourself for achieving your study goals on schedule. For some free goodies, make a Pleasant Events List.

Be Flexible
Allow yourself some flexibility. After all, your schedule is intended to serve you, not to rule you. You may not be able to change the times that classes meet, but you may (occasionally!) find it worthwhile to cut a class because you're finally making excellent progress on a term paper that's been aging you prematurely. If you've got a part-time job, you have to show up regularly or else you may be fired. But you may be able to postpone a study session to a free period if you have the chance to spend some time with the man or woman of your dreams. It might also make sense to put off the laundry during final exams. Use your judgment and make sure that you're not using "flexibility" as an excuse for indefinitely postponing some of the less pleasant tasks on your schedule.

Set Down Priorities and Long-Term Assignments
List your top priorities and your long-term assignments at the top of each week's schedule. The priorities are the least flexible items. If you must do some switching around, these are the things you'll make up fast.

Check syllabi or class notes for long-term dates when papers are due and tests will be given. Note important long-term dates on a monthly calendar. Transfer some of the long-term dates from the calendar to your weekly schedule. Having your long-term assignments in front of you prevents you from forgetting about them and encourages you to do something about them on a weekly basis.

Carry Your Schedule with You
Put your schedule in a notebook that you can carry along. A schedule is like a wristwatch: It does no good to have either of them waiting for you in the room.

Scan Your Schedule
Briefly scan your schedule from time to time even when there's nothing that has to be done. These glances will help you track your priorities and keep long-term assignments in mind.

Monthly Calendar. Students can note important long-term dates on a monthly calendar and transfer them to their weekly schedules.

OCTOBER

Sunday	Monday	Tuesday	Wednesday	Thursday	Friday	Saturday
	1 *math quiz*	2	3	4 *Complete term paper Outline*	5 *Psychology quiz*	6
7	8 *Spanish quiz*	9 *Fresh comp paper due*	10 *Chris's birthday*	11	12	13 *Home game*
14	15	16	17	18 *Complete term paper draft*	19 *Pick up J. (4:15 pm)*	20
21	22 *Midterms: Spanish + Math*	23 *Fresh comp paper due*	24 *Psychology mid term*	25	26	27 *Home game*
28	29	30	31			

How to Set Up a Schedule: The Specifics

1 Map out a schedule like the one in Bernie's schedule. Notice that the days of the week go across the top row, and the hours of the day go down the left column. Start with the hour you get up in the "Time" column. Give yourself enough hours to reach bedtime.

2. Fill in the hours you are in class. If you are piecing together a trial schedule for an upcoming term, try to leave some time between classes to review what you have learned and to preview the material that will be discussed in the next class.

3. Enter all other fixed activities such as part-time work, dropping off or picking up the kids, meals,* athletic practices, athletic events, and appointments.

---

*If they're fixed, that is. If mealtimes are flexible for you, let them go for a while.

4. Enter mealtimes. Be realistic: If your stomach starts grumbling or you get the "shakes" at 11:30 A.M., don't write in lunch at 1:00 P.M. Or at least pencil in an earlier snack (preferably nutritious!)*

5. Put in the times when you plan to get to sleep. Don't be a hero and try to limit yourself to four hours of sleep a night. If you believe that you need more than nine hours, why not talk things over at the college health center?

6. Enter study periods.

7. List the weeks priorities in the box at the upper left. Priorities include upcoming exams, important assignments that have to be completed in the near term, and appointments, such as dental cleanings.

8. Note long-term assignments in the box at the upper right. These are things like term papers and big tests that lie a few weeks ahead. The idea is to include some time to work on them each week.

9. Consider allowing yourself a bit of time—perhaps a half hour or so—to unwind before getting to bed. Some students find that there's no point to hopping into the sack with theorems on the brain.

10. Try to allow yourself at least a little free time every day. Don't book yourself solid for many days in a row. You'll find yourself wasting time on the lighter days and dreading the heavier days. Moreover, if a problem prevents you from meeting your work goals on the heavy days, you'll have a hard time playing catch-up.

11. Check items off as you complete them. If an unexpected problem or chore prevents you from studying or carrying out an assignment, pencil time in for it later in the week.

Sample Schedule

Now that you've considered guidelines for filling out a schedule and have made a schedule for yourself, let's consider if it has some strengths and some weaknesses.

How to Handle Distractions

The Scottish poet Robert Burns wrote, "The best planned schedules of mice and college students go oft awry."** Despite the creation of a logical schedule and the best of intentions, "things" have a way of intruding when we are trying to complete assignments and study. First, indicate the types of things you do to prevent people from distracting you from your work. Then check the suggestions offered below.

Make Arrangements with Roommates

Make arrangements as to what times of the day will be quiet study periods. Use some of the methods as discussed in class to resolve conflicts. For example, negotiate differences, or make exchanges. Try, "I'll stay out of the room from 3:00 to 6:00 on Monday afternoons, if you'll honor a quiet study period from 7:00 to 10:00 on Mondays, Tuesdays, and Thursdays."

---

*Look, someone's got to act *in loco parentis,* so it might as well be us.
**All right! We confess that Burns actually wrote: *The best laid schemes o' mice an' men, Gang aft a-gley.*

If you live at home, try asking your family for quiet time in the house. Tell them specifically what hours you want for yourself. Help give them the resources they need to give you this time. Prepare meals in advance, have frozen pizzas available, or send everybody (but you!) to the fast-food restaurant. If your family knows exactly what you need, they may surprise you by cooperating.

If your family insists upon intruding, you might say something like, "Tell me your preference. Do you want me home for dinner or do you want me to stay on campus? If you want me home, you've got to pretend that I'm not here after dinner till 8:00. I'll put you to bed at eight, but you've got to get ready for bed yourself or else have your father help you. What'll it be?"

Keep the TV Off!

You may think that you can watch TV and work at the same time, but unless you're just treating the TV like background noise (that is, not really watching it), you're fooling yourself. Some students find that they can work with soft music in the background. Perhaps, perhaps not. If you suspect that music may be interfering with your ability to concentrate, you're probably right. Turn it off.

Handle Internal Distractions

If you're hungry, get a small, preferably nutritious, snack.* If you're uncomfortable, move to another spot. If some important ideas come to you, jot them down so that you can think about them later, during the first free time period that comes along. Then let them go.

Place a *Do Not Disturb!* Sign on Your Door

You'd be surprised. Many people really honor these signs. Of course, someone occasionally barges in and says, "Did you put up the sign now or leave it up from before?" or, "Listen, I'll only take a minute of your time."

Our advice is to be assertive and . . .

Just Say No

Say, "I'm in the middle of something and can't get distracted. You'll have to stop back later." It's better to give a specific time than to say "later," because people are more likely to follow concrete suggestions and instructions.

If you have a hard time saying no, consider why. Is it because you're terribly afraid the intruder won't approve of your saying no or won't like you anymore? Psychologist Albert Ellis notes that many of us hold the mistaken belief that we cannot survive unless other people approve of us all the time. And this belief makes us just plain miserable! *You don't need everybody's approval all the time!* You can be polite, but firm, with intruders. You can also offer a *brief* explanation ("I'm in the middle of something important.") If the intruder gets miffed, tell yourself that the problem lies with him or her, not with you . People who care about you want you to do well and respect your right to study without intrusion. If the intruder has no concern for your welfare, why should you worry about his or her approval?

---

*Too many students go through bag after bag of potato chips or half a jar of peanuts while they're working. If this sounds like you, read the section on eating a nutritious diet.

Believe that you are a valuable person and that your time is important. *Believe* that people who are worthwhile will respect your rights. Work on saying no. Practice doesn't always make perfect, but most of the time it helps. And if you have tried and tried and you really can't say no* study someplace where intruders won't find you.

Control Phone Calls

You know not to make telephone calls when you're studying, but how do you handle incoming calls? After all, the person on the phone couldn't read the *Do Not Disturb* sign on the door and didn't know that this time is important to you. And of course you don't want to be rude. So it's not your fault if you get trapped in conversation, right? Wrong. You chose to have a telephone, so it's up to you to handle it.

One way to handle phone calls is to tell the truth. Say, "I really wish I could talk now, but I'm in the middle of _____ (you fill it in)." If the person says, "Really, this'll only take a minute," you can say, "I really can't interrupt what I'm doing right now: I'll call you back later." If you repeat the last sentence three or four times, the message will get through. If the caller then says, "Wow, you're in a mood, aren't you?" don't take up the challenge or you'll never get back to work. You can say something like, "Call me back after eight or I'll call you." Then hang up.

If you really have trouble with phone calls while you're studying, unplug the contraption until you're finished, or study in the library or a study lounge.

Students are sometimes most inventive in the way they handle obtrusive callers. One student remarked, "The greatest invention in the world is my answering machine. I listen to who's calling and call back later unless it's an emergency. If I want to talk to the person, I break in and say, 'Hi! I just got in! Wait until the recording goes off and then we'll talk.'"

Another student noted, "I just say, 'Oops, So and So's calling me—gotta run! I'll talk to you later.'"

A third student occasionally solves the problem by saying, "Hello, hello! Listen, something happened and I can't hear you. If you can still hear me, call me back later. I'm going out now."

How to Move Ahead When You're Stuck:
Ways of Accomplishing Something When You Can't do Anything

Sometimes you get to your study place and have all your equipment set up, and then you get stuck. You try to force yourself to do something, but nothing seems to work. Following are some ideas for getting past these blocks.

Do Something—Anything

If you can't force yourself to read the chapter, try skimming the table of contents, the preface, the index, or even the bibliography or references. Try leafing through the pages, dwelling on anything that catches your eye. If you can't force yourself to write the paper, jot down the random ideas about the topic that are swimming in your head.

---

*Oh, come on! Sure, you can. Try it. Really, it won't hurt. Well, not too much.

Trial Schedule

Priorities for the Week		
Course	Task	Due

Long-Term Assignments		
Course	Assignment	Due

Days / Time	Monday	Tuesday	Wednesday	Thursday	Friday	Saturday	Sunday
7:00							
8:00							
9:00							
10:00							
11:00							
12:00							
1:00							
2:00							
3:00							
4:00							
5:00							
6:00							
7:00							
8:00							
9:00							
10:00							
11:00							

Bernie's Schedule. What strengths do you see in this schedule? What weaknesses?

Time \ Days	Monday	Tuesday	Wednesday	Thursday	Friday	Saturday	Sunday
7:00	Get up and get ready	Get up	Get up and get ready	Get up	Get up and get ready	Get up and get ready	Get up and get ready
8:00	Child Development	Exercise	Child Development	Exercise	Child Development	Study	Study
9:00	Review Break Preview	Freshman composition	Review Break Preview	Freshman composition	Review Break Preview	Exercise	Exercise
10:00	College math	Term	College Math	sition Term	College math		
11:00	Spanish	Paper	Spanish	paper	Spanish	Free	Free
12:00	Chemistry		Chemistry	Chemistry			Watch Bears vs.
1:00		Study		Lab	Study	attend	Cowboys football
2:00	Study		Study	Chores: Shopping		football	game on TV
3:00				Laundry etc.	Dentist	game	Watch Jets vs.
4:00				Free			Raiders football
5:00							game on TV
6:00	Job	Job	Job	Job			Free
7:00					Free	Free	
8:00	Free				(Social)	(Social)	Study
9:00	Watch 49ers	Study	Study	Study	Activity	Activity	
10:00	vs. Dolphins						
11:00	football game	Sleep	Sleep	Sleep			Sleep

Write down some of the strengths and weaknesses you find in your schedule in the spaces provided. Then check some of our thoughts in the key at the end of the chapter.

Strengths of Your Schedule   ## Weaknesses of Your Schedule

_____   _____

_____   _____

_____   _____

_____   _____

_____   _____

_____   _____

_____   _____

_____   _____

_____   _____

_____   _____

_____   _____

_____   _____

_____   _____

_____   _____

_____   _____

_____   _____

_____   _____

_____   _____

_____   _____

_____   _____

_____   _____

Or jot down a list of things to do for the paper. Or even switch to another subject: be flexible and switch slots on your schedule for the week.

Doing something accomplishes these goals:

1. You feel that you have accomplished something and haven't wasted all your time.

2. Sometimes doing something leads to doing more. When something catches your eye in the middle of the assigned chapter, or in another chapter, you may start reading around it and spend your time in a very worthwhile way.

3. You cut the big job down in size, even if just a little.

Look for Interference

Are you being distracted by thinking about your big date, or about what you need to do for another course? Get out your schedule and look for the next free period. Write in. "Worry about date!" or "Do *a*, *b*, and *c* for math class." Of course, if you have a real inspiration for math, consider making a switch. Get to work on math and change the next scheduled period for working on math to the course you let go.

Review Reasons for Being in College

Write down a list of reasons for being in college. Keep the list with you. When you can't get to work, review the reasons. They'll remind you that you're not being "victimized" by college. Even if the workload sometimes gets you down, there's a method to the madness. That is, your college education will help you meet your life goals. So reviewing your reasons for attending college will help motivate you.

Some students have told us that they've tried this method but haven't been able to come up with the list. Most of the time, they were not giving the list their full attention or were feeling sort of down about things in general at the time. But a couple of students had never really examined whether or not college was right for them. We don't recommend going into a week-long mental retreat to examine this question in the middle of a busy term, but you can always deal with it when the term is over.

Remind Yourself That the Assignment Is Time-Limited

Look at your schedule and note that you'll be finished working on this course in, say, 35 minutes. Then you don't have to deal with it again for, say, two days. Moreover, if courses in this field really turn you off, you don't have to take too many more of them. (To meet most core requirements, you don't have to take more than two courses in any particular area.)

Try to keep an open mind, too. It may be that you'll come across something in this subject that you really enjoy. If not this week, perhaps next week or next month.

Compromise

If you have 40 minutes left to go on the subject, study hard for 20 and then quit. Twenty may not be as much as 40, but it's a lot more than none! You can occasionally compromise on the quality rather than the quantity of your work. Read an annoying novel less closely, or skimp on writing parts of the body of a paper rather than not doing them at all. To make this kind of concession, perfectionistic students will have to live with the notion that some of their work can be less than exemplary.

Don't Catastrophize!

Failure to study during this time block, this day, does not mean that you're a terrible student and that it's only a matter of time until you drop out or flunk out of college. All of us have periods when we just can't get anything done. Don't blow things out of proportion so that you believe that you'll be doomed to more of the same every time you sit down to work.

Learning to live within your means doesn't have to be a catastrophe, either. That's the topic of the next chapter—handling money. But before we get into that extravagant subject, let's do some summing up.

TRUTH OR FICTION? REVISITED

- Sad to say, half of all college students spend two hours a week or less studying in the library.

- Yes, one-third of all college students do spend at least seven hours a week watching TV. But we're sure that 90 percent of it is educational television.

- Some students do study most effectively in the morning, and others are more efficient in the afternoon. We all have internal rhythms, and we may be at our peaks at different times of the day.

- Yes, you do forget about half of what you learn within half an hour. This is why it is worthwhile to review what you have learned soon afterward.

- All study with no breaks is enough to dull and discourage most Jacks and Jills. Breaks should be scheduled every hour. Free time and recreational activities also need to be built into students schedules.

- Actually, rather than stubbornly adhering to a schedule, it helps to be flexible. By being flexible, we take advantage of opportunities that arise and cope with unforeseen problems. The trick is to understand the difference between flexibility and neglect.

- Saying "No" and "Later" help students cope with people who distract them from their work and waste their time.

- Sometimes it is better to do less-than-perfect work rather than to let an assignment go completely. You accomplish something, or you hand something in. The trick is not to let slipshod work become a habit.

SUMMING UP

1. How do you waste time?

2. How can you find out how you spend your time?

3. What is your attention span for studying various courses, writing papers, and so on?

4. What problems did you encounter in creating your own schedule? Did you need to make any changes in your trial schedule to get it to work right for you?

5. Are you flexible in adhering to your schedule? Do you think of your schedule as being carved in stone? Is your attitude toward your schedule somewhere in between these extremes?

6. In what ways can you reward yourself for sticking to your schedule?

Bibliography

Flemming, Laraine E. and Judith Leet, *Becoming a Successful Student*, New York, Harper Collins College Publishers, 1994.

Rathus, Spencer A. and Rathus-Fishner, Lois, *Making the Most of College*, Englewood Cliffs, New Jersey, Prentice Hall, 1994.

Tips on Improving Study Skills

Overview

The development of effective study skills and habits is fundamental to your successful academic achievement. You must be able to locate, organize, and demonstrate knowledge of information quickly. Since there is insufficient time to prepare each of you for every university course you plan to pursue, it is vital that you learn to be flexible and adapt the basic learning skills to courses. Consequently, in order to effect your smoother matriculation through courses pursued, it is essential that you develop critical study skills designed to maximize learning and minimize failure.

Objectives

The purpose of this unit is to:

- introduce you to study strategies designed to make learning easier, more interesting, and ultimately lead to the acquisition of success;

- help you develop a systematic procedure for a more effective use of study skills in the various disciplines in the college curriculum;

- help you examine your attitudes about college (studying, test-taking, and taking responsibility for your own learning);

- help you focus attention on effective study methods as they relate to mastering information in the content area; and

- introduce test-taking skills that will help you score well on objective tests, subjective tests, standardized tests, and graduate/professional school entrance examinations.

PRE-TEST EVALUATION TOOL

Use the following checklist to evaluate your use of the study skills. When you have read through the list and have checked the appropriate columns, notice particularly your responses in Columns 2 and 3. They remind you of those areas where you need more work. Remember that your answers will be of value only if the statements are answered *honestly* and *accurately*.

Column 1:	Use Regularly	
	either since learning the technique or from past experiences	
Column 2:	Used A Few Times	
	and found helpful, but no time or willpower to continue to use.	
Column 3:	Intend To Use	
	but haven't yet.	
Column 4:	Didn't Try	
	because my own system works as well.	

	1	2	3	4
Adapting To Classes				
1. Analyze the organization of each class	___	___	___	___
2. Analyze your responsibilities in each class	___	___	___	___
3. Take advantage of outside help	___	___	___	___
Assignments				
1. Understand and record assignments accurately on assignment sheets	___	___	___	___
2. Write due date for each assignment	___	___	___	___
3. Divide long assignments into short steps	___	___	___	___
4. Do assignments regularly and on time	___	___	___	___
5. Keep the quality of assignments consistently high	___	___	___	___
Concentration				
1. Have a regular place to study	___	___	___	___
2. Recite and write while studying	___	___	___	___
3. Reward yourself for starting and finishing a job	___	___	___	___
4. Set goals and work to achieve them	___	___	___	___
5. Set priorities for jobs	___	___	___	___
6. Work to finish a job rather than to put in time	___	___	___	___
7. Avoid distractions while taking notes or studying	___	___	___	___
8. Read summary of previous class just before next class	___	___	___	___
9. Label lecture notes in lefthand margin to force concentration	___	___	___	___
10. Take marginal notes while reading	___	___	___	___

	1	2	3	4

Exams, Preparing For and Taking

1. Make table of contents sheets to organize your exam studying ____ ____ ____ ____
2. Make study sheets by topic whey studying for exams ____ ____ ____ ____
3. Read all questions thoroughly, noting important words ____ ____ ____ ____
4. Answer the questions you know first ____ ____ ____ ____
5. Proofread exams carefully ____ ____ ____ ____
6. Show all your work on quantitative exams ____ ____ ____ ____
7. Use what you have learned from the test itself to help answer difficult questions ____ ____ ____ ____
8. Write brief outlines for essay questions ____ ____ ____ ____
9. Manage your time during an exam ____ ____ ____ ____
10. Come right to the point in essay answers; don't pad or digress, but do support your answer ____ ____ ____ ____

Lecture Note-Taking

1. Make notes into chapters with title at top ____ ____ ____ ____
2. Outline lecture notes as much as possible ____ ____ ____ ____
3. Be an active, aggressive note-taker ____ ____ ____ ____
4. Always attend lectures ____ ____ ____ ____
5. Take complete lecture notes ____ ____ ____ ____
6. Develop abbreviations and symbols for note-taking ____ ____ ____ ____
7. Put your own ideas into your lecture notes ____ ____ ____ ____
8. Write in ink and on one side of paper ____ ____ ____ ____
9. Revise notes within 24 hours ____ ____ ____ ____
10. Label notes in margin, cover notes, then learn, using labels as cues ____ ____ ____ ____
11. Write brief summaries of your notes ____ ____ ____ ____

Library Research

1. Know how to find books, articles, and other materials in the library ____ ____ ____ ____
2. Ask questions whenever you get confused or can't find something in the library ____ ____ ____ ____
3. Survey a book or article before taking research materials from it ____ ____ ____ ____
4. Evaluate how competently written your research sources are ____ ____ ____ ____

	1	2	3	4

Math and Problem-Solving Courses

1. Write in lecture notes both problems on blackboard and verbal explanations given by professor _____ _____ _____ _____
2. Make math strategy cards _____ _____ _____ _____
3. Make math fact cards _____ _____ _____ _____
4. Write definitions of math symbols and specialized vocabulary on definition sheets _____ _____ _____ _____

Memory

1. Look for a logical pattern of ideas in material you wish to remember _____ _____ _____ _____
2. Associate the unfamiliar with the familiar _____ _____ _____ _____
3. Make lists, diagrams, or "maps" of materials to be learned _____ _____ _____ _____
4. Write and recite when you study more than you read and listen _____ _____ _____ _____
5. Visualize and draw diagrams and pictures _____ _____ _____ _____
6. Think up your own examples _____ _____ _____ _____
7. Memorize facts for some classes _____ _____ _____ _____
8. Make up sentences, rhymes, or words to help you remember _____ _____ _____ _____
9. Memorize just before you go to sleep
10. Review every week or two _____ _____ _____ _____

Motivation

1. Have a reason for going to college _____ _____ _____ _____
2. Try difficult jobs to improve confidence _____ _____ _____ _____
3. Find something interesting in boring classes _____ _____ _____ _____
4. Work yourself out of dead ends _____ _____ _____ _____

Oral Reports

1. Give all oral reports in oral style _____ _____ _____ _____
2. Speak from a speech outline when giving an oral report _____ _____ _____ _____
3. Rehearse all oral presentations _____ _____ _____ _____
4. Enliven oral reports with visual aids _____ _____ _____ _____

Organizing Ideas

1. Perceive the organization of a course _____ _____ _____ _____
2. Perceive the organization of a lecture _____ _____ _____ _____
3. Perceive the organization of a book _____ _____ _____ _____

| | 1 | 2 | 3 | 4 |

4. Perceive the organization of a chapter   ____   ____   ____   ____

5. Organize your own ideas in writing a paper   ____   ____   ____   ____

6. Organize your own ideas in doing a speech or oral report   ____   ____   ____   ____

7. Organize material by topics on study sheets for exam preparing   ____   ____   ____   ____

8. Organize essay exam answers before you begin to write   ____   ____   ____   ____

Organizing Study Materials

1. Organize lecture notes, class materials, and reading materials so you can find them   ____   ____   ____   ____

Original Thinking

1. Put own ideas in [square brackets] in lecture notes   ____   ____   ____   ____

2. Write own ideas in margins and on flyleaves of textbooks   ____   ____   ____   ____

3. Write own ideas before doing research for a paper   ____   ____   ____   ____

4. Write own ideas on study sheets   ____   ____   ____   ____

5. Present original material in exam answers   ____   ____   ____   ____

6. Think about what you are learning both inside and outside of class   ____   ____   ____   ____

Reading

1. Survey a book before you read it   ____   ____   ____   ____

2. Survey a chapter before you read it   ____   ____   ____   ____

3. Identify the main idea in paragraph or section of material and note how it is developed   ____   ____   ____   ____

4. Jot down main ideas in margin   ____   ____   ____   ____

5. Note how ideas in a chapter are organized   ____   ____   ____   ____

6. Write summaries at end of each section of textbook material   ____   ____   ____   ____

7. Recite main points in a chapter as soon as you've read it   ____   ____   ____   ____

8. Isolate and define unfamiliar concepts in your textbooks   ____   ____   ____   ____

9. Take summary notes on library reading   ____   ____   ____   ____

10. Develop a range of reading and skimming speeds   ____   ____   ____   ____

Time Use

1. Learn during class time   ____   ____   ____   ____

2. Study when you're most alert   ____   ____   ____   ____

3. Use small amounts of time such as hours between classes   ____   ____   ____   ____

4. Find enough time to put in one, two, or three hours outside of class for every hour in class   ____   ____   ____   ____

           1   **2**   **3**   **4**

Vocabulary

1. Isolate, write on vocabulary sheets, and learn the specialized and general vocabulary for each course   —— —— —— ——
2. Know and use vocabulary terms when taking exams   —— —— —— ——
3. Use a dictionary regularly   —— —— —— ——

Writing Papers

1. Choose and narrow down to manageable size a subject for a paper   —— —— —— ——
2. Do some initial planning before you begin research   —— —— —— ——
3. Make a rough outline to guide research   —— —— —— ——
4. Take all research notes on cards   —— —— —— ——
5. Make note cards with direct quotes, paraphrases, and your own ideas   —— —— —— ——
6. Make an outline to guide your writing
7. Compose rapidly when writing a paper   —— —— —— ——
8. Revise for organization, sentence structure, words, and punctuation   —— —— —— ——
9. Read paper aloud when revising   —— —— —— ——
10. Proofread all written work for mechanical errors   —— —— —— ——

USE THE RIGHT STUDY EQUIPMENT

A job is easier to do when you have the equipment that is needed to do the task efficiently. The "Study Equipment Checklist" may include some items that you need to purchase.

Study Equipment Checklist

Put checks in front of the items you own.

_____ Desk or table		_____ Notebook	
_____ Desk chair		_____ Notebook paper	
_____ Reading lamp		_____ Typing paper	
_____ Required textbooks		_____ Index cards	
_____ Dictionary		_____ Pencils	
_____ Calculator		_____ Pens	
_____ Pencil sharpener		_____ Highlight pens	
_____ Paper clips		_____ Eraser	
_____ Transparent tape		_____ Rubber bands	
_____ Stapler and staples		_____ Staple remover	
_____ Ruler		_____ Scissors	
_____ Hole punch		_____ Clock or watch	

- You can add paper to a ring binder. As a result, you can always have enough paper in your notebook for courses in which teachers give many long lectures.

- A ring binder is a safe place to keep materials your teachers distribute.

- If you are absent, you can insert notes you copy from a classmate exactly where they belong.

- You can have an assignment section in a ring binder, so you don't have to have a separate assignment book.

When a desk is too small to accommodate a ring binder comfortably, remove some paper from the binder at home, take notes on loose-leaf paper that you carry in a folder with double pockets, and insert the notes where they belong in your ring binder when you return home.

If you decide to use spiral notebooks, it is a good idea to purchase a separate notebook for each class. Buy notebooks with pockets on the inside covers so you will have a place to keep papers your teachers distribute. Write the names of your courses in large print on the outside front covers of your notebooks to ensure that you take the right notebooks to your classes.

STRATEGIES FOR TEST TAKING

   a.   The longest multiple-choice answer is often correct.

   b.   The most complete and inclusive multiple-choice answer is often correct.

   c.   A multiple-choice answer in the middle, especially one with the most words, is often correct.

   d.   If two multiple-choice answers have the opposite meaning, one of them is probably correct.

   e.   Answers with qualifiers, such as *generally, usually, probably, most often, some, may,* and *sometimes*, are usually correct.

   f.   Answers with absolute words, such as *all, always, everyone, everybody, never, no one, nobody, none*, and *only*, are usually incorrect.

General Tips Before An Exam

   1.   Study right before sleep.

   2.   Take materials needed to the exam.

   3.   Be on time for the exam.

   4.   Sit in a quiet spot.

   5.   Read all directions carefully.

   6.   Budget your time.

Getting Ready for Objective Exams

   1.   Memorize as necessary.

   2.   Ask instructor about makeup of test.

   3.   Look at similar tests.

   4.   Review carefully all main points of course.

   5.   Make up practice test items.

Taking Objective Exams

   1.   Answer all easier questions first.

   2.   Do difficult questions in time remaining.

   3.   Answer all questions.

   4.   Ask instructor to explain unclear items.

   5.   For difficult questions, think of the instructor's point of view.

   6.   Mark key words in difficult questions.

7. State difficult questions in your own words.

8. Use all the time given.
   Use the specific hints given for multiple-choice, true-false, fill-in, and matching questions.

ACTIVITY

Practice the basic strategy for answering multiple-choice questions by circling the correct answers to the following questions.

1. Scotch, wine, and vodka are
   a. drinks for kids.
   b. reddish in color.
   c. healthful foods.
   d. alcoholic beverages.

2. The bass drum and triangle are
   a. melodic instruments
   b. made mostly of metal.
   c. percussion instruments.
   d. band instruments.

3. Tuna and sardines are
   a. saltwater fish.
   b. large fish.
   c. flying fish.
   d. equally popular.

4. Baseball, hockey, and basketball are
   a. usually played outdoors.
   b. the most popular sports.
   c. played on a field.
   d. three team sports.

5. Sofa, chairs, and benches are
   a. furniture for sitting.
   b. pieces of furniture
   c. cloth-covered furniture.
   d. four-legged furniture.

6. Los Angeles and San Francisco are
   a. well-known cities.
   b. cities in California.
   c. cities of the United States.
   d. known for trolley cars.

7.   *Time* and *Newsweek* are
     a. sold only in the United States.
     b. two news magazines.
     c. the best-selling magazines.
     d. little-known magazines.

Practice the basic strategy for answering true-false questions. All the following statements are true except the ones that state a reason.

T   F   1.   People gain one additional pound of body weight for every 3,500 calories they consume but do not use in physical activity.

T   F   2.   The number of physicians in the United States is increasing more rapidly than the population.

T   F   3.   The reason colleges require students to take physical education courses is so they will enjoy watching athletic competition more when they are older.

T   F   4.   Over half of the world's known tungsten reserves are located in China.

T   F   5.   Americans today enjoy longer life spans mainly because of genetic factors.

T   F   6.   Patients should not ask doctors questions because this develops poor relationships between doctors and patients.

T   F   7.   The Old Testament does not report an incident in which a woman was put to death for sleeping with a man other than her husband.

T   F   8.   Since the family (a group) is an important agent of socialization, children find it difficult to function as individuals in society.

T   F   9.   Social change usually lags behind scientific and technological change.

T   F   10. College freshmen are more romantic than college seniors.

T   F   11. New Delhi is a better location for the capital of India than Calcutta because it is a better outlet for international commerce and trade.

T   F   12. There are at least seven thousand people in the United States who are more than one hundred years old.

T   F   13. The reason Tropical Africa has a very good agricultural economy is that there is a very long growing season there.

T   F   14. Most of the parents who abuse their children actually need them and love them.

T   F   15. Group health insurance policies are better than individual policies because they are less expensive and cover more types of illness and injury.

T   F   16. There are approximately 25,000 different occupations available for workers in the United States.

STUDY TIPS

The following study tips will enable you to maximize your academic potential.

Developing your study skills can make the passage to college life considerably easier. The attitude and approach to classes are different in college; classes do not meet every day and many classes are so large that the professors cannot monitor progress as closely as teachers could in high school. Because you won't be able to rely on your parents and teachers to check your school work and enforce your study habits, you must discipline yourself to do the work.

STRATEGIES TO IMPROVE YOUR ABILITY TO CONCENTRATE

Definite Study Periods start by making your study periods short, and planning brief periods of rest or relaxation in between.

Good Physical Conditions to study can help considerably in your efforts to work effectively on a schedule and accomplish what you want to do.

1. The best place to study is at a table or desk that is clean and clear of everything not connected with the work.

2. You should have good lighting that floods the entire working area.

3. The table or desk you use should face the wall or be away from other people or objects in the room.

Where to Study

Whenever you can find the best combination of conditions at just described, this is the place to study.

If you have a room all to yourself that you can arrange to meet these conditions, and if it is located in a quiet area where other people will not distract you with their noise or conversation, that is a good place.

Suggestions for Helping You Study

1. Budget your time.

2. Listen in class.

3. Preview the material before reading.

4. Have a definite study period.

5. Have adequate conditions of study.

6. Develop good note-taking skills.

7. Improve concentration skills.

8. Remember the SQ3R's, SQ4R's, and the SOAR study formula.

ACTIVITY

Budgeting Your Time Wisely

Prepare a list of what you need to do next week. Include chores, social obligations, and other things you want to accomplish.

Things To Do Next Week

_____

_____

_____

_____

_____

_____

_____

_____

_____

_____

_____

_____

_____

_____

_____

Bibliography

Deese, James and Morgan, Clifford T. *How to Study*. New York. McGraw-Hill Book Company, 1970.

 Friday, Robert A. *Create Your College Success*. Belmont, California. Wadsworth Publishing Company, Inc., 1988.

Langon, John. *Reading and Study Skills*. New York. McGraw-Hill Book Company, 1989.

Park, Walter. *How to Study in College*. Boston. Houghton Mifflin Company, 4th ed., 1989.

Shepherd, James F. *College Study Skills*. Boston. Houghton Mifflin Company, 1985.

Shephere, James. *The Houghton Mifflin Study Skills Handbook*. Boston. Houghton Mifflin Company, 1982.

Usova, George M. *Efficient Study Strategies*. Pacific Grove, California. Brooks/Cole Publishing Company, 1989.

GLOSSARY

Abilities

Absolute

Achievement tests

Acronym

Active listening

Affixes

Analysis

Antonym

Anxiety

Appendix

Aptitude tests

Author order

Base word

Bibliography

Blue book

Call number

Card catalog

Causes

Comparison

Comprehensive tests

Contrast

Copyright page

Course outline

Derivative

Diagnostic tests

Diagram

Direction word

Discussion

Distractor

Effects

Endnote

Essay question

Evaluate

Example

Extreme modifier

Exposition

Fact

Fill-in Question

Footnote

Glossary

Guide words

Highlighting

Index

Infer

Interest

Interest Inventory

Introduction

Long-term goal

Matching questions

Memorization

Memory

Mental block

Motivation

Newspaper Index

Option

Organization

Outline

Paraphrase

Pictorial ads

Plagiarism

Preface

Prefix

Prime study time

Priorities

Preview

Reading

Reading Rate

Reciting

Reference area

Reserve books

Reviewing

Rewards

Sentence Completion questions

Sequence

Short-term goal

Skill

Skim

SQ3R

SQ4R

Stem

Study cards

Study guide

Studying

Study notes

Subject label

Suffix

Summary

Survey of a book

Standardized test

Syllabus

Table

Table of contents

Take-home test

Terminology

Test anxiety

Textbook

Time control

Title page

Topic sentence

True-False questions

Underlining

Attending Classes

Overview

College is a time of choices or options and freedom-attendant to this premise is how you use opportunities. Attending class can be a freedom in that many professors allow you to cut but expect you to keep up on your assignments and related academic work.

Objectives

1. Class attendance assist students in the development of areas of personal discipline.

2. To develop desirable attitudes toward educational pursuits.

3. To facilitate wholesome adjustment to the educational program through class attendance.

    Most college professors do not endorse the practice of coercing students to come to class. They relate to students who desire to be there and participate in a wholesome learning experience. In addition, most professors accept the idea that college students are young adults who are free to make choices— including the choice of attending class with the learning chances being improved.

There are many reasons:

1. You're paying for them. Even if you're on a scholarship or your family is footing the bill, you're paying for classes by spending years of your life in college. Time is your most precious asset.

2. Much of what you learn in college stems from personal interaction with professors, not textbooks. Professors not only know about subjects: they represent their disciplines. That is, your chemistry teacher is a chemist as well as a teacher. You have the opportunity to get to know someone who is devoted to chemistry and may help advance the field. As a rule, we should enjoy relating to people who are successful in our chosen fields. In other words, if you don't enjoy relating to chemists, you may not be suited for a career in chemistry.

3. You give your professors a chance to get to know you, which can influence them to think positively about you. *Trap*: If you're going to snooze or chat with neighbors in class, you may be better advised not to attend. The professor will probably develop a negative attitude toward you if you show up to write letters and do your nails rather than learn.

4. Professors tend to highlight the key terms and concepts. They often explain essential terms and give examples. If you don't catch on at first, you have the opportunity to ask questions—something you can't do with a textbook or with a friend's notes.

5. Attending classes gives you an opportunity to get inside your professors' minds to figure out what they consider most important. This helps on tests and perhaps helps you understand the subject matter better. Look for cues (and clues) such as the professor's saying. "The major reason that . . ." "The important thing to know about this is that . . ." "My view is that . . ."

6. Attending classes is an efficient use of time. It might take you two or three times as long to learn the same amount of subject matter from the textbook or from a friend's notes. Even then, you won't be sure about what your professor considers important. *By investing time in class, you may wind up saving time.*

Focusing Your Attention

So you've decided to come to class. (Pat on the back.) What do you do now? You pay attention. Paying attention in class or in the lecture hall is not like paying attention elsewhere. When we listen to our friends at lunch, we're often thinking more about the food or watching the leaves turning and falling outside the cafeteria window. When we listen to our families at home, sometimes we're filtering their words through the blabber of the television set. But if we give our professors only part of our attention, if we allow ourselves to drift, we may be squandering time and losing the chance to gather information that can help us "ace" the course.

The point is that listening in class should be goal-oriented and purposeful not passive. Even though your professor may be doing most or all of the talking, you can be an alert, dynamic seeker and integrator of information.

What *can* you do to focus your attention on the lecture? Many things.

HEAD OFF ATTITUDE PROBLEMS First, head off possible attitude problems with courses you may not particularly like. Rather than thinking, "Ugh, I hate this course," think something like, "I may not be crazy about this course, but the subject matter is part of my general education." Also remind yourself that the grade for the course is important. Connect it to your eventual goal of landing a good job or getting into graduate school, both of which can be highly competitive. Moreover, your attitude about the course may change as you find out more about it.

You can work toward changing your attitudes about the course by relating the subject matter to your own life. Doesn't the discussion of social stratification in sociology relate to your own family's background? Doesn't the discussion of compound interest in math relate to your own eventual retirement funds? Doesn't the discussion of neurotransmitters in biology relate to your own changes in mood? Later we shall see that relating material to things you already know not only motivates you, but also helps you remember it.

SIT FRONT AND CENTER! Second, sit front and center (and hope everyone else in the class isn't following the same advice!). In this location, the professor's voice will be loudest. Audiovisual displays will be clearest. You will have the opportunity to make eye contact with the professor. Nodding off, writing a letter to a friend, and talking to the person sitting next to you are also most likely to be noticed by the professor when you sit up front, so you re less likely to fall into these traps.

PREVIEW LECTURE MATERIAL

Third, preview the material to be discussed in the class. Check the syllabus or course outline to see what topic or topics will be covered. Or ask your professor what will be covered next time at the end of the class.

Leafing through the pages of a "whodunit" to identify the killer is a guaranteed way to destroy the impact of a mystery novel, but it can help you learn class and textbook material. Many textbooks have devices that can help you survey the material, such as chapter outlines, section heads, and chapter summaries. In a literary work, it makes sense to begin at the beginning and read page by page. But with textbooks, it is usually more effective first to examine the chapter outlines, skim the minor heads not covered in the outlines, and read the summaries. Familiarity with the skeletons or advance organizers of the chapters provides you with frameworks for mastering the meat of the chapters.

If you don't have time to read the whole chapter before class, at least check the chapter outline (or table of contents for the chapter) or read the chapter summary. Thus, you will enter the class with the bare bones of the material in mind and be prepared to flesh it out.

QUESTIONNAIRE

Reasons for Not Paying Attention in Class

Over the years we have collected reasons students have given us for not paying attention in class. For a while we were going to donate them to a museum of excuses but we thought better of it and saved them for this questionnaire.

In completing this questionnaire, consider each of the following reasons. Write a checkmark if you have ever used the reason, or a similar reason, for not paying attention. Then there's room for you to add reasons you've used that aren't on the list. When you are finished, see the following "What-Do-You-Do-Now?" exercise.

_____ 1. An important practice session is coming up for the big game.

_____ 2. I drank too much beer last night.

_____ 3. I'm way ahead in this course.

_____ 4. I'm way behind in this course.

_____ 5. The trees outside the window are really gorgeous at this time of year.

_____ 6. I really don't want to be in college

_____ 7. I have to write that letter to.

_____ 8. I'm wiped out from that all-nighter.

_____ 9. I'm never going to use the subject matter in this course anyhow.

_____ 10. I got an F on the last test, so what's the point?

_____ 11. I got an A on the last test, so what's the point?

_____ 12. My girlfriend (boyfriend) is angry with me.

_____ 13. Everything's going great with my girlfriend (boyfriend).

_____ 14. I hurt my knee during the track meet.

_____ 15. The carburetor has to be fixed.

_____ 16. I'm starved!

_____17. I'm stuffed!

_____18. I didn't get the part-time job at the hamburger place.

_____19. The professor is a bore.

_____20. I don't know what the professor's talking about.

_____21. I know what the professor's talking about.

_____22. I didn't read the chapter in time for class.

_____23. I'm sitting all the way in the back of the room.

_____24. I have to study for a test in another course.

_____25. I have to listen to the nerd sitting next to me who wants to tell me about the weekend.

_____26. It's 8:00 in the morning!

_____27. It's just before lunch (dinner) and I'm starved!

Now it's your turn. Add your own reasons here. Then go on to the following "What-Do-You-Do-Now?" exercise.

_____28. _____
          _____

_____29. _____
          _____

_____30. _____
          _____

WHAT DO YOU DO NOW?

Changing Attitudes that Encourage you to Cut Classes and Allow Your Attention to Wander

Now you have identified some reasons for not paying attention in your classes. The following exercise will help you to challenge them and see if they're accurate or if they're simply excuses for sloughing off.

Let's say that you find yourself thinking, *I don't know what the professor's talking about,* and so you drift off in class. Here we have a self-defeating way of responding that can pervade every area of life—not just college. Rather than evading the classroom challenge, you can take charge of the situation—and your life—by thinking: "What can I do so that I will know what the professor is talking about? How can I better prepare myself for class? I'm letting events control me rather than taking charge of things myself."

A couple of additional examples of self-defeating attitudes and suggested alternatives follow. Then there's some space for you to list excuses and attitudes that have been getting in your way and alternatives that you come up with.

Excuses and Attitudes That Encourage You to Cut Classes and Allow Your Attention to Wander	Alternative Attitudes That Encourage You to Make Optimal Use of Classes
"This Professor is a bore"	So if I wanted entertainment, I should have stayed home watching soap operas and listening to the stereo all day. The issue is whether I can gather information from class that will help me get good grades and get on with my life."
"I have no idea what's going on in this class. So why bother?"	"So it's time to make a decision rather than just let things happen to me. I have to figure out what the problem is. Maybe I should get some tutoring or work harder. I've got to make concrete plans to do better.
Now write in the attitudes that are causing you problems, and suggest some alternatives:	
_____	_____
_____	_____
_____	_____
_____	_____
_____	_____
_____	_____
_____	_____

PICK OUT KEY TERMS AND CONCEPTS Fourth, pay particular attention to new vocabulary in the text. If you check the meanings of these terms before class, you will follow class discussion better. Even if the professor carefully defines new terms, the professor's efforts will allow you to check the accuracy of your definitions and will reinforce your memory. If the professor uses a new term without explaining it, ask for a definition. If necessary, ask the professor to provide some examples of usage of the term. *Don t worry about looking ignorant. You are in college to learn. Moreover, if you didn't understand the term, other students might not have grasped it either.*

REVIEW Fifth, reread or at least skim the notes from the previous lecture before class. They will fine-tune your expectations for the lecture and set the lecture within your growing understanding of the subject.

Participating

It may not be possible to have discussions in large lecture halls, but it is valuable to participate in regular classroom meetings or in discussion sections. Discussion sections—also referred to as recitation sections—frequently accompany large lecture sections. The professor may lecture 120 or 1,000 students in lectures that are held once or twice weekly. But students may then discuss the material and take tests in small groups that are led by teaching assistants (TA's). TA's are usually graduate students who are earning their way through their programs by assisting in classes or laboratories.

There are excellent reasons for participating in discussion groups, even if you're not graded on class participation.

1. Knowing that you will be participating encourages you to preview the material and to take notes.

2. Participating helps you organize the subject matter in your mind as well as in your notes.

3. Participating provides you with practice in speaking before groups of peers (fellow students) and supervisors (in this case, professors or TA's). You develop skills that will help you in the "real world"—for example, in business meetings—after college.

4. Participating underscores your presence to the professor or TA. As noted earlier, this is a double-edged sword. When you make your presence known, you want to do so in an appropriate, helpful fashion. Most professors and TA's may grade you on the basis of assignments and tests, and not on the basis of whether or not they like you. But if you have a borderline grade, it doesn't hurt to have professors or TA's develop positive attitudes toward you. Both in academia and in the workplace, your performance may be evaluated on the basis of the general impression you make and the amount of effort you put in, as well as on your test scores (or on your job performance).

Improving Test Taking Skills

Overview

Students at Southern University, like their peers across the nation, are being confronted more and more by standardized tests. These tests are being used to determine such important aspects of one's life as scholarships, entrance into colleges and professional schools, jobs, promotions, etc. If you expect to be successful or even competitive, you must learn how to successfully perform on standardized tests. The suggestions included on this outline are designed to provide you with a basic guide for taking standardized tests. This information is general. There is no substitute for studying the specific materials available for any given test. If you practice these suggestions you will greatly enhance your performance on standardized tests.

Goal

Upon completion of this unit you will have been exposed to information and exercises that will help you to improve your performance on standardized tests.

Objectives

When you have successfully completed this unit you will:

1. be able to identify what the various tests are designed to measure.

2. initiate preparation for standardized test months in advance.

3. demonstrate the ability to read and follow directions accurately.

4. budget your time wisely, allowing you to complete the tests.

5. use logical reasoning to answer multiple choice items.

6. determine when guessing is appropriate.

TEST-TAKING TIPS

Please get a sheet of paper and follow the directions:

1. Read all of the directions before doing anything else.

2. Write your name in the upper right-hand corner of the paper.

3. Fold the paper in half, lengthwise.

4. Write your name on the outside of the folded paper.

5. Print the letters of the alphabet beneath your name.

6. Open the paper up and write your teacher's name beneath your name.

7. Place your folded paper on the floor.

8. Do not do anything asked for in 2 through 7. Raise both hands up and smile. Do not say anything.

Hopefully, you followed the directions before taking this test. It could have prevented you from looking very foolish!

The previous exercise demonstrates the importance of following directions; following directions is one of several skills necessary for successful test-taking. The test-taking tips presented are not designed to serve as a substitute for knowledge. These tips, however, are designed to assist persons who may have difficulty taking tests or who may tend to lose points because of carelessness.

There are several areas that tend to cause persons to score poorly on tests. These areas are:

1. improper attitude toward testing

2. lack of general preparation for testing

3. not reading and following directions of tests

4. careless marking of answer sheets during tests

5. not managing time during tests

6. not understanding what is read on tests

7. poor guessing on tests

8. not using logical reasoning on tests

9. not changing wrong answers on tests

10. not recognizing question formats

Improper attitude toward testing

A person's life is a series of tests. Athletic tournaments, job evaluations, even interviews are tests. Realize that testing is a part of life and your approach to test taking will be more positive. School is the place where these skills can be developed and refined.

Lack of general preparation for a test

Two of the least effective methods of preparing for tests are cramming and "all nighters." A person should regularly review the material and begin studying several days prior to the exam. The night before is not the time to begin learning new material. A person should get a good night's sleep and eat a light breakfast prior to the test. These practices help to lower the stress.

Not managing time

Good test takers budget their time wisely. Each question is worth the same amount of points on the majority of standardized tests; it is important not to spend too much time on the first part of the test at the expense of the last part. Remember:

- If you work too fast, you make careless mistakes

- If you work too slowly, you may not have time to finish

Here are some ways to help you budget your time:

1. Find out how much time you have to finish the test. Check yourself with a clock or watch.

2. Before beginning the test, scan through it to see the number and types of questions. This will help you to budget your time.

3. Set up a schedule for working through the test. Work as quickly and as carefully as possible. Answer the easier questions first; skip the harder ones and return to them later. When you finish the test, always review it. At the end of the first half of the testing period, you should be at least halfway through the test.

Not understanding what you read

Most tests involve some reading. How well you read the test can make a difference in how well you score. These are important points to keep in mind when reading the test:

1. Read and follow all directions very carefully.

2. After reading a question, stop and think about what is being asked. If you are not sure, reread the question. If you are still not sure, go on to the next question and come back to this one later.

3. Be on the lookout for small but important words like only, always, all, and may. These words indicate that some exceptions may be possible. Examples of other key words are no, not, and none. These words are easily overlooked and can change the meaning of the question. For example:

    _____A desert *may* be
       1. cold
       2. dry
       3. hot
       4. all of the above

    _____ Which of the following cities is *not* in the United States?
       1. London
       2. Houston
       3. Los Angeles
       4. New York

4. Read for a purpose. Instead of simply reading words, read for ideas. Stress comprehension over speed.

Poor guessing

When you take tests, there may be some test questions which you are not able to answer. This is not surprising; the people who make standardized tests include some very difficult questions which they really do not expect all students to be able to answer. If you are not sure whether or not you should guess, ask your teacher how the test will be scored. Most standardized tests that you will be taking do not have a "penalty" for guessing. This means that the wrong answers are not subtracted from the number of right answers. So unless there is penalty, go ahead and guess at questions you don't know. You can only help your score. Here are some tips to guessing:

1. After reading the question, read each of the possible answers.

2. Some of the answers will look wrong to you. Eliminate all those answers that you know are incorrect. This should leave you with two or three possible answers that may seem right.

3. If you still are not sure of the answer after eliminating one or two answers, make the best educated guess you can (the one you *think* is right).

4. If you read all the possible answers and they all seem right, go ahead and make a stab at the answer. If there is no penalty for guessing, you have nothing to lose and everything to gain. *Don't leave any question unanswered.*

Not using logical reasoning

You may be able to find the right answers to difficult questions on a test if you are willing to work at them. So don't give up on a question because it *looks* too difficult or asks about things that are not familiar to you. You may be able to "reason out" the correct answer by using the following strategies:

1. Eliminate the answers that you know are wrong. Choose your answer from the choices that are left.

2. Compare the possible answers with each other. Eliminate choices that have the *same* meaning. For example:
   a. Rhode Island is smaller than Texas
   b. Texas is smaller than Rhode island
   c. Rhode Island has more land area than Texas
   d. Rhode Island is larger than Texas

Choices b, c, and d all have the same meaning (Rhode Island is larger than Texas). So, you should be able to eliminate these choices and choose "a" as the correct answer.

3. Generally, choosing the answer that *includes two or more* of the choices is a safe bet, particularly if you know the meaning of one of the words. For example:

The word *myth* is synonomous with
   a. legend
   b. lyric
   c. tale
   d. both a and c

If you do not know the meaning of the word myth, legend, or lyric, but you know the meaning of the word tale, then there is a greater than average chance that "d" is the correct choice.

Not changing wrong answers

Do not be afraid to change your answer, if you think you should. Some people think that their first response is the best. But research studies show that *students get more items right than wrong when they change their answers.*

So if you have a fairly good reason why your second choice may be better than your first choice, go ahead and change your answer. You will get more questions right in the long run.

These test-taking tips are not of much value if you don't study before the test. They are designed to help maximize your ability in communicating the material you have learned.

Practice Exercise:

Directions: Read the following directions before continuing. The questions below differ from the preceding questions in that they all contain the words *not, least,* or *except.* So that you fully understand the basis that is to be used in selecting each answer, be sure to read each question carefully.

1. Which of the following is the *least* important consideration in establishing criteria for the certification of teachers?
    a. Research findings regarding teaching
    b. The demands of special–interest groups
    c. The requirements of state constitutions and legislatures
    d. The needs of learners
    e. The needs of society

2. According to current theory and professional practice, it is appropriate to assign homework in all of the following circumstances *except* when
    a. the assignment is made because of inappropriate conduct in class
    b. a class assignment expected to be finished in school is not finished
    c. a special arrangement has been made for parents to assist their child in a weak skill area.
    d. a child has asked to be able to earn bonus points as part of a special lesson
    e. a child needs additional practice to develop a skill that requires memorization

3. A teacher who restricts a student's expression or personal style probably is *not* violating the student's constitutional rights if the student is
    a. causing serious disruption of the learning environment
    b. violating the dress code developed by a duly elected student government
    c. offending the moral values of some other students in the school
    d. opposing the foreign policy of the United States government
    e. advocating the overthrow of the United States government

4. A teacher's sponsorship of which of the following student activities could *least* easily be defended in the face of parent or community protest?
    a. Discussing the issues in a local political campaign
    b. Assisting the League of Women Voters in urging citizens to register to vote
    c. Extending an invitation to candidates in a local election to address the class
    d. Having the class vote to decide which of two local candidates the class will actively campaign for
    e. Holding a mock presidential campaign and election

5. Which of the following classroom characteristics is *least* likely to influence the nature of social interaction in the classroom?
    a. Location of the room
    b. Size of the room
    c. Location of the teacher's desk
    d. Arrangement of the students' desks
    e. Placement of learning centers

6. Since the Civil War in the United States, all of the following have at one time or another been major objectives of groups seeking civil rights for Blacks *except*
    a. passage of affirmative–action legislation
    b. desegregation of public educational facilities
    c. passage of the Thirteenth, Fourteenth, Fifteenth, and Twenty-fourth Amendments to the Constitution
    d. creation of a third party in national politics
    e. passage of antilynching laws

Directions: Each of the questions or incomplete statements below is followed by five suggested answers or completions. Select the one that is best in each case and then fill in the corresponding lettered space on the answer sheet with a heavy, dark mark so that you cannot see the letter. Remember, try to answer every question.

7. All of the following statements about nutrition are correct *except*:
    a. During pregnancy, proper nutrition for the mother protects the unborn child.
    b. Only carbohydrates count when a reducing diet is being planned.
    c. Obesity is a major health risk among United States residents.
    d. Cooking food destroys some nutrients.
    e. Lack of iron is the most common mineral deficiency among women in the United States.

8. In the nineteenth century, the English sparrow was introduced into the United States. Within 65 years it had become common in almost all of the states. Factors that contributed to the sparrow's success in the United States probably included all of the following *except*
    a. appropriate locations for nesting
    b. availability of food
    c. suitable range of temperatures
    d. suitable moisture conditions
    e. absence of all natural enemies

9. Which of the following statements represents the most economically sound strategy to apply in consuming the energy resources of coal, oil, wood, and solar energy?
    a. For as long as possible, we should use all four sources as nearly equally as possible in meeting energy needs.
    b. Emphasis should be placed on the most renewable resource.
    c. Energy requirements should be met by using coal since coal reserves are very extensive.
    d. Decisions on the use of energy resources should be based solely on current costs.
    e. Oil should be used as long as it is available since it is so easily transported by pipelines.

10. The observation of which of the following properties of an unknown material would support the hypothesis that the material represented a life form?

I. Cellular structure

II. Metabolic functions

III. Crystalline structure
   a. I only
   b. III only
   c. I and II only
   d. II and III only
   e. I, II, and III

11. After coming to school one day, a middle-school teacher begins to feel ill. Professionally responsible procedures that the teacher could follow until a substitute arrives include which of the following:

I. Assigning primarily written work that requires little direction

II. Having students do library research

III. Allowing students to work on individual projects or in small groups

IV. Appointing student monitors to handle discipline
   a. I and II only
   b. II and III only
   c. III and IV only
   d. I, II, and III only
   e. I, II, III, and IV

Directions: Each of the questions of incomplete statements below is followed by five suggested answers or completions. Select the one that is best in each case and then fill in the corresponding lettered space on the answer sheet with a heavy, dark mark so that you cannot see the letter. Remember, try to answer every question.

12. In each of the following, if the solid bar () represents $200,000, in which case does the striped bar () most likely represent $300,000?

   a. ▰▰▰
      ▱▱▱

   b. ▰▰
      ▱▱▱

   c. ▰▰
      ▱▱▱▱▱

   d. ▰▰
      ▱▱▱▱▱▱

   e. ▰▰▰
      ▱▱▱▱▱▱▱▱

13. On the dial below, the arrow points most nearly to which of the following readings?

    a. 11-1/2
    b. 15
    c. 20-1/2
    d. 25
    e. 30

    If M is twice N, then N is
    a. one-half M
    b. twice M
    c. two less than M
    d. two more than M
    e. M minus one-half

Questions 14–15 are based on the following cartoon.

14. The cartoon illustrates an economic condition known as
    a. inflation
    b. tight money
    c. overproduction
    d. a stock market collapse
    e. a trade war

15. In a period characterized by the condition depicted in the cartoon, which of the following persons would be economically the worst off?
    a. A disabled person living on a fixed income
    b. A retired federal employee whose pension is subject to a cost-of-living adjustment
    c. A person engaged in importing and exporting goods
    d. A bank officer
    e. A person who borrowed a substantial sum of money several years ago.

EVALUATION

Having completed this section on taking standardized tests, complete the following questions. Select the letter of the most appropriate answer.

1. All of the following represent areas that tend to cause persons to score poorly on tests except:
    a. improper attitude toward testing
    b. failure to read and follow directions
    c. lack of general preparation
    d. managing time wisely

2. Two of the least effective methods of preparing for tests are:
    a. reviewing regularly and studying in advance
    b. getting a good night's sleep and eating a light breakfast
    c. cramming and "all nighters"
    d. reviewing basic math and reading extensively

3. Which of the following does not apply to following directions:
    a. Do not assume you know what is being asked.
    b. Ask for assistance if needed
    c. Quickly skim over directions
    d. Do exactly what the directions tell you to do!

4. All of the following should be included in budgeting your time except:
    a. Find out how much time you have left to finish the test
    b. Before beginning the test, scan through it to see the types of questions
    c. Skip the harder questions and return to them later
    d. Spend a lot of time on the first part of the test

5. Which of the following are small words that indicate exceptions that may affect the answer of a question?
    a. only
    b. always
    c. may
    d. all of the above

6. If you are not sure about some questions you may guess if:
    a. you think you are good at guessing
    b. there is no "penalty" for guessing
    c. you want to take a chance
    d. none of the above

7. When you "reason out" the correct answer to a difficult question you are:
    a. guessing
    b. using a positive attitude
    c. recognizing formats of questions
    d. using logical reasoning

8. Eliminate the statements that have the same meaning: Which answer is left?
   a. Rhode Island is smaller than Texas
   b. Texas is smaller than Rhode Island
   c. Rhode Island has more land area than Texas
   d. Rhode Island is larger than Texas

9. When reading directions which of the following are words that change meaning?
   a. not
   b. least
   c. except
   d. all of the above

10. When studying for a standardized test one should:
    a. Keep the ultimate exam in mind
    b. Practice on sample tests
    c. Improve on vocabulary, spelling, grammar, etc.
    d. All of the above

Additional Test Strategies:

1. Determine where and when the next test will be held and what material will be covered. The course syllabus frequently offers some information, so check there first. But the syllabus may only offer dates and not indicate what you need to know.

2. If you and other students must take another test on the same day, ask if your professor would mind moving the test back a class.

3. Ask what types of questions will appear on the test. This question is most important before the first test, when you don't know what to expect. There are different strategies for answering short-answer and essay questions, and it helps to know what's coming.

4. Ask your instructor what will be most important for you to know, and check with students who have already taken the course to determine the sources of test questions—chapters in the text, lecture notes, student study guides, old exams, and so on. Old tests are valuable sources of information. They show the type of question that the professor likes to ask on a topic, and professors often repeat questions, even when they are making them up for each test. (There are just so many ways to phrase questions on a topic!) Fraternities and sororities frequently file old tests. If these tests are not available to you, go to the instructor and say, "Several students in the class are studying your old tests in the fraternity and sorority test files. Would you allow me to look over some of your old examinations so that I'm not at a disadvantage?" Fair is fair.

5. "Psych out" tests by generating possible test questions from the reading assignments and your notes. If you're going to have multiple-choice questions, ask yourself what kinds of distractors (e.g., things that are only partly true) the professor might use.

6. Plan study periods during which you will generate questions from lecture notes, old exams, the student study guide, and so on.

7. Plan for weekly study periods during which you will compose and take practice tests. During these practice tests, define the key terms. Explain how they relate to one another. Outline the answers to practice essay questions, setting down key words in your outlines.

8. Take the practice quizzes and tests in the student study guide. Many instructors reinforce use of the study guide by adopting some exam questions from them. The authors of the study guide also try to provide questions that cover the main points of each topic.

9. Arrange study groups in which students share possible test questions and quiz one another. Answering essay questions verbally is excellent preparation for writing them. This type of group also offers social stimulation (which is an incentive for being there) and social support. But beware: When study groups seem in danger of degenerating into bull sessions or Let's-go-out-for-pizza-now-that-we've-studied-for-15-minutes groups, bow out and prepare for tests on your own.

10. Keep a diary or log in which you record your progress, including when, where, and how long you study, and how well you perform on practice tests. A diary motivates you to perform more consistently and helps point out your weak spots. It helps you keep in touch with whether or not you are achieving what you think you are achieving.

11. Write your name on the test! Yes, this means *you*.

12. Wise up! Become test-wise, that is: Know what to bring! Read the directions! Know how to be a good guesser on multiple-choice questions! Know how to make a good impression on essay questions, even when you're not sure of the material! Many instructors and students believe that there is something underhanded about being test-wise. They argue that if you study hard and learn the material, you shouldn't have to worry about other ways of making a good impression or about "tricks." They are not necessarily wrong. However, test-wiseness also helps you optimize the presentation of what you know. And there's something else: If you're not test-wise, you can bet that other students in the class will be. And when grades depend on your performance relative to theirs, why be at a disadvantage? Again: Fair is fair.

Which brings us to our next point—what to bring to a test.

WHAT TO BRING

One of the most concise ways of informing your instructor that you're not a serious student is to ask to borrow a pencil or a pen during a test. This is the message you communicate: "I'm not prepared. I don't take this seriously. I'm in college because somebody put me here, not because I have concrete goals and want to be here."

So: Be prepared, whether or not you're a Boy Scout. Here are the types of things to bring to quizzes and tests:

- *Sharpened pencils.* The old standard number 2 pencils are ideal for electronic scoring methods.

- *Pens.* Pens should be blue or black because these colors are legible and create the impression that you are a serious student. Green is also possible because it's bright and doesn't look frivolous. Red and orange do look frivolous. Professors also like to use red and orange to grade papers and make comments, so they're out.

- *Paper.* You should always have 8 1/2-by-11-inch loose leaf paper available, if only as scrap paper. Some professors or institutions provide "blue books" for examinations: others require that you purchase them in the bookstore and bring them to essay examinations. Even when they are provided in class, it can be helpful to bring along a couple of extra blue books.

- *A watch.* You want to keep track of time, and there may not be a strategically placed clock in the testing room.

- *A dictionary.* Ask the professor whether you can use a pocket dictionary so that you can check your spelling (and be sure that you're using the right word) on essay questions. Simply asking the question will show that you are a serious student and make a positive impression. Professors in advanced foreign language courses will sometimes allow you to use foreign language-English dictionaries in writing essays. This is especially so when they are focusing on your knowledge of the literature of the language and your compositional abilities, rather than on your memorization of vocabulary.

- *Calculators and computers.* These may be allowed for math, science, and business tests, especially when the important issue is whether you know how to approach a problem, not how to do the calculations. Check with the instructor.

- *Formulas.* You may ask whether or not you can bring a list of formulas for math, science, and business tests. Some instructors believe that it is more important to know when and how to use a formula than to memorize it. If your instructor is one of them, you can focus your studying on applying formulas in practice problems, not on memorization.

Enhancing Your Vocabulary Skills

Overview

The primary aim of this section of your study guide is to help you enlarge your vocabulary. The most profound question one must ask is: why should I want to do this? There are many reasons for wanting to enlarge your vocabulary. One is that college students should have a broad vocabulary. Why? It helps you to read better, pass examinations, speak better, and makes employment opportunities better. But, perhaps the most important reason is that a good vocabulary makes you a better thinker. You will be better able to receive ideas and to communicate your ideas to others.

What can you do to improve your vocabulary? You can improve your vocabulary with this module because it will quickly enable you to understand roots, suffixes, and prefixes. You will learn that a knowledge of synonyms, antonyms, and analogies will almost magically multiply the number of words you have at your command. You will learn how our language includes foreign words and phrases and how a knowledge of these will increase your word power. Finally, you will become more aware of the words that should not be used in formal writing and speaking such as colloquialisms. Not only will you be better able to define new terms, but you will also learn an easy way to improve your ability to spell.

The improvement of vocabulary is the key that unlocks the door to better reading because you increase comprehension when you know the words that make up the composition.

Identifying Analogies

Overview

The enhancement of vocabulary skills must include the ability to identify and understand analogies. An analogy is a statement of comparison between two or more things that are different, but have something in common that makes them related or alike. There are various types of relationships expressed in analogies. Some of the types of relationships that are analogous will be used as examples in the activity outline that follows.

Student Objectives

The student will be able to communicate effectively by developing the vocabulary skill of identifying and understanding analogies, and the relationship between words.

ACTIVITY OUTLINE

The analogy may be expressed in various types of relationships. These are some examples:

1. Purpose to Function
   Scissors: cut: towel: dry

2. Time—Sequence
   Dawn: Twilight: Morning: Evening

3. Tool and User
   Scissors: Cloth: Knife: Bread

4. Part and Whole Relationship
   Toes: Foot: Fingers: Hand

5. Cause and Effect Relationship
   Laziness: Failure: Industriousness: Success

When you identify an analogy, you look for something which two very different things have in common. For example, a leaf is to a tree what a wheel is to a car. These two sets are completely different, but they have one thing in common. The leaf is part of a tree and the wheel is part of the car.

Now examine the relationship which is presented in this statement.

Red is to color as apple is to fruit.

Why is it an analogy? Red is a kind of color. Apple is a kind of fruit. There is a relationship between the two parts of the statement.

Magic Johnson is to basketball as Michael Jackson is to music. It is an analogy because Magic Johnson is a great star of basketball, and Michael Jackson is considered a great star of music.

SUGGESTED ACTIVITIES

For practice you can:

1. Look at sets of four words that are related and one word that does not belong because it is not related to the other four. Select the one that is not related.

2. Form word relationships and see whether other students can identify the relationship.

3. Perform exercises in analyzing word relationships from different content areas.

Evaluation

1. Teacher-Made Test

2. Observation of group work

3. Evaluation of exercises taken from reference books

EXAMPLE OF TEST

Directions: Check the word which completes the analogy.

1. Washington, D.C. is to the United States as Paris is to
   a. Europe
   b. London
   c. France
   d. DeGaulle

2. Nut is to tree as grapes are to
   a. bunch
   b. vine
   c. fruit
   d. jelly

3. A hospital is to doctor as a courtroom is to
   a. judge
   b. policeman
   c. detective
   d. criminal

4. Arena is to sport as theater is to
   a. city
   b. play
   c. actor
   d. audience

5. Wine is to grapes as
   a. cheese is to milk
   b. beef is to meat
   c. cake is to pie
   d. flour is to bread

6. Canoe is to Indian as
   a. ship is to captain
   b. car is to driver
   c. dog sled is to Eskimo
   d. sleigh is to reindeer

7. The Great Wall is to China as the Grand Canyon is to
   a. Arizona
   b. the Colorado River
   c. the desert
   d. America

8. A conductor is to an orchestra as
    a. a driver is to a bus
    b. an author is to a book
    c. a coach is to a team
    d. a make-up man is to an actor

9. Wall is to mortar as nation is to
    a. family
    b. people
    c. patriotism
    d. geography
    e. boundaries

10. Fish is to seal as
    a. elephant is to giraffe
    b. bird is to cage
    c. mouse is to cat
    d. snake is to frog

Synonyms and Antonyms

You can enhance your ability to communicate by increasing the number of words that you are able to use. Each word has a number of other words that have the same definition. By learning the words that mean the same, not only do you increase the number of words you now know, but you also add the beauty of variety that a good college student should have. Words that are pronounced differently, but have the same meaning are called synonyms. For example, *obsolete, antiquated, archaic*, and *obsolescent* all have the same meaning.

On the other hand, you can find just as many words that have just the opposite meaning. These words are called antonyms. The word "large" is an antonym of small, little, minute or tiny.

To increase your knowledge of antonyms and synonyms, you must own the best book on this subject, the thesaurus; it looks like a dictionary, but deals only with synonyms and antonyms.

EVALUATION

1. Organize word games that could be used for contests, such as Jeopardy.

2. Develop practice exercises where students can find immediate answers in locating the synonym or antonym from a cluster of words.

EXERCISE

Directions: Write the letter of the word that is most opposite in meaning to the other words in the group.

1.   a. immaturity
     b. adolescence
     c. senility
     d. nonage
     e. childhood

2.   a. cleansed
     b. tarnished
     c. expurgated
     d. sublimated
     e. purged

3.   a. transgression
     b. breach
     c. overstepping
     d. retrogression

4.   a. commplace
     b. dull
     c. pedestrian
     d. diverting

5.   a. dejection
     b. conjecture
     c. sadness
     d. depression

6.   a. vilify
     b. slander
     c. induce
     d. calumniate

7.   a. deathless
     b. moribund
     c. everlasting
     d. immortal

8.   a. block
     b. impede
     c. obstruct
     d. expedite

9.   a. dependent
     b. conditional
     c. abject
     d. contingent

10. a. diffidently
    b. aggressively
    c. fearfully
    d. apprehensively

Foreign Words and Phrases

FRENCH

Culinary Terms

a la mode	served in a certain style, usually pie with ice cream on top
aperitif	alcoholic drink taken before meals
au gratin	with a crust of crumbs and grated cheese
au jus	served in its natural juices, usually a meat in its own gravy
canape	cracker with a spread of cheese, etc., as an appetizer
cuisine	a style of cooking
hor d'oeuvres	appetizers served before a meal
julienne	in thin strips; potatoes are commonly served this way
pièce de resistance	the most remarkable achievement in a series (of courses); it does not always refer to food
sauté	to fry quickly
a la carte	a separate price for each item on the menu

Other Terms

au naturel	in the natural state; nude
avant garde	leaders in a new movement (generally an art movement)
blasé	bored (ex: He was blasé about the trip to Europe.)
bon ami	good friend
bourgeois	middle class (not a compliment—it refers to someone being very conventional and humdrum)
camaraderie	close fellowship among friends
carte blanche	white card (it means that the person with carte blanche be given full authority to do anything he wishes)
cause celebré	celebrated case (usually a controversial one)
cherchez la femme	watch out for the woman (the misunderstanding or mystery will be cleared up when the involvement of the woman is understood)

connoisseur	one who has expert knowledge in a given field
coup de grâce	death-dealing blow. Act, stroke, etc., that ends something. (ex: The coup de grace of the trip was the flat tire.)
coup d'etat	the takeover of a government by sudden, illegal means
crème de la crème	the elite, the very best (often refers to people in "high society")
dejà vu	trite, unoriginal, boringly familiar. Psychologically it's the illusion of having previously experienced the present situation.
de rigeur	required of, by custom or etiquette (often coats and ties are de rigeur in nicer restaurants)

GERMAN AND HUNGARIAN

| eratz | inferior substitute or imitation; of inferior quality |

JAPANESE

| banzai | forever! (Japanese battle cry) |
| hara kiri | suicide, especially by a soldier, with patriotic intent |

LATIN

ad infinitum	to infinity (ex: And so on and so on, ad infinitum)
alma mater	fostering mother (the school from which a person graduated)
alter ego	second self (an intimate friend)
alumnus	member or former member of any learned establishment
ante bellum	before the war (in the U.S., this refers to the Civil War)
a priori	reasoning from cause to effect, deductively, without material evidence or experience. (ex: The murder was solved a priori.)
bona fide	authentic; sincere; genuine (ex: It was a bona fide disaster.)
caveat emptor	let the buyer beware (the buyer is responsible for the quality of what is bought)
cum laude	with praise or honor (graduates with a certain grade average will graduate cum laude)
de facto	actually, in fact, whether legal or not
E Pluribus Unum	one (made) out of many (motto of U.S.A., referring to our country: one country made out of many peoples)
ergo	therefore
in absentia	in the original place; on the spot (ex: The body was left in situ until the police arrived.)

ipso facto	by the very fact
magna cum laude	with great praise or honor (graduates who have a higher grade average than those who graduate cum laude will graduate magna cum laude)
magnum opus	a great work, masterpiece, usually applied to an artist's greatest work. (ex: Many people think DaVinci's Mona Lisa was his magnum opus.)
modus operandi	mode of operating; way in which a person works. (Many robberies are solved by knowing the robber's modus operandi.)
pater familias	male head of the household
per diem	by the day (Many people are paid operating expenses per diem)
per se	by or in itself (ex: It was not a date per se.)
persona non grata	an unacceptable person (ex: As far as we're concerned, he's persona non grata.)
pro rata	in proportion (ex: Everyone should get his pro rata share of the money.)
quid pro quo	something in return for something; one thing in exchange for another
sic	thus spelt; thus written; thus said. Used after a quotation to indicate that it is accurately reproduced to make clear that any error (i.e., grammar or spelling) is in the original, and not caused by inaccurate copying. (ex: It's two (sic) late to turn back now.)
sine qua non	an indispensable thing necessary for achievement of some person, condition, etc., (ex: The attache case was sine qua non.)
status quo	present state of affairs; prevailing, existing conditions. Always used to describe the continuation of existing state of affairs (ex: Everything is status quo.)
summa cum laude	(graduating) with highest honors
verbatim	word for word (ex: He recited the report verbatim.)
vice versa	conversely (ex: She like him, and vice versa (he liked her).

YIDDISH

chutzpah	audacity, nerve (ex: He showed chutzpah by cutting in line.)

Foreign Words and Phrases

As paradoxical as it seems, in order to express oneself well in English, one must also speak other languages. Fluency in another language is not necessary of course, but a command of foreign words and expressions is.

The preceding passage is a list of the most commonly used foreign words and expressions, alphabetized according to the languages from which they are borrowed. In addition to an English definition of the phrases, examples or explanations, when necessary, are included.

A command of these expressions will greatly increase your awareness of the English language and ability to express yourself more clearly.

EXERCISE
Foreign Words and Phrases

Directions: This is a true and false test. It is designed to test your knowledge of foreign phrases and expressions. In the blanks provided, write the word true next to the statements that are true, write false if the statements are false.

_____ 1. Cuisine is a French word that means a style of cooking.

_____ 2. If a person is very conventional and humdrum in terms of class, he is middle class or bourgeois.

_____ 3. One's alma mater is the school from which he or she graduated.

_____ 4. When something is referred to as a bona fide, generally it is not authentic or genuine.

_____ 5. Modus operandi is a mode of operating, or a way in which a person works.

_____ 6. Pro rata does not mean the same as an equal share.

_____ 7. To be au naturel is the same as being fully clothed.

_____ 8. To sauté onions, a cook must fry them quickly.

_____ 9. Crème de la crème most nearly means the worst people in society.

_____10. In order to commit hara kiri, a Japanese soldier would murder for the love of his country.

MULTIPLE CHOICE
Foreign Words and Phrases

Directions: In the exercise below, pick the correct meaning of the word by placing the letter of the best answer in the blank space provided.

_____1. _Incognito_ is
   a. open
   b. in a disguised state
   c. authorship
   d. real
   e. known

_____ 2. _Fiasco_ is the same as
   a. soft, sweet
   b. loud
   c. accented
   d. in moderate time
   e. difficult situation

_____ 3. *Status quo* is
   a. the head of the household
   b. one's mode of operating
   c. a style of cooking
   d. existing conditions, present state of affairs
   e. by the day

_____ 4. An *aperitif* is a
   a. hot broth with chunks of meat
   b. mixed bag
   c. alcoholic drink taken before meals
   d. potato cooked with cheese
   e. appetizers served before meals

_____ 5. A *chutzpah* is
   a. a brawl, fight
   b. a large stadium, sports arena
   c. a wine-tasting ceremony
   d. audacity, nerve

_____ 6. A *magnum opus* is
   a. a great work, masterpiece
   b. member of a learned establishment
   c. a graduate degree of high honor
   d. time before the Civil War
   e. an intimate friend

_____ 7. *A la mode* is a French term which means
   a. with a crust of crumbs
   b. served in a certain style, usually with pie and ice cream on top
   c. cut in thin strips and served with cheese
   d. one who has expert knowledge in a given field
   e. a separate price for each menu item

_____ 8. To graduate *summa cum laude* is to
   a. graduate with highest honors
   b. barely finish college
   c. finish only high school
   d. graduate in absentee
   e. not participate in formal graduation ceremonies, just have your degree mailed to your home

_____ 9. *Ipso facto* is
   a. Greek and it means second self
   b. Latin and it means by the very fact
   c. Japanese and it means forever
   d. French and it means close fellowship among friends
   e. English and it means middle class

_____ 10. To be *avant garde* is to be
- a. nude, in the natural state
- b. an inferior substitute
- c. leaders in a new movement
- d. bored silly
- e. glamorous and appealing

EXERCISE

Foreign Words and Phrases

Some foreign words and phrases have been anglicized foreign—that is, they have become accepted as part of the English language. These should not be underscored or italicized but treated as any other English word.

In the exercise below mark through the misspelled anglicized foreign words and write the word correctly above.

New Voe Reesh

When Mike Johnston opened his restaurant on Fifth Avenue in New York, he was aware that all the chick shops catering to the rich and famous would provide him with customers looking for the finest cuisine from hors d'oeuvres to soup de jour, entrays, and French aclairs. He knew that the slightest foe paw on the part of a naive waiter could make his elegant fasade strictly passay among the elegantly gowned and quaffured women who come in chauffeured cars to dine. He knew, too, that the busy executives would institute a laissay fare policy unless his mater dee could perform the daily feat of providing a choice table on short notice.

Mike is a believer in the old cleshay that customers go where they are invited and stay where they are appreciated. Mike Johnston is a millionaire.

EXERCISE

Words Often Confused

This is an exercise in distinguishing between homonyms and other "sound alikes" often confused by writers, secretaries, and public speakers. Underline the correct word in each set of parentheses in the story below.

A Tribute to Walt Disney

If the nations of the word should get together (to, too, two) establish a World Hall of Fame for the (great, grate) men who have contributed to the pleasure of mankind, Walter E. Disney would (commend, command) a place of honor. Among the (hordes, hoards) of people who have entertained us in the (course, coarse) of a lifetime, Walt Disney became a (medal, metal, mettle) winner around the world.

Such characters as Mickey Mouse, Donald Duck, and Pluto are better known (then, than) many kings. (Their, There) voices have been (heard, herd) via radio, television, and movie screens every place. Every child (nose, nos, knows) that a Walt Disney cartoon will provide unforgettable (sights, cites, sites) and his familiar characters have become (cymbals, symbols) of entertainment.

Walt Disney was a perfectionist. As such, he (set, sit, sat) a high standard for each production. A tour of Disneyland or Disney World will (confirm, conform) Disney's mastery in the field of entertainment. His work had a (dual, duel) purpose—to entertain in order to make it easier to (bare, bear) the daily cares of (current, currant) living and (to, too, two) set (fourth, forth) some (principles, principals) for living the good life. People expected nothing (fowl, foul) when they saw a Disney picture. He had great (insight, incite) into popular taste. Even now you may (canvas, canvass) any major city in the United States and (find, fine) people (buying, bying) tickets to a Walt Disney movie.

Abused Words and Expressions

The majority of abused works and expressions occur in conversation. A person learns to speak the way those around him speak; later, he will write what he hears. It is in this manner that abused words and expressions are perpetuated. Most misused words and expressions fall into the following categories: *colloquialisms, comparisons, superfluous words, redundancies*, and *commonly confused word pairs*. Each will be explained and followed by examples.

Colloquialisms

Colloquialisms are misused expressions that are so common that many people think of them as acceptable. In the business word, however, most of these expressions are not acceptable. Practice using the correct substitute, so that proper usage will become automatic when you are dealing with professionals. The following are some examples:

Wrong	Right	Don't Say
a	of	What time a day
all kinds of	many; much	All kinds of trouble
anywhere near	nearly	He wasn't anywhere near ready
nowhere near	nearly	He wasn't nowhere near ready
as like as not	likely	He'll as like as not get it
bank on	rely on	You can bank on it
broke	without money	I'm flat broke today
can't seem	seem unable	They can't seem to see it
don't never	never	They don't never go out
expect	suppose	I expect so
funny	strange	There was a funny smell
overly	too	He was overly curious
shape	condition	He's in bad shape
sooner	rather	He'd sooner eat than sleep
worst way	very much	He wanted it in the worst way
disremember	forget	Don't disremember to go
would seem	seems	It would seem they like it
a few	few; some	There are still a few left
between you & I	between you & me	Between you & I, he's fired
whether or no	whether or not	I'm going, whether or no he is

Wrong	Right	Don't Say
who	whom	To whom do you refer?
if I were her	if I were she	If I were her, I'd go
try and come	try to come	Try and come tomorrow
at best	at the best	At best she'll get second
that's him	that's he	That's him who did it
feel badly	feel bad	I feel badly that it happened
a long ways	long way	The store is a long ways from here
back down	withdraw	They backed down from the fight
irregardless	regardless	I'll go irregardless of the weather
prioritize	to make a priority	Please prioritize these duties
like	as	It tastes like medicine should taste
summarization	summary	Here is a summarization of the day
alright	all right	Is it alright to go?
orientate	orient	Please orientate yourself with this material
author	write	He authored this book
backwards	backward	He fell backwards into the pit
exit	leave	He exited through that door
amidst	amid	He lay amidst the flames
lay	lie	Lay down on the bed

Comparisons

The following words represent the highest degree, and generally should not have any other adjective added:

accurate	eternal	perfect
complete	exact	real
correct	genuine	wrong
dead	impossible	full

Superfluous words

A superfluous word is a word that is added to the original word yet does not add to the context or meaning of the word. Because a superfluous word does not help clarify the word to which it's added, it should be omitted.

For example, the following words do *not* need the word "up" added to them:

burn	finish	run
buy	fix	scratch
cripple	hurry	settle
divide	mix	start
eat	end	open
write	even	pay

The following words do not need the "in":

among	around	back of
between	under	up

The following do not need the word "of":

outside	inside

Redundancies

Redundant words are words that have the same meanings. Because they have the same meaning, it is unnecessary to use them both. When using a redundant word, you are repeating yourself; you are not communicating as effectively as possible. In this situation, it takes less effort to speak or write correctly than to do it incorrectly. For example,

Incorrect	Correct
revert back	revert
widow man	widow (a male would be a widower)
universally by all	universally
totally demolish	demolish
tiny little	small
great big	big
repeat again	repeat
return back	return
3 PM in the afternoon	3 PM
totally destroy	destroy
this goes without saying	don't use this phrase—If it "goes without saying," then don't say it!
an advance notice	notice
ago since	since
also . . . too	also
assembled together	assembled
at about	about
both equally	equally
cancel out	cancel
enclosed herewith	enclosed
equally as good as	as good as/equally good
etc., etc.,	etc.,
finish off	finish
first before	before
first began	began
follows after	follows
joint partnership	partnership
over with	over
pretend like	pretend
up above	above

Commonly Confused Word Pairs

Because most people drawl their speech (at least in Texas), many words are pronounced alike that are spelled differently and have different meanings. Many of these words are homonyms; some are word pairs whose spellings are almost identical. As an educated person, you must be able to differentiate between the following words in both conversation and writing:

complement	the amount needed to fill or complete (The gloves complement the outfit.)
compliment	something said in praise
beside	by or at the side of
besides	in addition; as well
brake	stop
break	come apart
course	part of a meal, a school subject, direction, certainly (of course)
coarse	rough
its	belonging to it (it hurt its paw.)
it's	abbreviation of "it is," or "it has"
principal	main; a person in charge of a school
principle	a law or standard
than	used in comparison (I am taller than she is.)
then	at that time (We then went to the store)
their	belonging to them
there	at that place; used with verbs "is, are, was"
they're	contraction of "they are"
to	a verb part
too	overly (too hot)
two	the number
your	belonging to you
you're	contraction of "you are"
weather	atmospheric conditions
whether	if it happens that; in case; if
accept	receive; agree to
except	exclude; but
affect	a verb meaning "to influence" (How will this affect the race?)
effect	a verb meaning "to bring about something," a noun meaning "results" (The waves had a soothing effect.)
quiet	peaceful
quite	entirely, really, rather

The use of these abused words and expressions is a matter of habit, and with concentrated effort and practice, you can break this bad usage habit. Whenever possible, converse with people who use these words and expressions correctly, and read material of literary merit. The result will be well worth the effort.

References

Berry, Thomas Elliot. *The Most Common Mistakes in English Usage*. New York: McGraw Hill Company, 1971.

Hutchinson, Lois. *Standard Handbook for Secretaries*. New York: McGraw Hill Company. 1979.

Langam, John. *English Skills*. New York: McGraw Hill Company, 1981.

Abused Words and Expressions

Many misused expressions are so common that they are often assumed to be correct. In the exercise below, select the alternative that agrees most closely with the word given.

_____ 1. *Accurate* most closely means
   a. almost correct
   b. somewhat sure
   c. careful and exact
   d. on the mark
   e. distinct

_____ 2. *Admidst* means
   a. friendly
   b. easygoing
   c. determined
   d. in the middle of
   e. ceaseless

_____ 3. To *revert* means
   a. move forward
   b. to disgust someone
   c. to look back
   d. to change one's mind or opinion
   e. to go back

_____ 4. *Regardless* means the same as
   a. in spite of
   b. conforming to rule
   c. to regulate
   d. without regret
   e. to feel sorrow

_____ 5. To *demolish* is the same as
   a. to demonstrate
   b. to carefully think out
   c. to wreck
   d. to deliver at once
   e. to build from the foundation up

_____ 6. A *summary* is
   a. a brief review
   b. a final decision
   c. a re-write after proofreading
   d. a measure of one's level of pain
   e. a position in state government

_____ 7. *Complement* is the same as

      a. a greeting, given in passing

      b. something said in terms of praise

      c. in addition to

      d. as well as

      e. the amount needed to fill or complete

_____ 8. A *principle* is

      a. a person in charge of a school

      b. used in a play to complete the production

      c. a law or standard

      d. used to maintain one's interest

      e. another name for supervisor

_____ 9. The word *whether* most closely means

      a. in case; if it happens that

      b. entirely

      c. exclude from participating

      d. to pretend like

      e. atmospheric conditions

_____10. *Affect* most closely means

      a. a verb meaning to bring about

      b. a verb meaning to influence

      c. artificial, not real

      d. too familiar

      e. something that causes other circumstances to occur

Root Words

Overview

Alex Haley has made many of us very conscious of the word "roots." We are therefore familiar with the term *root* as the history, origin or foundation of one's heritage. The concept is the same when speaking of roots as the foundation of words. Every word in English has a root or basic meaning. You have learned that a *prefix* is a part in front of a root or base word. It is used to change the meaning of the word. A *suffix* is a word part added after the base or root and is used to change the word to a noun, verb, adjective, or adverb.

Many different words with different meanings can be formed merely by adding prefixes and suffixes to a root. These new words are called *derivations*. Many words in our English language are built on smaller words of Greek and Latin origin. You will be introduced to these Greek and Latin roots and will learn how to combine these word parts to form many words in English. In fact, you will be able to figure out the meanings of large words by using your knowledge about roots. Our language is complex, subtle, and ever-changing. Therefore a knowledge of these basic roots and their combinations will help you understand vocabulary—old and new— more effectively in your everyday life. The approach you take to learning the roots presented is the key to your successful mastery. Your study of roots will be easier if you remember:

1. that some roots have several meanings such as "ped." (ped = foot, child or teach)

2. that some roots have several spellings, such as "ped."

    pod—foot
    ped—foot

3. that some words are made up of the same letters as some affixes and roots but in fact do not contain any combining forms.

    pretty (not pre)
    size (not ize)

In spite of the problems associated with learning roots, having a key to the meanings of thousands of words far outweighs the disadvantages. Although many roots have been presented, these are not all of the roots an educated person should know. These roots merely serve as a foundation upon which to add a new root each time you encounter it. Thus, an important function of this unit is to help you to become "root conscious."

Your Fourteen Master Words*

The words in the table below contain twelve of the most important Latin roots, two of the most important Greek roots, and twenty of the most important prefixes. Why are they so important? Because over 14,000 relatively common words—words of desk dictionary size—contain one or more of those elements. They will provide you with a truly remarkable shortcut to word power!

Words	Prefix	Common Meaning	Root	Common Meaning
Uncompli-cated	un-com-	(not) (together with)	plicare	(fold)
Non extended	non-ex-	(not) (out of)	tendre	(stretch)
Precept	pre-	(before)	capere	(take, seize)
Repro-duction	re-pro-	(back) (again, forward)	ducere	(lead)
Detain	de-	(away, from)	tenere	(hold, have)
Indisposed	in-dis-	(not) (apart, from)	ponere	(put, place)
Inter-mittent	inter-	(between)	mittere	(send)
Offer	ob-	(against)	ferre	(bear, carry)
Over sufficient	over-sub-	(above) (under)	facere	(make, do)
Insist	in-	(into)	stare	(stand)
Monograph	mono-	(alone, one)	graphien	(write)
Epilogue	epi-	(upon)	legein	(say, study of)
Mistran-scribe	mis-trans-	(wrong), (across, beyond)	scribere	(write)
Aspect	ad-	(to, towards)	specere	(see)

References

*Brown, James I. *Reading Power*, alternate ed. (Lexington, Massachusetts: D. C. Heath, and Company, 1978), p. 37.

Objectives

After careful study of the fourteen master words you wil be able to:

- combine twelve (12) of the most important Latin roots, two (2) Greek roots and twenty (20) prefixes to form more than 200 relatively common words.

- supply words that are formed by combining roots and prefixes in the appropriate sentences.

ACTIVITIES

Directions: In the space provided, write the letter of the word *not related* in meaning to the other words in each group.

_____1.
    a. controllable
    b. tractable
    c. refractory
    d. obedient
    e. manageable

_____2.
    a. gay
    b. convivial
    c. festive
    d. inhospitable
    e. jovial

_____3.
    a. inhuman
    b. tortuous
    c. winding
    d. curving
    e. bending

_____4.
    a. hasty
    b. abrupt
    c. restricted
    d. unexpected
    e. sudden

_____5.
    a. delicate
    b. weak
    c. feeble
    d. fragile
    e. fractious

_____ 6.
    a. trustworthy
    b. accredited
    c. credible
    d. believable
    e. incredulous

_____ 7.
    a. disclosed
    b. revealed
    c. shone
    d. evinced
    e. displayed

_____ 8.
    a. satiable
    b. ravenous
    c. voracious
    d. devouring
    e. greedy

_____ 9.
    a. stringent
    b. inflexible
    c. pliable
    d. rigid
    e. firm

_____ 10.
    a. distorted
    b. corrupted
    c. admonished
    d. contorted
    e. falsified

Directions: In the space provided, write the letter of the word that has most nearly the *same meaning* as the underlined word.

_____ 11. *fragile* flower
    a. fragrant
    b. broken
    c. colorful
    d. frail

_____ 12. cling *tenaciously*
    a. stubbornly
    b. dangerously
    c. hopefully
    d. timidly

_____13. beyond *credence*
   a. detention
   b. doubt
   c. belief
   d. recall

_____14. *omnipotent* ruler
   a. almighty
   b. wise
   c. cruel
   d. greedy

_____ 15. *mandatory* increase
   a. deserved
   b. required
   c. temporary
   d. substantial

_____ 16. Surprising *impertinence*
   a. firmness
   b. unreliability
   c. impatience
   d. rudeness

_____ 17. *breach* of trust
   a. atmosphere
   b. testing
   c. breaking
   d. abundance

_____ 18. *unvanquished* foe
   a. defeated
   b. exhausted
   c. treacherous
   d. unbeaten

_____ 19. in a *fiduciary* capacity
   a. confidential
   b. special
   c. professional
   d. important

_____ 20. refused to *genuflect*
   a. admit
   b. kneel
   c. cooperate
   d. disclose

Directions: Choose the letter of the correct answer.

_____ 21. An *omnivorous* creature
    a. hunts only at night.
    b. eats both plant and animal substance.
    c. has no enemies more powerful than itself.

_____ 22. What does an *astringent* lotion do?
    a. It binds the skin tight.
    b. It loosens the skin.
    c. It makes a person look younger.

_____ 23. Tim is *credulous*
    a. too readily believing
    b. dull or stupid
    c. too easygoing

_____ 24. On April 15, Ruby will have twenty years of " _____ " in this office.
    a. tenure
    b. tenacity
    c. tenancy

_____ 25. He was punished very severely for a minor " _____ " of the rules.
    a. fraction
    b. infraction
    c. fractious

Prefixes

Overview

Certainly there have been times when you have attempted to read a paragraph which contained many words that you knew at first glance. Somehow as you continued to read several words probably caused you so much frustration that you felt desperate. The change in the structure at the beginning and ending of the word probably caused the trouble. Knowledge or prefixes and suffixes will serve as an aid in learning new words; however, at this time we will focus primarily on the function of prefixes as they relate to the formation of new words.

A prefix is a word part that is added to the beginning of a word (called the base or root word) or a word part such as a combining form or root word. For example, the word *prefix* is made up of the prefix *pre* (before, in front) and the root word *fix* (to attach) and prefix means "to attach before or in front." A prefix has a meaning which is added to the meaning of the base word, root word or combining form to which it is attached.

Unabridged dictionaries (the very large ones) list thousands of derivatives that begin with the common prefixes. For example, most unabridged dictionaries list more than 10,000 words that begin with *non-* and more than 400 words that begin with *pseudo-*. If you know the meanings of *non-* and *pseudo-*, you know something important about the meaning of more than 10,400 words. Imagine that! Your receptive vocabulary can be increased by hundreds, or even thousands of words in a very short time through mastery of the aforementioned prefixes.

Objectives

After careful study of the nineteen basic prefixes, you will:
- be able to recognize and define some of the most common prefixes through the use of context clues.
- be able to demonstrate this knowledge of the use of appropriate prefixes for base words.

ACTIVITIES

Directions: Choose the answer you think is correct.

_____ 1. Eyeglasses that help a person see better both near and far are called
  a. bimanual
  b. bifocals
  c. binoculars

_____ 2. A machine whose operation required the use of two hands is
  a. bimanual
  b. bilateral
  c. bicuspid

_____ 3. A song for two voices is a
  a. dual
  b. duet
  c. duo

_____ 4. A tooth having two points is called
  a. biped
  b. binary
  c. bicuspid

_____ 5. A reproduction is a
  a. dual
  b. duplicate
  c. bimanual

_____ 6. A baseball player who plays for money, but who does not do so full-time, is known as
  a. a rookie
  b. a semi-professional
  c. an all-star

_____ 7. In the word _semiautomatic_, the prefix _semi-_ carries the meaning of
  a. half
  b. almost
  c. partly

_____ 8. Kareem Abdul-Jabbar's legendary status in the world of basketball has placed him among that sport's
   a. semi-gods
   b. demigods
   c. hemispheres

_____ 9. We perceive the equator as dividing the planet into
   a. spheres
   b. hemispheres
   c. unispheres

_____ 10. If you are a person who has more training that an unskilled laborer, but less than a skilled laborer, you are probably
   a. semiskilled
   b. self-employed
   c. unqualified

_____ 11. If *ultima* means the last syllable in a word, the last syllable of ultima is
   a. ul
   b. ti
   c. ma

_____ 12. The primitive beings who were the first humans are sometimes called
   a. protohumans
   b. protagonists
   c. protozoans

_____ 13. The Times Square shuttle, a subway line in New York City, originates at Times Square and ends at Grand Central Station, which means that Grand Central Station is the shuttle's
   a. ultimatum
   b. terminus
   c. protagonist

_____ 14. If you know that *ultimate* means last and that *pen* means almost or next to, what do you think *penultimate* means?
   a. before the first
   b. next to the last
   c. never-ended

_____ 15. Outer space has been called the last, or ultimate,
   a. frontier
   b. playground
   c. battlefield

Directions: Mark each statement as either true or false.

_____ 16. When the town of Greenville was two-hundred years old, it celebrated its centennial.

_____ 17. An event that takes place gradually occurs all of a sudden, usually without warning.

_____ 18. The word *retrograde* refers only to the backward motion of celestial bodies.

_____ 19. A high school graduate has completed all the steps involved in earning a high school diploma.

_____ 20. A retro-rocket produces thrust in a direction opposite to the motion of the main missile, causing the missile to slow down.

Directions: On the line before each sentence, write the letter of the definition appropriate to the way in which the word is used in the sentence.

resolve

      a. (n) a firm decision
      b. (v) to settle or find an answer to
      c. (v) to reach a firm decision
      d. (n) determination
      e. (v) analyze

_____ 21. I *resolved* to get more exercise.

_____ 22. When Hans quit smoking, it was a difficult test of his *resolve*.

_____ 23. Let's *resolve* this dispute before it gets out of hand.

_____ 24. Andrew made a *resolve* to spend more time with his family.

_____ 25. Dr. Thomas will *resolve* the results of the experiment.

Suffixes

Overview

When the meaning of a word is not stated in or implied by a context, you may determine it by analyzing the base word and the word's suffix. A suffix is a letter or group of letters that is added to the end of a base word. For example, in *truthful*, the base word is *truth* and the suffix is *-ful*. Words that are unfamiliar to you may sometimes consist of a base word you know and an added suffix. For instance,

How many years was her mayoralty?

    Mayoralty is a word that does not appear often in print; it may be unfamiliar to you. However, by locating the base word in *mayoralty* you can easily understand that the question is, "For how many years was she mayor?"

Words you know may be the base words for five, ten, fifteen, or more other words that you do not read often. For example, adapt (v)

adaptable	adaptation	adapter
adaptableness	adaptational	adaptive
adaptability	adaptationally	adaptiveness

If you know that *adapt* means "to make suitable," you know the essential meaning of these nine words, even if you have never seen some of them in print before. Notice that some of the words contain two suffixes. For instance, *adaptableness* contains two suffices -*able* and -*ness*.

A suffix usually identifies the part of speech of a word without giving important information about the word's meaning. For example, *adapt* is a verb, *adaptable* is an adjective, and *adaptation* is a noun. These three words represent different parts of speech but have similar meanings. Since they are different parts of speech, they cannot be used correctly in identical grammatical constructions.

She can *adapt* to difficult situations.

She is *adaptable* to difficult situations.

She can make *adaptations* to difficult situations.

Though *adapt* is a verb, *adaptable* is an adjective, and *adaptation* is a noun, all three of the sentences have very similar meanings.

Following are the most common adjective, noun, verb, and adverb suffixes.

The Most Common Adjective, Noun, Verb, and Adverb Suffixes

Adjective Suffixes	Examples
-able	approachable, comfortable, transferable
-al	classical, critical, mystical
-ent	absorbent, dependent, insistent
-er	taller, harder, shorter
-est	tallest, hardest, shortest
-ful	fearful, truthful, wasteful
-ible	corruptible, inflexible, suggestible
-ic	angelic, artistic, realistic
-ish	childish, foolish, girlish
-ive	assertive, attractive, possessive
-less	lifeless, meaningless, shapeless
-ous	dangerous, hazardous, poisonous
-y	sleepy, squeaky, speedy

Noun Suffixes	Examples
-ance	annoyance, deliverance, inheritance
-ence	conference, difference, existence
-ion	expression, profession, prevention
-ist	journalist, novelist, perfectionist
-ity	humidity, reality, sexuality
-ment	appointment, commandment, punishment
-ness	bitterness, greatness, weakness
-s	boys, girls, persons

Verb Suffixes	Examples
-ed	called, played, worked
-ing	calling, playing, working
-ify	falsify, glorify, simplify
-ize	idealize, socialize, verbalize
-s	calls, plays, works

Adverb Suffixes	Examples
-ly	quickly, slowly, thoroughly
-ward	afterward, backward, homeward

Objectives

After careful study of the most common adjective, noun, verb, and adverb suffixes, you will:

- be able to demonstrate this knowledge of the use of the appropriate suffixes for base words.

- be able to recognize and define some of the most commonly used suffixes through the use of context clues and knowledges of base words and prefixes.

EXERCISE

Directions: Answer the following questions true or false.

_____ 1. A *disclosure* can reveal what was not known before.

_____ 2. The result of a *reformation* can be a fresh start.

_____ 3. An *abomination* is anything greatly prized.

_____ 4. A *docile* child is one who refuses instructions.

_____ 5. *Portly* people usually look as if they need a good meal.

_____ 6. Horses and cows live almost exclusively on *roughage*.

_____ 7. Anything *inhibiting* growth is likely to produce greater size.

_____ 8. A *convivial* party is one at which everyone refuses to mingle with others.

_____ 9. *Banal* remarks are clever and witty.

_____ 10. Anything *fluorescent* gives off light.

Directions: Place the letter of the best answer in the blank space.

_____11. An *amorist* is likely to be an expert at
   a. finance
   b. love-making
   c. public debate
   d. military strategy

_____12. A *superannuated* person is
   a. hostile
   b. immature
   c. old
   d. penniless

_____13. *Avian* characteristics are
   a. hospitable
   b. naive
   c. suggestive of death
   d. birdlike

_____14. An *incarnate* creature is one who is
   a. fiendishly evil
   b. hideously misshappen
   c. in bodily form
   d. approaching death

_____15. A *centenaria* is
   a. a celebration
   b. a military hero
   c. a legal statement
   d. an aged person

_____16. A person without *credibility* is
   a. untrustworthy
   b. very emotional
   c. insolvent
   d. commonplace

_____17. A *fiduciary* is a
   a. relative
   b. priest
   c. trustee
   d. fortune-teller

_____18. A *confraternity* is a
      a. subversive political party
      b. unified group of people
      c. class reunion
      d. collection of immigrants

_____19. *Egregious* behavior is likely to be
      a. polite
      b. shocking
      c. irrational
      d. clever

_____20. A *rejoinder* is a
      a. military person
      b. type of weld
      c. clever reply
      d. stupid blunder

_____21. *Perjury* involves
      a. doing good for others
      b. a careful avoidance of mistakes
      c. dressing according to the latest styles
      d. lying under oath

_____22. *Loquacious* individuals are
      a. moody
      b. jealous
      c. taciturn
      d. talkative

_____23. An *emissary* is
      a. an immigrant
      b. a representative
      c. a philosophical statement
      d. a spy

_____24. To *mortify* is to
      a. embellish
      b. irritate
      c. embarrass
      d. adjust the tone or pitch

_____25. A *pensive* expression suggests
      a. a military background
      b. apprehension
      c. selfishness
      d. wistfulness

Spelling

Overview

The importance of correct spelling cannot be overestimated because your spelling represents you. A misspelled word denotes inefficiency and carelessness to your instructor or employer. A paper neatly written with correct spelling marks you as a person of value and precision. An employer thinks of you as a representative of his firm; therefore, he naturally wants to show the best. In business you must be 100 percent accurate—competition and society demand it. Misspelled words stand out like a sore thumb; they break the flow or continuity of ideas. They give readers a poor impression of you.

Many students are poor spellers because their enunciation and pronunciation are incorrect.

Upon completion of this unit you should be able to:

- improve your spelling skills

- use correct enunciation and pronunciation to improve your spelling ability

- use visualizations to improve spelling skills

- improve your spelling of troublesome words in content areas

Spellings

If you own a good dictionary, you own an excellent spelling textbook. Modern desk dictionaries give the answers to virtually all your questions about spelling.

This chapter explains how to locate correct spellings in a dictionary and how to use a dictionary to improve your spelling ability. Most of the words in this chapter are frequently misspelled by college students.

Pronunciation and Spelling

If you pronounce words carelessly or incorrectly, you may misspell them or have trouble locating them in the dictionary.

For example, if you refer to the second month of the year as (feb'you-er'e) you are more likely to misspell the word than if you pronounce it (feb'roo-er'e); it is spelled February, not Febuary. Similarly, if you say (disgard'), meaning "to throw away," you may have difficulty finding the word in a dictionary; it is pronounced (dis-kärd') and spelled discard.

The following exercise is a quiz you may take to determine whether mispronunciations cause you to misspell words.

Exercise

Pronunciation Quiz

Directions: The italicized words in the following phrases are misspelled in ways that persons who mispronounce them, or who do not pronounce all the syllables in them, tend to misspell them. Without referring to a dictionary, write the correct spellings of the italicized words on the lines that are provided.

1. a loving *famly*   _____
2. a *dimond* ring   _____
3. the city *goverment*   _____
4. a chemistry *labratory*   _____
5. *quite*, not loud   _____
6. a *pitcher* on a wall   _____
7. a *canidate* for mayor   _____
8. a *libary* book   _____
9. a great *quanity* of food   _____
10. to *roconize* her face   _____
11. a *sophmore* in college   _____
12. a *suprise* birthday party   _____
13. the *strenth* of a bull   _____
14. a *choclate* cake   _____
15. a *factry* worker   _____
16. a *grocrey* store   _____
17. a *miniture* doll house   _____
18. an old *bachlor*   _____
19. the state *boundries*   _____
20. a *familar* story   _____
21. a *kindergarden* pupil   _____
22. to *excape* from a fire   _____
23. a *literture* course   _____
24. beautiful *scenry*   _____
25. some *vegtable* soup   _____

If you misspelled five or more of the words, it is likely that careless pronunciation is causing you to spell many words incorrectly.

When you locate the spellings of words in a dictionary, study their pronunciation, as well as their correct spellings. Knowing the correct pronunciations will often help you to spell the word correctly.

Visualization and Spelling

If you are not in the habit of visualizing how words are spelled, you are likely to misspell many of them. The homophone quiz in the following exercise will help you determine if you visualize spellings accurately.

Homophones are words that are spelled differently but sound alike; *cite, site,* and *sight* are homophones. They are often spelled incorrectly by persons who do not visualize words.

Among the most frequently misspelled homophones are *to* and *too* and *their* and *there*. If you ever misspell these words, study their definitions and usages in a good desk dictionary. If you take the time to learn what the words mean and how they are used, you should never confuse them. *Its* and *it's* are also commonly confused. The only meaning of *it's* is "it is"; always use *its* unless you want to write "it is."

Exercise: Homophone Quiz

If you have mastered the most commonly used homophones, you probably have the habit of visualizing the spellings of words. Without referring to a dictionary, write the correct spellings of the pronunciation spellings in the following sentences. For instance, in the first sentence decide if the correct homophone is *bare* or *bear* and write the word on the line provided.

1. a baby's (bâr) bottom _____
2. to (ber e) the dead _____
3. to be (bôrd) and tired _____
4. the (sent) of flowers _____
5. a (sit) for a home _____
6. to pay bus (fâr) _____
7. to receive good (koun'sel) _____
8. bread made form (flaúer) _____
9. chicken and other (faúel) _____
10. to (gron) from pain _____
11. to have (its) own way _____
12. a (lon) traveler _____
13. a (pal) face _____
14. a (pes) of candy _____
15. to (pîr) at someone _____
16. to (rit) a letter _____
17. a (sem) in a shirt _____
18. to (stâr) at someone _____
19. to tell a (tal) _____
20. (thâr) coming with us _____
21. not (too) tall _____
22. (thâr) coming with us _____
23. to eat (thâr) food _____
24. (yoor) coming with us _____
25. eating some (stak) _____

If you misspelled five or more of the words, you have sufficiently developed the habit of noticing the relationships between spellings and meanings.

Troublesome Spelling Words in Content Areas

A man who owns a diesel-powered car refuses to have his car repaired at a garage with the sign DEISEL EXPERTS. He says, "If they can't even spell their specialty, do they really know much about it?"

Maybe he is wrong, but he is not alone in believing that all men and women should be literate in at least their own special fields. College level is certainly the appropriate point at which a student can begin to expand upon improving his spelling skills. Most of the words included here, however, are so widely used that most people—not only specialists—should know how to spell them.

Practice Exercise

Directions: Look at each of the words carefully. Pronounce it aloud if possible. Then practice spelling the word aloud and, finally, on paper.

A. Troublesome Words in Business
1. addressee
2. corporation
3. disbursement
4. equity
5. invoice
6. lessee
7. quarterly
8. remittance
9. requisition
10. warranty

B. Troublesome Computer-Related Words
1. access
2. analog
3. binary
4. compatible
5. interface
6. microprocessor
7. processing
8. processor
9. recursive
10. terminal

C. Troublesome Words in Literature
1. allegory
2. ballad
3. biography
4. epic
5. epigram
6. imagery

PLEASE PRINT

NAME: _
              Last   First   M.I.

SOCIAL SECURITY NO. _ _ _ _ _ _ _ _ _ _ _ _ _ _ _

ADDRESS (HOME): _ _ _ _ _ _ _ _ _ _ _ _ _ _ _ _

CITY: _ _ _ _ _ _ _ _ _ _ _ ZIP CODE _ _ _ _ _

ADDRESS (CAMPUS): _ _ _ _ _ _ _ _ _ _ _ _ _ _

CITY: _ _ _ _ _ _ _ _ _ _ _ ZIP CODE _ _ _ _ _

PHONE: (HOME) — ( ) _ _ _ _ _ _ _ _ _ _ _ _

PHONE: (CAMPUS) — ( ) _ _ _ _ _ _ _ _ _ _ _

BOOK NO.

DO NOT TEAR OUT
UNTIL TOLD TO DO SO!!!!

7. lyric
8. personification
9. simile
10. soliloquy

D. Troublesome Words in Music
1. accompanist
2. ballet
3. cadence
4. concerto
5. encore
6. ensemble
7. octave
8. prelude
9. serenade
10. sonata

E. Troublesome Words in Social Science
1. alien
2. bipartisan
3. caucus
4. census
5. fiscal
6. inauguration
7. judicial
8. legislative
9. naturalization
10. preamble

F. Troublesome Words in Mathematics
1. circumference
2. diameter
3. equation
4. exponent
5. perpendicular
6. radius
7. sine
8. sphere
9. symmetry
10. tangent

G. Troublesome Words in Science
1. acoustics
2. alloy
3. barometer
4. luminous
5. opaque

6. osmosis
7. oxidation
8. radioactive
9. respiration
10. turbine

H. Troublesome Words in Mechanics and Electricity
1. carburetor
2. conduit
3. diesel
4. differential
5. gasket
6. insulation
7. ohm
8. resistor
9. thermostat
10. watt

I. Troublesome Words in Home Economics
1. antique
2. buffet
3. chandelier
4. croquette
5. hors d'oeuvre
6. lacquer
7. provincial
8. quiche
9. synthetic
10. veneer

Evaluation

Directions: Each item contains several spellings of a word. Select the correct spelling.

1. a. addressee
   b. adressee
   c. addresee
   d. addresse

2. a. access
   b. acess
   c. acces
   d. aces

3. a. semilee
   b. semile
   c. simile
   d. similee

4. a. onsembel
   b. onsemble
   c. ensomble
   d. ensemble

5. a. inauguration
   b. inauguriation
   c. inarguration
   d. inaugurasion

6. a. symmetry
   b. symetry
   c. symettry
   d. symmettry

7. a. carbarator
   b. carburator
   c. carburetor
   d. carbureter

8. a. deisle
   b. deisel
   c. deisle
   d. diesel

9. a. chandaleir
   b. chandaleer
   c. chandelier
   d. chandilier

10. a. croqette
    b. croquette
    c. croquete
    d. croquett

11. a. abcence
    b. abence
    c. abcense
    d. absence

12. a. axiliary
    b. auxiliary
    c. auixliary
    d. auxliary

13. a. calander
    b. calender
    c. calendar
    d. caldener

14. a. disastrous
    b. disasterous
    c. disasterious
    d. dissterous

15. a. fascinate
    b. facinate
    c. faiscinate
    d. fasniate

16. a. resistence
    b. resitence
    c. resistance
    d. resistense

17. a. symmetrical
    b. symmetircal
    c. symetrical
    d. symetricel

18. a. vegnence
    b. vengenance
    c. vengance
    d. vengeance

19. a. weird
    b. wiered
    c. wierd
    d. wried

20. a. vilain
    b. villian
    c. villain
    d. vialin

SPELLING DEMONS

Spelling Demons are words that are frequently misspelled. Most of the words in this unit are spelling demons for college students; they are words that students frequently misspell when they write papers for college credit.

Your spelling demons are the words that you misspell. Keep a list of your demons; record the way you misspell them and their correct spelling. If you keep a record of this type, you may find that some of your misspellings follow patterns. For example, you may discover that you have special difficulty with words that contain "ie" or "ei", words that end with "e", or words that contain deemphasized vowels. If you identify a pattern of errors, you can concentrate on improving your specific weaknesses.

A list of 335 words that are spelling demons for college students follows. Notice that the misspellings include such common words as *across, although, calendar, lose,* and *quiet.* If you ever misspell everyday words such as these, you are not alone.

absence	appearance	cemetery	curiosity	eligible
absorption	appropriate	certain	cylinder	embarass
accidentally	Arctic	changeable	dealt	enemy
accommodate	arguing	chief	decide	environment
accomplish	argument	choose	decision	equipped
achievement	around	chose	definite	especially
acquire	arouse	clothes	desirable	etc.
across	arrangement	column	despair	exaggerate.
advise	article	coming	destroy	excellent
affect	ascend	committed	develop	excerpt
against	athlete	committee	development	exercise
all right	athletic	comparatively	difference	existence
almost	author	conceive	different	expense
already	auxiliary	conceivable	dining	experience
although	beginning	conscience	disappoint	experiment
altogether	believe	conscientious	disastrous	explanation
amateur	benefit	conscious	discipline	extremely
among	benefited	consistent	disease	familiar
analysis	breathe	continuous	dissatisfied	fascinate
analyze	brilliant	controle	distinction	February
angel	business	controlled	divide	finally
annual	calendar	convenience	divine	financier
answer	careful	counsel	easily	foreign
apparatus	carrying	criticismn	effect	foresee
apparent	ceiling	criticize	psychology	suppress
forty	later	optimism	pursue	surprise
fourth	led	origin	pursuit	syllable
friend	leisure	original	quantity	symmetrical
fundamental	length	paid	quiet	temperament
further	library	parallel	realize	temperature
generally	license	particularly	receipt	their

102

government	likelihood	peculiar	receive	than
governor	likely	peaceable	efficient	
grammar	livelihood	peculiar	recognize	their
grateful	loneliness	perceive	recommend	then
guarantee	lose	perform	regard	there
guard	magazine	permanent	relieve	therefore
guidance	maintenance	personal	religious	they're
height	maneuver	perspiration	repetition	thorough
heroes	many	persuade	resistance	thought
heroine	marriage	pertain	rhythm	through
hoping	mathematics	piece	ridiculous	together
humorous	meant	planned	safety	too
imaginary	medicine	playwright	scene	tragedy
imagination	miniature	pleasant	schedule	tries
immediately	morale	poison	science	truly
incidentally	muscle	politician	seize	undoubtedly
independence	naturally	possess	sense	until
independent	necessary	possession	separate	unusual
indispensable	neighbor	possible	sergeant	using
influential	neither	practical	several	usually
intellectual	nickel	precede	shepherd	vacuum
intelligence	niece	prefer	shining	vegetable
intelligent	ninety	preferred	shoulder	vengeance
interest	ninth	prejudice	significant	villain
interfere	noticeable	preparation	similar	weather
irrelevant	obstacle	prepare	simile	Wednesday
island	occasion	prevalent	sophomore	weird
it's	occasionally	primitive	specimen	where
its	occur	principal	speech	whether
jealous	occurred	principle	stopped	wholly
judgment	occurrence	privilege	straight	whose
kindergarten	official	probably	strength	woman
knowledge	omit	procedure	strenuous	women
laboratory	omitted	proceed	stretch	writing
laid	opinion	professor	studying	written
larynx	opportunity	prove	succeed	you're

PRACTICE EXERCISES

Spelling Demons: This exercise makes it possible for you to estimate how many of the 335 spelling demons are words that you spell correctly. Number a sheet of notebook paper from 1 through 21. Then have a friend give you the following test. After you have taken the test:

    1. Count the number of words you spelled correctly

    2. Multiply this number by 16.

For example, if you spell 15 words correctly, multiply 15 by 16 ($16 \times 15 = 240$). The 240 is an estimate that you spell approximately 240 of the 335 spelling demons correctly. Learn the correct spellings of any of the demons that you are likely to spell incorrectly.

Spelling Demon Test

Directions: Read a word on the left and the sentence that follows it; then reread the word on the left. For example: "Absence. Your absence is excused. Absence."

1.	absence	Your absence is excused.
2.	altogether	Altogether ten people were present.
3.	business	She works for a big business.
4.	committee	The committee made no decision.
5.	curiosity	Curiosity promotes learning.
6.	disappoint	The movie will not disappoint you.
7.	equipped	The car is equipped with a spare tire.
8.	February	February is the second month of the year.
9.	guarantee	We guarantee you satisfaction.
10.	influential	We have an influential senator.
11.	laid	He laid the book on the table.
12.	maneuver	Pilots maneuver aircraft.
13.	ninety	She is ninety years old.
14.	origin	Evolution explains the origin of species.
15.	piece	Have another piece of cake.
16.	prepare	What shall I prepare for dinner?
17.	quiet	The streets were dark and quiet.
18.	schedule	Schedule classes early in the day.
19.	speech	Her speech is clear and distinct.
20.	until	I will not return until five o'clock.
21.	woman	Mary is a young woman.

Using the Library

"Knowledge is of two kinds; either
we know a subject ourselves, or we know
where we can find information upon it."
Samuel Johnson

Overview

Some college assignments that you are given can be mastered by way of self knowledge, but there are others that require a bit of research. When research is necessary, you should go to the most valuable resource on the campus—the library.

Every successful college student constantly draws upon its facilities. It is of utmost importance that you learn to use the library efficiently. Once you have mastered the basic library skills, you will have more time to concentrate on your research. The primary purpose of this guide is to keep you from wandering about the library in a puzzled state.

Student Objectives

As a result of mastering the material in this guide, you will be able to:

    a. understand the basic format of your college library;

    b. locate desired information in magazines and newspapers;

    c. locate library books through the efficient use of the card catalog; and

    d. identify and utilize various reference sources related to particular disciplines (subject areas).

Library Format

Oftentimes students only encounter the inside of a library when a research assignment is due. To avoid mental anguish, you should learn the hours and layout of your library prior to embarking upon future research.

Learning your way around libraries—any kind of library—makes you your own teacher. New materials are always being added.

Southern's library, the John B. Cade Library, has a Quick Glance Guide that explains its four floor formats. Library hours when school is in session are as follows:

Mon-Thurs.	8am–12 midnight
Friday	8am–5pm
Saturday	9am–5pm
Sunday	2pm–12 midnight

All departments/resource areas may not be open for public access after 5 pm or on weekends.

One extremely helpful feature of the library is an information desk located on the first floor as you come into the main entrance. It's usually staffed by a professional librarian to direct and assist students in locating appropriate materials needed in their research.

DEPARTMENTS/RESOURCE

Information Desk .... All Floors

Student Areas .... All Floors

General Collection .... 2nd, 3rd, & 4th Floors

1st Floor	Card Catalogs
	Reference/Interlibrary Loan
	Electronic Periodical Indexes
	Computerized Research
	Circulation
	Reserve
	Technical Services
	Collection Development

2nd Floor	Administration
	Government Documents
	Educational Media Services
	PC Access Center
	Video Center
	Micrographics Center
	Exhibit/Lecture Hall, Rooms 1 & 2
	Periodicals
	Electronic Periodical Indexes
	Microforms
	Magazines
	Newspapers

3rd Floor	Archives
	Black Heritage/Special Collection
	Music Listening Center
	Rooms A & B

| 4th Floor | General Collection |

BRANCH LIBRARY

Art & Architecture

Engineering West – Room 207 (2nd Floor)

Another important attribute of the library is the Circulation Desk which is located on the first floor. It is not only the place where you check out books; it is also the place where records are kept on all books that are not on the shelves: those that are checked out on reserve, or are being repaired. The staff people behind this desk can usually tell you where books are and when you can expect to use them.

The *reference desk*, located in the Reference Reading Room on the first floor, is always staffed with a professional librarian. The reference librarian has been trained to help you, knows the resources of the library's collection, and can give you suggestions to enable you to use the resources to the fullest.

The Reference Librarian is there to answer your questions, no matter how simple or how complex. Do not hesitate to ask for assistance. A good many research papers owe their success to the suggestions offered by reference librarians.

ASK FOR HELP!!

In the reference section you will find such general resource materials as indexes, encyclopedias, atlases, dictionaries, and yearbooks. The resource books in this area are generally large, expensive volumes that cannot be taken out of the library; they must be used on the premises.

These materials are used by thousands of patrons in the course of a semester to fulfill research needs.

Most resource books and journals owned by the library are purchased in single copies and have a shelf–life expectancy of many years. Therefore, it's extremely important that students handle library material with care and respect. When using library materials, be considerate of others who will be using the same material after you. These materials are often impossible or very costly to replace.

Organization is the key to any venture. A research assignment cannot be performed properly unless you have given your charge some direction. By going to the aforementioned desks for assistance, you will be given very beneficial aid. Interaction with the library staff, prior to engaging in research, will provide you with some very helpful pointers. The librarians are there to help you—ASK FOR HELP!!

ACTIVITY 1

Directions: On your answer sheet, indicate the most appropriate answer for the following questions.

1. The reference section of John B. Cade Library is located
   a. On the third floor
   b. On the first floor
   c. On the second floor
   d. On the fourth floor

2. The primary responsibility of a librarian is
   a. to locate books
   b. to check out books
   c. to help the individuals desiring to use the library
   d. to conduct research

3. The electronic periodical indexes are located in _____ areas of the library.
   a. Two
   b. Four
   c. Five
   d. Three

4. If you wanted to know where newspapers were housed in the university library, you would go to
   a. the information desk
   b. the reference desk
   c. the circulation desk
   d. the newspaper desk

5. Prior to searching for a book, one can find out if it has been checked out by
   a. asking at the reference desk
   b. asking at the circulation desk
   d. asking the reference librarian
   d. asking at the information desk

The Periodical Section of the Library

Periodicals are magazines, journals, and newspapers that are printed at periodic intervals during the year. Because these materials contain current information, they are often particularly valuable when you are doing research. It is suggested that when you research a topic in the library, you should begin by researching the current information published in magazines, journals, and newspapers. Justification for this suggestion lies in the fact that the papers you write in college will be closer to the length of articles than the length of books. For this reason, articles are more likely to give you some good ideas about the ways you can discuss a topic in a paper for a college course.

Southern's **current** periodicals are housed on the second floor of the library in the periodical room. Some of the periodicals are kept in stacks. "Stacks" is the library term for books arranged on shelves one above the other. The stacks are both open and closed. Open stacks are available to all users of the library; whereas, closed stacks are not. In order to retrieve items from the closed stacks, you must wait for a library staff person to secure it for you.

A. The Readers' Guide to Periodical Literature

There are several periodical guides or indexes to locate a specific article in a magazine or other publication. Just as an index in a book helps you find a topic in that book, periodical indexes are used to find out what may have been written on a subject, from a whole range of magazines, journals, and newspapers. The most common periodical index, however is *Readers' Guide to Periodical Literature*. Articles are listed from over 180 popular magazines, journals, and newspapers.

Some students are confused by the format used in the *Readers' Guide*. However, all the abbreviations used in an entry are explained at the front of each issue. Here, for example, is a typical entry:

1 COLLEGE and school journalism

2 School newspapers have the right to freedom
   of the press. a. Karp. *Seventeen* 35:88 Je'76

                         3   4   5   6   7

1. subject
2. title
3. author
4. magazine
5. volume
6. page
7. date

The *Readers' Guide* is published (in paperback) monthly in February, July, and August, and semi-monthly the rest of the year. During the year there are four cumulated issues (interfiled alphabetical lists) and a bound annual volume. Whether you are using a current paper issue or a bound volume, the date is clearly stated on the cover, so that you know exactly what period of time is included in that particular issue. You may need to consult several volumes of an index. The university does not subscribe to all the magazines that are listed in an index. A list of all the magazines housed in the library is available to you. If a periodical you want is *not* available, the librarian may be able to locate it elsewhere. ASK FOR HELP!!

B. Specialized Indexes

There are also indexes for articles that appear in periodicals that publish scholarly articles and articles about specialized topics. The *Art Index*, for instance, lists articles about fine arts, architecture, photography, film, and many other related subjects. Other indexes to specialized periodicals include the following:

- *Applied Science and Technology Index*
  a subject index to periodicals in the field of aeronautics, automation, chemistry, electronics, physics, telecommunication, etc.

- *Business Periodicals Index*
  a subject index to periodicals in the area of accounting, advertising, banking, economics, etc.

- *Education Index*

  a subject index to education periodicals.

- *Humanities Index*

  an excellent source for articles on literary figures and their works.

- *New York Times Index*

  an index to articles appearing in the *New York Times* newspaper. It is a comprehensive digest of the world's events. It can be used to help you locate the date of an important event, so that you can look it up in other newspapers.

- *Facts on File*

  a weekly digest of world news. It is an excellent source of information on current affairs.

It is important for you to consult indexes such as these. For example, if you write a research paper for a business course, you should consult the *Business Periodicals Index.* If you are uncertain about which specialized index to use, ASK FOR HELP!!

The periodical indexes are located in the Reference Reading Room on the 1st floor.

Although periodical indexes are usually the best guide to current information, they are usually about two months behind. Therefore it is necessary to know which periodicals would be most useful. For general and current events, the following lists of periodicals are helpful.

CURRENT EVENTS:	*Facts on File*, Weekly. REVIEWS
	Manchester Guardian Weekly, Weekly. BOOK REVIEWS.
	Nation, Weekly. REVIEWS: Books, Drama, Films, Records
	New Republic, Weekly. BOOK REVIEWS.
	The New York Times Magazine, Weekly.
	Newsweek, Weekly. BOOK REVIEWS.
	Time, Weekly. REVIEWS: Books, Drama, Movies, Records.
	U.S. News and World Report, Weekly.
GENERAL:	*Atlantic Monthly*, Monthly. REVIEWS: Books and Records
	Bulletin of the Atomic Scientist, Monthly. BOOK REVIEWS
	Ebony, Monthly
	Harper's Bazaar, Monthly, BOOK REVIEWS
	New Yorker, Weekly. REVIEWS: Art, Books, Movies, Theater.
	Reader's Digest, Monthly.
	Saturday Evening Post, Monthly (except Jan., June & Aug.)
	Times Literary Supplement, Weekly. BOOK REVIEWS.
	Virginia Quarterly Review, Quarterly. BOOK REVIEWS
	Yale Review, Quarterly. BOOK REVIEWS.

ACTIVITY 2

Directions: Indicate the most appropriate response to the following questions.

1. The most common periodical index is
   a. *The New York Times Index*
   b. *The Business Index*
   c. *Readers' Guide to Periodical Literature*
   d. *The Humanities Index*

2. A newspaper is a
   a. Journal
   b. Index
   c. Periodical
   d. Specialized Index

3. Information listed in recent periodical indexes is
   a. Complex
   b. Lengthy
   c. Detailed
   d. Current

Use the following entry to answer the next question.

> Thomas, Lester
>
> > The gas shortage in America
> > *Newsweek* 9: 12–16 April 11, '89

4. The volume of *Newsweek* where this article appears is
   a. Twelve (12)
   b. Nine (9)
   c. Twelve–Sixteen (12–16)
   d. Eleven (11)

5. The most appropriate index to locate information on building styles would be
   a. The House Index
   b. The Humanities Index
   c. The Art Index
   d. The Readers' Guide

The Card Catalog

The heart of any library is its card catalog. The card catalog is an index to all of the books in the library, and is located on the first floor. The card catalog is an alphabetical list of cards, representing books, filed by author, title, and subject, with information on the location of the book on the shelves. It is based on a classification system. This system serves the same purpose as a map does for a tourist. It provides the information and proper directions needed to locate a book.

By utilizing the classification systems, a call number is assigned to all books in the library. Without the use of these systems and the skills in using them a student would find himself in a vast wilderness of unmanageable and unattainable materials. The university library employs the two types of classification systems: *The Dewey Decimal System* and T*he Library of Congress System*. The system in use determines the call number of any book.

The Dewey Decimal System divides books into ten major subject categories with subdivisions in each denoted by tens, ones, and succeeding decimal places. A valuable feature of this method of classifying books is that all books on the same subject are given the same class number and may be placed together on the library shelves. Once you have learned the class number of the subject you are interested in, you can find most of the books in the library on this subject grouped together in one place.

The division of *The Dewey Decimal System* is as follows:

000–099.	General Works (encyclopedias, periodicals, etc.)
100–199.	Philosophy (includes psychology)
200–299.	Religion (includes mythology)
300–399.	Social Sciences (economics, law, etc.)
400–499.	Languages (dictionaries, grammar, etc.)
500–599.	Science (mathematics, chemistry, etc.)
600–699.	Technology (agriculture, engineering, etc.)
700–799.	The Arts (sculpture, painting, music)
800–899.	Literature (poetry, plays, etc.)
900–999.	History, Travel, Biography

The *Library of Congress System* designates categories by capital letters. The division of the Library of Congress system is as follows:

A	•	General Works
B	•	Philosophy and Religion
C	•	History: Auxiliary Science
D	•	History: General and Old World
E-F	•	History: American
G	•	Geography, Anthropology, Folklore
H	•	Social Sciences
J	•	Political Science
K	•	Law
L	•	Education
M	•	Music
N	•	Fine Arts
P	•	Philosophy and Literature
Q	•	Science
R	•	Medicine
S	•	Agriculture
T	•	Technology
U	•	Military Science
V	•	Naval Science
Z	•	Bibliography and Library Science

The Library of Congress System, designates categories by capital letters, with the subdivisions designated by combinations of letters. For example:

Language and literature is the *P* series. Greek and Latin literature is *PA*. Modern European languages is *PB*. Romance languages is *PC*, German languages is *PD*. English is *PE*.

Regardless of the classification system used, for each book in the library you will find three cards in the card catalog: an *author card*, a *title card*, and a *subject card*. All three cards contain the same information about the book. The only difference is the information on the top line. The following are examples of a title, a subject, and an author card.

LIBRARY OF CONGRESS CLASSIFICATION SYSTEM

TP	The technology of food preservation.
311.2	Desrosien, Norman W.
.D47	Westport, Conn., AVI Publishing, Co., 1963.
	405 p. illus.

TITLE CARD

TP	Food Preservation, The technology of
311.2	Desrosien, Norman W.
.D47	Westport, Conn., AVI Publishing, Co., 1963.
	405 p. illus.

SUBJECT CARD

TP	Desrosien, Norman W.
371.2	The technology of food preservation.
.D47	Westport, Conn., AVI Publishing, Co., 1963.
	405 p. illus.

AUTHOR CARD

DEWEY DECIMAL SYSTEM

664.8	The technology of food preservation.
D474	Desrosien, Norman W.
1963	Westport, Conn., AVI Publishing, Co., 1963.
	405 p. illus.

TITLE CARD

664.8	Food Preservation, The technology of
D474	Desrosien, Norman W.
1963	Westport, Conn., AVI Publishing, Co., 1963.
	405 p. illus.

SUBJECT CARD

664.8	Desrosien, Norman W.
D474	The technology of food preservation.
1963	Westport, Conn., AVI Publishing, Co., 1963.
	405 p. illus.

AUTHOR CARD

Books having the same class number may be distinguished from one another by the author's name. For instance, all books on food technology are given the number 601. This number appears on the spine of the book. This number is known as the book's call number. To find the call number of a book, you must look the book up in the card catalog. This call number will appear in the upper left–hand corner of the card. All parts of the call number are important in order to locate a specific book.*

	601	The technology of food preservation.
*Call	D46	Desrosien, Norman W.
Number	1963	Westport, Conn., AVI Publishing, Co., 1963.

An **author card** is filed according to the surname or last name of the author. A **title card** is filed according to the first main word of the title. If the title of the book begins with "A," "An," or "The," it is filed according to the next word. For example: *The Arabian Nights* would be filed under Arabian, the first main word.

You will probably find listings in the card catalog for more books on your topic than you can possibly read in the time available to you. You should not try to read them all, or even to get hold of them all. Instead, you should choose the books that seem likely to be most useful for your project.

After obtaining the call number of the book, students may use the following guide in determining where that book is shelved.

*   *   *   *

LOCATION GUIDE

Library of Congress Classification

A-K	*	2nd Floor
L-P	*	3rd Floor
Q-Z	*	4th Floor

Dewey Decimal Classification

| 000-999 | * | 4th Floor |

ACTIVITY 3

Directions: Indicate the most appropriate response to the following questions.

1. The title card for a book entitled *An Enterprising American* would be filed under the letter
   a. V
   b. A
   c. E
   d. N

2. The three types of cards in the card catalog are the title card, author card, and
   a. publisher's card
   b. card catalog card
   c. subject card
   d. author/title card

3. The three cards found in the card catalog contain
   a. factual information
   b. same information
   c. different information
   d. research information

4. The purpose of book classification systems is to
   a. give credit to the author
   b. provide a means for locating a book on a library shelf
   c. distinguish the difference between Library of Congress and the Dewey Decimal System

5. The Dewey Decimal System utilizes _____ subject categories.
   a. Nine (9)
   b. Eleven (11)
   c. Seven (7)
   d. Ten (10)

Bibliography

Lannon, John M. "The Library Research Report." *The Writing Process*. Boston: Little, Brown and Co., pp. 329–366.

Maker, Janet. "How to Use a Library." *College Reading*. Belmont, Calif.: Wadsworth Publishing Co., pp.112–153.

Yuthas, Ladessa and David Smith-Gold. "Library Skills." *Reading and Other College Survival Skills*. Iowa: Kendall / Hunt Publishing Co., pp. 165-178.

ACTIVITY KEY

Activity 1

1. b
2. c
3. a
4. a
5. b

Activity 2

1. c
2. b
3. d
4. b
5. c

Activity 3

1. c
2. c
3. b
4. b
5. d

FINAL EVALUATION

Directions: Indicate the most appropriate response to the following questions.

1. The number in the upper left hand corner of a card catalog card is the _____ number.
   a. subject
   b. call
   c. concise
   d. specialized

2. The way a library is arranged is called its
   a. plan of study
   b. reference section
   c. format
   d. position

3. The Information Desks in Southern's library are located on
   a. four floors
   b. two floors
   c. three floors
   d. five floors

4. The name of Southern's library is
   a. Smith-Brown Library
   b. The J.C. University Library
   c. The James Seymore Library
   d. The John B. Cade Library

5. To place a book on reserve in the library, instructors go to the
   a. information desk
   b. reference desk
   c. periodicals' desk
   d. circulation desk

6. The primary responsibility of a librarian is
   a. to check out books
   b. to help individuals
   c. to locate books
   d. to conduct research

7. Periodicals contain
   a. current information
   b. indexed information
   c. detailed information
   d. illustrated information

8. *Stacks* is a library term for _____ arranged on shelves one above the other.
    a. film
    b. supplies
    c. books or magazines
    d. *Readers' Guide*

9. Periodicals are published
    a. at the library
    b. during the fall semester
    c. at various periods of time
    d. primarily for student use

10. The *Readers' Guide* is published in _____.
    a. the library
    b. the Southern states
    c. volumes
    d. indexes

11. The popular newspaper index is
    a. *New York Times Index*
    b. *Morning Advocate Index*
    c. *Readers' Guide to Periodical Literature*
    d. *Facts on File*

12. To locate periodicals on chemistry, the most suitable index to use would be
    a. *Social Sciences Index*
    b. *Applied Science and Technology*
    c. *Business Index*
    d. *Natural Science Index*

13. A newspaper is a
    a. periodical
    b. index
    c. classification Item
    d. journal

14. The Library of Congress system designates categories by
    a. topic
    b. length of topics
    c. spelling
    d. capital letters

15. A title card is filed according to the
    a. second word of title
    b. first main word of the title
    c. first word of the title
    d. spelling of the title

Improving Reasoning and Critical Thinking Skills

Learning to comprehend what you read is learning to associate meaning. To understand the ideas in college textbooks, you have to work harder than you do when reading newspapers or magazines. Absorbing the meaning from college texts frequently requires a laborious, step-by-step analysis of details and their relationships to the whole.

Each time you master a textbook, you have learned how to think about a subject. There are both immediate and future benefits. For example, after struggling through and finally understanding an introductory text, the same habits of thinking of and getting meaning transferred to the next course makes it easier to understand because of the previous experience. Another example of future benefit is the ability to apply the learned thinking skills to a new and different task. Thinking, like everything else, requires practice, and the more you do, the better you get. Consequently, you gradually develop the ability to educate yourself.

There is a famous quotation about thinking by the British philosopher Bertrand Russell, who said, "Most people would rather die than think—and most do!" Thinking is a process that enables us to understand what is happening in our lives and to make informed decisions based on our understanding. Yet, as Russell aptly pointed out, most of us do not take full advantage of our thinking abilities, and thus often suffer the unpleasant—and sometimes fatal—consequences of this failure. Fortunately, thinking is an ability, like other abilities, that can be improved through proper guidance and practice.

Objectives

After completing this module, you will be able to:
- classify terms and ideas to determine their relations to each other and recognize when ideas are improperly related.
- draw valid conclusions from properly related statements or premises and recognize conclusions incorrectly drawn from the argument on which they are based.
- identify the underlying assumptions on which an argument is based, whether they are stated or not, in order to determine whether the reasoning is sound.
- recognize assumptions that are false, are based on insufficient evidence, or that contain undefined terms.
- identify illogical cause-and-effect reasoning and arguments based on irrelevant issues, emotional appeal, exaggeration, and false analogy.
- distinguish between valid evidence and false evidence and know when an inference drawn from evidence is reasonable.
- understand the relevance of selected college courses to your own life.
- stress the importance of background information in problem solving and decision making.
- explore devices of persuasion commonly used in the media, advertising, and propaganda.
- emphasize techniques related to critical and effective thinking.
- recognize that "how to think" is much different from "what to think."
- employ the basic steps involved in logical thinking.

Terms of Logic—Key Words

Before you consider the principles of logic, examine the following list of some of the important terms of logic. Read them carefully now so that they will be familiar when you encounter them.

Agreement
> Ideas that correspond.

Ambiguous
> Words having more than one distinct meaning and the reader is not sure which meaning is intended.

Analogy
> A comparison or relation of two things that are superficially different on the basis of a common underlying similarity.

Argument
> The reason or reasons offered in support of an assertion; the process of reasoning which has led to the statement or conclusion presented.

Causation
> A relationship of ideas or events in which one is a direct result or consequence of the other.

Classification
> The process of grouping items or ideas in classes and sub-classes so that each class includes all members that belong to it.

Conclusion
> A final statement in a chain of reasoning that is reached on the basis of the evidence or premises presented.

Connotation
> The meanings associated with a word in addition to its literal or central meaning.

Deductive Reasoning
> A form of reasoning that proceeds from a general truth or premise to a conclusion about a particular instance.

Definition
> A clear statement of the specific meaning of a term as it applies in the context in which it is being used.

Evaluation
> To make a judgment or decision about something through examination of all of its parts.

Fact
> That which is known to exist or to have occurred in the past.

Fallacy
> Faulty or invalid reasoning or a conclusion reached by faulty reasoning.

Generalization
> A general statement about the whole made from information about the specific parts.

Hypothesis
> A proposition set forth to explain a set of facts.

Inductive Reasoning
> A form of reasoning that proceeds from particular observation of facts to a general conclusion.

Inference

    A reasonable guess about something unstated on the basis of what has been stated.

Judgment

    An evaluation in terms of some subjective or objective standard or criterion of value.

Opinion

    A belief, judgment, or attitude.

Premise

    An assertion or generalization, either stated or implied, on which a conclusion is based.

Reasoning

    The logical progression from a set of ideas or facts to a conclusion based on them.

Sampling

    Selection of particular examples for objective examination as a basis for inferring some conclusion or generality about the whole.

Truth

    A statement that has been verified by reasonable objective proof.

Validity

    The logical correctness of a statement or the reasoning on which it is based.

Thinking

    An active, purposeful, organized, process whereby we make sense of the world through solving problems, working toward our goals, locating and understanding information, and making sense of people.

Critical Thinking Skills

You have been using critical thinking skills all your life. The purpose of this activity is to make you aware of some of the critical thinking skills you already use and to help you sharpen them. Below are the names of the critical thinking skills you use daily without being cognizant of how you practice them. Next to each skill is an example of how you use this skill in your daily lives.

Anticipating Probabilities

    You are preparing for a job interview. You make a list of questions you might be asked. You compare the prices of products of different sizes. You now have a tool for determining the best value.

Classifying

    Your room has gradually filled up with clothes and books. It is hard to find what you need when you need it. You decide to divide everything according to purpose.

Communicating Ideas

    You disagree with a review you read in the newspaper about a music video. You write a letter to the critic giving your own opinion.

Developing Criteria

    You want to open a charge account. You make a list of the interest rates, minimum balances, and service charges for each store you are considering. Then you decide which is the best for you.

Distinguishes Fact from Reality

You read a newspaper article about comets, stars, or extraterrestrial ships. You are aware that you are reading something about some real things. You see the movies or horror shows, but you know it is fantasy.

Distinguishing Opinion from Fact

You read an article about a famous rock star. If the writer says this star is a great artist, you know that it is an opinion. However, if the article says he has cut 3 platinum albums in the last two years, you know that it is a fact.

Drawing Conclusions

You are watching a football game on television. The score is 7–0. You are called to the telephone. When you return to the television, the score is 7–7. You draw the conclusion that the team that was behind made a touchdown while you were on the telephone.

Estimating

It is the end of the month and your cash flow is extremely low. You have made a list of some things you would like to buy. You estimate how much each one will cost. They you decide whether or not you can afford the entire list or need to reduce it.

Forming Hypotheses

You notice that in the summer you frequently get headaches in the afternoons. However, you also notice that you do not get headaches in the mornings or on cool days. You hypothesize that the hot afternoon sun causes your headaches.

Giving Definitions and Examples

You tell your child that a skyscraper is a very tall building. You are giving a definition of the word. You show the child the Empire State Building or Sears Tower. You are showing him or her an example of the word.

Identifying Main Ideas

You read an article entitled, "Making the Most of Your Leisure Time." You figure out that one of the main ideas of the article is that most Americans watch too much television.

Making Generalizations

"All basketball players are tall." You know this is not a valid generalization because one basketball player you watched on television is very short.

Making Inferences

You wake up in the morning and see that the ground around your house is wet. You infer that it rained during the night.

Ordering Steps in a Process

You decide to repair your own roof. You go to the library and get information on do-it-yourself roof repair. You make a list of all the steps you will need to take. You put the steps in order. You list the materials you need and their approximate cost.

Outlining and Summarizing

You are studying for a social studies test. After you read a chapter of the book, you make an outline or write a summary to help you understand and remember what you have read.

Planning Projects

You need to put together a piece of furniture you bought unassembled. You read the directions carefully before you begin. Then, you follow the directions step by step.

Identifying Relationships

You know that leaving your car lights on when the car is parked may cause your battery to malfunction.

Identifying Mood of a Story

You read an Edgar Allen Poe story. You are aware that the author creates a mood of fear or terror.

Identifying Story Elements

You talk with a friend about a story you have both read or a movie you have both seen. You talk about different things you liked or didn't like: the setting, the plot, the characters.

Identifying Structure

You examine a bicycle and determine the function of the various parts.

Identifying Values

You have a chance to take a job in another city for more money. But you will have to leave your family and friends. You decide not to take the job because family and friends mean more to you than a bigger paycheck.

Judging Completeness

You read an article/ad for a piece of jewelry. It looks like a real bargain, but you decide not to buy it. The ad does not mention the size of the jewelry.

Judging Accuracy

You read an advertisement about something you need to buy. You try to get straight information. You ignore the parts of the ad that are trying to sway your thinking.

Judging Sentence Sequence

You write a letter to a friend. You tell the most interesting things that happened since you last wrote. You put your sentences in the order that the events occurred.

Making Comparisons

You go to the jeans store. You know whether you want fashion jeans or work jeans. You find the right section of the store. You compare the different types of jeans.

Making Decisions

You compare two job offers you have received. You talk to people you know from both companies. You study salaries and benefit plans. You talk to your family. You decide which of the two you will accept.

Recognizing Fallacies

You recognize that the following thought is a fallacy: The weather was chilly last night. I woke up with a cold. That is proof that the chilly weather caused my cold.

Recognizing Meaning

You go to a football game and watch the Chicago Bears. You know these Bears are not the kind that live in the wilds. They are real people. You understand that words, in general, take their meaning from the situation.

Recognizing Relevance and Irrelevance

You are talking to some friends about the meaning of pets in their owners' lives. Someone goes on and on about a monkey he saw at the zoo. You realize his comments are irrelevant.

Critical Thinking Abilities

- *Actively* using one's intelligence, knowledge, and skills to deal with ourselves, others, and life's situations effectively rather than passively receiving information or merely "having thoughts."

- Developing a *questioning* and *reflective* attitude that penetrates beneath the surface of what is simply being presented.

- Creating and using ideas that are *one's own* rather than critically imitating or borrowing the thoughts of others.

- Being *open* to other views and new ideas and *flexible* enough to change or modify one's ideas in light of the new information or better insight.

- Imagining *other possibilities* than those being presented; attempting to identify with *other points of view* and different perspectives.

- Developing solid *reasons* and *arguments* for one's views.

- Showing evidence *logically consistent* with one's beliefs.

- Engaging in substantive *dialogue* and *discussion* with others: thus, systematically exchanging, exploring, and clarifying ideas with others.

- *Analyzing* and *evaluating* complex issues and situations through critical reflection and dialogue with others.

- Translating critical understanding into thoughtful and effective *planning* and *decision making*.

Problem-Solving Abilities

Developing the general ability to approach and analyze complex problems in a systematic fashion for the purpose of making informed decisions include the following components:

- Identifying and defining the *"real" problem*.
- Gathering, organizing, and evaluating relevant *information*.
- Conceptualizing and evaluating *alternatives, approaches*, and *strategies*.
- Specifying the *goals* and determining the underlying *values*.
- Assessing the *risks* and identifying the *constraints*.
- Synthesizing this material into a general *conclusion*, including the planning of *specific steps* to be taken.

Language

The purpose of this section is to explore the relationships between thought and language, and to demonstrate that clarity in language leads to clarity in thought and communication. The relationship between thinking and language is extremely complex. However, it is clear that thinking and language are closely related, interdependent processes that must be addressed together. Clear language and clear thinking go together.

Structure of Language

1. Language can be "dead"—a collection of static formulas and used meaning.

2. Language can be "alive"—dynamic, creative, personal.

3. Language has "meaning"—symbolism.

4. Language has "pitfalls"—ambiguity, vagueness, euphemisms, clichés.

5. Language influences life experiences—meanings of words and expressions sometimes are changed either to get around or to take advantage of laws, rules, or customs. (Example: calling an employee a subcontractor to avoid paying a minimum wage or social security.) The English language contains features that mirror sexist attitudes of the past.

6. Language can influence (positively and negatively). Con artists use the emotive side of language to mask cognitive meaning by whipping up emotions so that reason is overlooked, to dull the force of language, and to promote propaganda.

7. Language influences advertising.

Conclusion

In addition to being influential with regard to the clarity of your thinking, language influences the way that we think about the world. The particular language that we use to describe our experiences both reflects and influences how we perceive the beliefs that we form, and the decisions we make. Consequently, the insights gathered regarding the development of effective thinking and language use should be reinforced throughout your academic experiences so that you become articulate thinkers, writers, readers, and speakers.

ACTIVITY

SOURCE: *Create Your Own College Success*
Robert A. Friday

EXERCISE: Recording the Logic Around You

PURPOSE: Your world is filled with fallacious statements. Such statements abound in most of the public, electronic, and print media. Because you are exposed to media often, you may find yourself reacting to false conclusions, often referred to as propaganda. If you base your decisions on false conclusions, you may get into difficulty. The purpose of this exercise is to help you become more critical of the media messages that you consume daily.

Directions: Listen or watch for and record logical and illogical statements from the sources listed on thebelow. Write the statement in the space provided along with a brief explanation of why it is logical or fallacious!

Sources	Logical Statements	Fallacious Statement
U.S. Presidents		
Explanation		
Ad in Newspapers		
Explanation		
Commercial on TV		
Explanation		
Your Choice:		
Discussion with Roommate or Friend:		
Explanation		
Discussion with your parents		
Explanation		

Closure

This exercise should have demonstrated some of the fallacies that you are exposed to daily. Learn to watch for them, knowing whether a statement is sound or not is the sign of the well-educated person.

PRACTICE EXERCISE

DIVERGENT THINKING: LOOKING AT PROBLEMS FROM DIFFERENT PERSPECTIVES

In order to evaluate a problem or conflict, you need to take emotions and individual viewpoints into account. Before using a problem-solving procedure such as the one in Worksheet 1, you may sometime want to practice examining an issue from multiple perspectives.

Newsweek presents many "problem" stories. (In fact, news is inherently "problematic.") Below is a summary of one such story: The Baby M case. Ultimately, William and Elizabeth Stern won custody. But take yourself back, for awhile, to the early stages of the Baby M case. Imagine your reaction if you were one of the people involved.

To remind you of the case, here is a summary of the early events:

> William Stern's wife, Elizabeth, was advised not to try to have a child of her own for medical reasons. So, she and her husband signed an agreement to have Mary Beth Whitehead become a surrogate mother so that they could have a child.
>
> Mary Beth Whitehead, 29, gave birth to Baby M under a surrogate-mother arrangement in which she was artificially inseminated with William Stern's semen. However, following the child's birth, Whitehead decided she wanted to keep the child.
>
> The Sterns desperately wanted the child and sued for custody.

Different Perspectives

Answer the questions below as if you were the person involved. Use a separate sheet of paper for your answers.

1. You are Mary Beth Whitehead, the woman who agreed to bear a child for a New Jersey couple. You have decided you want to keep the child. Write a letter to Elizabeth and William Stern expressing your change of heart.

2. You are Elizabeth Stern. Write a letter to your sister telling her how you feel about the situation.

3. You are William Stern. Write a letter to Mary Beth Whitehead expressing your feelings.

4. You are Noel Keane, a Dearborn, Michigan, lawyer who has brought the Sterns and the Whiteheads together. Write a paper stating your position on the case.

5. You are Judge Harvey R. Sorkow. You must decide whether the contract signed by the Sterns and Whitehead was valid. You also must decide who will get custody of the child. What do you write in your diary after hearing the first few days of testimony?

6. You are Baby M—20 years from now. What has happened to you? Write an opening statement for your autobiography.

PRACTICE EXERCISE

A PROBLEM-SOLVING PROCESS

Some people panic when they face difficulties. They honestly have no idea how to begin solving their problems. Other people see problems as a challenge. They critically examine the situation and find logical solutions. The following questions can be useful for solving problems, from personal to global.

PROBLEM SOLVING

A. Selecting a problem

List some problems that your school or city faces.

_____

_____

_____

B. Solving the problem.

1. What problem would you like to solve?

_____

2. Why is this a problem?

_____

3. What are your goals? In other words, what would you as a problem-solver like to achieve as a result of solving the problem?

_____

_____

4. How can these goals be attained? In other words, how can the problem be solved? What course of action should be taken? Try to think of two potential solutions.

_____

_____

_____

a. What are the advantages of each solution?

_____

_____

_____

b. What are the disadvantages of each solution?

_____

_____

5. Predict the results. Which course of action is more likely to achieve the desired results?

_____

_____

PRACTICE EXERCISE

CREATIVE PROBLEM SOLVING

When guided problem-solving strategies don't seem to help, many people try creative problem-solving strategies. This exercise will give you practice using one of these techniques—comparative brainstorming.

Comparative Brainstorming

If you are trying to think through an idea or a problem and feel you are getting nowhere, stop and jot down every thought you have about the topic. For instance, if you were planning to write or speak about the topic "thinking skills," you might jot down the following ideas:

1. not everyone thinks the same way
2. not everyone will benefit from any one thinking strategy
3. good writing is the result of good thinking
4. effective speakers have thought about their topics carefully
5. to understand what they read, students need to think critically.

Now, try to relate any one idea on this list with another idea. For instance, think about item #4 in relationship to item #5. Ask yourself: What does the comment "to understand what they read, students need to think critically" have to do with the comment "effective speakers have thought about their topics carefully." At first, you might not see any connection, but after thinking for awhile, you might come up with: "By reading background materials carefully and critically, speakers will be more likely to consider their topic from many perspectives." This new idea might not have occurred to you if you hadn't juxtaposed the items on your list.

Directions: Practice "Comparative Brainstorming" by selecting a topic that interests you from a current issue of *Newsweek*. After reading the story about your selected topic, list eight ideas related to the topic that pop into your mind. Don't be critical; brainstorming should be free and open-ended.

READING LIST

Good Reasoning

Baker, Samm Sinclair. *Your Key to Creative Thinking*. New York: Harper & Row, 1962.

Blair, J. Anthony, and Ralph H. Johnson. *Informal Logic: The First International Symposium*. Inverness, Calif.: Edgepress, 1980.

Carroll, Lewis. *Symbolic Logic and the Game of Logic*. New York: Dover, 1958.

Damer, T. Edward. *Attacking Faulty Reasoning*. Belmont, Calif.: Wadsworth, 1980.

Gardner, Martin. *Science: Good, Bad, and Bogus*. Buffalo, NY: Prometheus, 1981.

Garner, Martin. *Fads and Fallacies in the Name of Science*. New York: Dover, 1957. (The classic debunking of pseudoscience.)

Henry, Jules. *On Sham, Vulnerability and Other Forms of Self-Destruction*. New York: Vintage Books, 1973.

Kahane, Howard. *Logic and Philosophy*. 4th ed. Belmont, Calif.: Wadsworth, 1982. (A mostly formal–logic test.)

Marks, David and Richard Kammann. *The Psychology of the Psychic*. Buffalo, NY: Prometheus, 1980.

Nickell, Joe. *Inquest on the Shroud of Turin*. Buffalo, NY: Prometheus, 1982. (An example of sanity on a foolishness-provoking topic.)

Peirce, Charles Sanders. "The Fixation of Belief," *Popular Science Monthly*. 1977.

Radner, Daisie, and Michael Radner. *Science & Unreason*. Belmont, Calif.: Wadsworth, 1982. (Explains a lot of pseudoscience.)

Randi, James (The Amazing). *Flim Flam! Psychics, ESP, Unicorns and Other Delusions*. Buffalo, NY: Prometheus, 1982.

Rice, Berkeley. "O Tempora, O Cult." *Psychology Today*. March 1979.

Twain, Mark. *Mark Twain on the Damned Human Race*. Edited by Janet Smith. New York: Hill & Wang, 1962.

III.
Enhancing Your Social Skills

Developing Social Skills

Managing Social Relationships

**Becoming Culturally Literate In
a Multicultural Society**

Enhancing Your Social Skills

Unit Concepts

The development of social skills and life management behaviors are vital to all of us. The term development includes a process that is sequential, progressive and often involves some type of "growing" on the part of students or individuals depending upon your own values, needs, goals, and lifestyle—many skills will be inclusive of the work-day, encounters with other people (including "significant others") that completely envelops and provide meaning to your life.

These skills are vital in today's society that is characterized by change. Social changes refer to myriad factions as technology, the organization of the family, the arrangements for earning a living and the growth and diversity (multiculturalism) characteristics of the population.

Developing Social Skills

Overview

Letitia Baldrige, in a revised edition of Amy Vanderbilt's *Complete Book of Etiquette*, states that "in the field of manners, rules are based on kindness and efficiency." She also believes that good manners and acceptable social skills are those qualities that make life and the workplace more livable. A revolution in the social mores has occurred. However, both men and women feel better about themselves and live more effectively when they are well-mannered.

Objectives

After studying and practicing skills in this module you will be able to:

1. Determine the importance of a positive first impression in organizational and social settings;

2. Understand how etiquette affects first impressions and socially acceptable behavior;

3. Cultivate basic social skills needed to improve your interpersonal relations; and

4. Assess your strengths and weaknesses through myriad activities while enhancing the college experience and your total development.

Manners and Etiquette in Organizations

The way you are treated in this world depends largely on they way you present yourself, the way you look, the way you speak and the way you behave.

Janet G. Elsea observes, "if people aren't quickly attracted to you or don't like what they see and hear in those first two or four minutes, chances are they won't pay attention to all the words you believe are demonstrating your knowledge and authority. They will find your client guilty, seek another doctor, buy another product, vote for your opponent or hire somebody else." This concept is expressed in more detail by Leonard and Natalie Zunin, coauthors of *Contact—The First Four Minutes*.

A study of manners (sometimes called etiquette) reveals a number of areas that potentially could serve as barriers to making a positive impression. Jonathan Swift, an advocate for good manners, states: "Good manners is the art of making people comfortable; whoever makes the fewest people uncomfortable has the best manners."

Making people feel comfortable is at the heart of good human relations. Good manners serve as a universal passport to positive relationships and respect. One of the best ways to develop rapport with another person is to avoid behavior that might be offensive. Selective strategies and guidelines that contribute to good manners and socially accepted behavior include:

1. **Establishing New Relationships in Professional and Personal Situations.**

   Avoid addressing people by their first names. Use titles of respect—Miss, Mrs., Ms., Dr., Professor, etc. until the relationship is well established. Too much familiarity can breed invitation. Informality should develop by *invitation*, not be presumption.

2. **Language and General Communication**

   Avoid obscenities and offensive comments or stories. In recent years, standards for acceptable and unacceptable language have changed considerably. Obscenity is used and more permissible in everyday conversation than it was in the past. However, it is still considered inappropriate to use foul language in educational institutions, with customers, clients, and in many cases with fellow workers or colleagues. If you broadcast it to people in general, you're telling them you don't care what their feelings might be.

   Never assume that another person's value system is the same as your own. Foul language and off-color stories can do irreparable damage to interpersonal relations.

3. **Never smoke in the presence of a fellow student, faculty member, client, or customer unless you are sure he or she will not be offended.**

   Most organizations and business facilities have restricted smoking areas. Some people are allergic to smoke or simply dislike the odor. People who do not smoke will appreciate your consideration for their comfort.

4. **Avoid making business or professional visits unless you have an appointment.**

   At the university, check a faculty member's office schedule prior to visiting. Walking into someone's office without legitimate reasons or without an appointment is generally considered rude.

   There are exceptions at the University during special activities such as Registration, Preregistration, and Examination Periods.

5. **Express appreciation at appropriate times.**

   A simple thank you can be very meaningful. Failure to express appreciation can be a serious human–relations blunder.

6. **Do not express strong personal views regarding issues that may be controversial.**

   It is usually not a good idea to express strong political views when you are attempting to establish a good relationship with others, particularly customers or clients.

   Personal beliefs regarding religious issues should also be restricted or avoided. There is seldom a "safe" position to take in the areas of religion or politics.

7. **Be Aware of Personal Habits that may be offensive to others.**

   Sometimes an annoying habit can be a barrier to establishing a positive relationship with someone else. Chewing gum is a habit that bothers many people, particularly if you chew gum "rigorously" or "crack" it. Biting fingernails, cracking knuckles, scratching your head and combing your hair in public are some additional habits to be avoided.

GENDER ETIQUETTE

Many of the rules of social etiquette arose from the traditional concept of chivalry, in which gentlemen were viewed as the protectors of ladies and were expected to accord them an extra measure of respect. Business etiquette requires, among other things, that:

1. before entering an elevator, men wait until all women present have entered. Also before exiting the elevator, they wait until all women who wish to leave have done so;

2. men stand up when a woman enters the room or office they are in, and continue to stand until she is seated;

3. ladies precede men when they are walking together, and men carry the ladies' packages;

4. men open doors for ladies. If necessary, a lady walking ahead of a man waits for him to catch up and open the door; and

5. men generally greet women with a compliment about their appearance.

Currently, many women are working side by side with men, and some women do not want to be treated differently because of gender. Yet many men feel that it is "improper" to treat women otherwise. The situation is just as awkward for women, who find it difficult to refuse such treatment without appearing to be discourteous or pushy.

The problem seems to be one of finding a middle ground—an organizational etiquette that preserves courtesy without distinguishing between male and female organizational members.

Values—Some Guides for Action

Many authors, inclusive of Richard L. Morrill, contend that "attitudes, feelings, beliefs, and ideas qualify as genuine values only when we consciously choose them." Others state that values are the "oughts" that guide behavior or ideas about what is desirable." Values shape the appreciation of beauty, human kindness, goodness, and the lovely things in life.

If, after some observation and deep introspection and evaluation of alternative choices, you elect to follow either a value taught to you, or one opposed to those taught to you, your actions will be *guided by your own values*.

ACTIVITY

Directions: Complete the following statements after reflecting on and possibly discussing them with family or close friends.

Values Toward Higher Education

1. Higher education (check one) _____ is or _____ is not a tradition in my family.

2. If I had complete freedom to do anything I wanted to do this year, I would have _____

_____

3. The decision for me to go to this college was _____% my parents' or guardians' decision, and _____% my decision.

4. Below is a list of 16 reasons for going to college. Rate the reasons from 1 (**most influential in your decision**) to 16 (**the least influential in your decision**).

_____ To be exposed to new ideas.
_____ To prepare for a job or profession.
_____ To gain problem-solving skills.
_____ To gain prestige or status.
_____ To prepare for good citizenship.
_____ To raise my economic status.
_____ To gain more maturity.
_____ To be a productive member of society.
_____ To get a degree.
_____ To please parents.
_____ To assimilate knowledge.
_____ To have something to do.
_____ To learn how to learn.
_____ To find a spouse or a mate.
_____ To make friends.
_____ To have fun.

5. List the six (6) key words out of all the preceding responses that name the values which have guided you into the role of a student at the university.

a. _____   d. _____
b. _____   e. _____
c. _____   f. _____

STUDENT ACTIVITIES

I. ROLE PLAYING INVOLVING STUDENT DEMONSTRATIONS ON CORRECT SOCIAL BEHAVIORS—ON INCORRECT OR INAPPROPRIATE SOCIAL SKILLS.

II. CONSULTANTS IN THE AREAS OF:
COSMETOLOGY
Male and Female Specialists

MAKEUP TECHNICIANS (Artist)

FASHION CONSULTANTS
Wardrobe and Color Coordination
(Possibly using students as models)

III. LEARNING TO IDENTIFY UTENSILS IN A FORMAL DINING PLACE SETTING.

GROUP ACTIVITY

(Personal Goals Auction)

Purpose: Making choices between one value (action) and another is the constant challenge of a free person, as Richard Morrill observed in *College Is Only the Beginning*. This activity is designed to force you to establish some priorities for yourself while getting a view of the priorities of your peers.

Directions: Each member of your class has $100,000 to bid for values in your class auction. Review the following list of life goals, which will be auctioned off in your class. Decide which values you want and how much you are willing to bid to obtain them. Bid in increments of $1,000. Only the highest bid will achieve the life goal.

After a careful review of the goals, distribute your money according to your priorities in the first column of the Budget Bidding Record, which follows the goals description.

Your instructor will auction off the life goals in a random order. If you are forced to overbid your budget to obtain a goal, you must adjust the amount you can bid on another goal. **Do not exceed $100,000.**

After each bidding, whether you win the goal or not, record the amount you bid and the sale price on the Budget Bidding Record.

(Personal Life Goals Description)

An Exciting Life: You will lead an exciting, stimulating life, encountering a wide range of new experiences with the confidence that you are equal to all challenges and able to enjoy whatever comes your way.

Financial Security: You will have sufficient money to support any material needs or desires you have, plus enough surplus wealth to use for any purpose of your choice, be it pampering others, contributing to charity, or assuring social status.

Personal Freedom: You will have a life of independence, always being able to do what you know is right for you in the here-and-now, without any interference from others.

Pleasure: You will lead an enjoyable, leisurely life. You will not be rushed by commitments, and all possible pleasures will be readily available.

Closeness to God: You will experience a communication with God, who will know that you are serving Him/Her, and you will achieve His/Her purpose for you.

A World of Beauty (Culture): You will live close to the beauty of nature and to the beauty of fine arts. (literature, music, and the theater.)

Job Satisfaction: You will be recognized by all as being the best in your profession, contributing more than you ever hoped and achieving everything you ever dreamed.

Long Life and Good Health: You will live far longer than the normal life expectancy, and your physical and mental health will be superb. You will benefit from both the vitality of youthfulness and wisdom born of experience.

A Comprehensive Personal Library: You will possess a personal library containing every bit of information ever recorded. The information will be totally accessible. You will be able to receive immediately any item you request, in printed or voice-recorded form.

An Ideal Setting: You will have a house overlooking the most beautiful scenery in the world. The house will have all the atmosphere, space, and facilities necessary to provide you and others of your choice with a perfect environment.

A Perfect Love Affair: You will experience an emotional and sexual relationship with a person of great physical and emotional attractiveness—a person who will have the same expectations of the affair as you. You will have absolute control over who is aware of the affair.

Universal Harmony: You will live in a world in which equal opportunity for all and the love of humanity are recognized as the primary value.

A Perfect Family Life: You and your family will experience ideal relationships together, each finding the needed love and security to assure personal growth within the family unit.

Inner-Peace: You will be free from all inner conflicts, secure in the knowledge that you will always make right decisions and continue effective personal functioning.

Intelligence: You will function at full mental capacity, being able to perceive solutions to critical problems and to understand logical relationships between ideas.

Productivity: You will have a feeling of satisfaction from completing numerous tasks successfully and making things happen.

Political Power: You will be in a position to control the destinies of most people in the civilized world. You will have absolute power to institute any program or policy you choose and will be able to gain the cooperation of any person or organization required by your purpose.

An Authentic World: You will live in a world in which all people are open, honest, and totally able to relate authentically with one another.

Fame: You will receive the respect and admiration of all and will be in demand at prominent social occasions and decision-making conferences.

Social Service: You will have the opportunity, the skill, and the resources to serve the sick and needy of the world. Full effort on your part will eliminate sickness and need in your lifetime.

Creativity: You will be able to formulate innovative ways of communicating perceptive understanding. You will have unusually fine command of several art media, as well as verbal creativity.

Self-Esteem: You will respect yourself, knowing that you are realizing your potential and that you are a person of great worth.

Deep Friendships: You will have many close and meaningful relationships with people you would choose to know well.

Mature Love: You will attain lasting spiritual and sexual intimacy with another.

Wisdom: You will have a mature understanding of life and will be sought out by others to furnish advice and counsel.

Success: You will feel and have others feel that your life is successful, perhaps including the materials and possessions to back that up.

BUDGET BIDDING RECORD

Item	Amount Budgeted	Amount Bid	Sale Price
An exciting life			
Financial security			
Personal freedom			
Pleasure			
Closeness to God			
A world of beauty			
Job satisfaction			
A long life			
Personal library			
An ideal setting			
A perfect love affair			
Universal harmony			
Perfect family life			
Inner peace			
Intelligence			
Productivity			
Political power			
An authentic world			
Fame			
Social service			
Creativity			
Self-esteem			
Deep friendships			
Mature love			
Wisdom			
Success			

Your top 3 life goal choices:	The top 3 goals you won:	The top 3 goals as indicated by bids:	Biggest surprise to you:
1. _____	1. _____	1. _____	1. _____
2. _____	2. _____	2. _____	2. _____
3. _____	3. _____	3. _____	3. _____

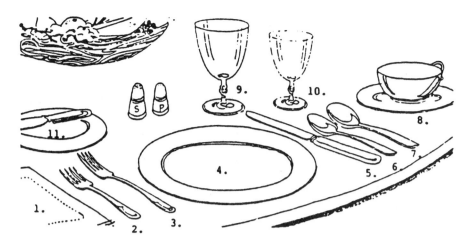

1. Napkin	6. Teaspoon
2. Salad Fork	7. Soup Spoon
3. Dinner Fork	8. Coffee or Tea Cup and Saucer
4. Dinner Plate	9. Water Glass
5. Dinner Knife	10. Beverage Glass
11. Bread and Butter Plate	

TABLE MANNERS

A. Use a *fork* to eat all food served on a plate except finger foods. The fork has three basic uses: to carry food to the mouth, to cut soft foods, and to hold foods when cutting them with a knife. You should hold the fork as you do a pencil, with the tines up when you carry food to the mouth.

B. You will frequently use the fork when you cut foods with a *knife*. Hold the knife in your right hand so that the handle rests in the palm of your hand and your forefinger is on the back of the knife blade. Place the knife on the edge of your plate with blade facing you, transfer the fork to your right hand and with tines up lift the food to your mouth.

C. At the end of the meal, place the knife across the center of the plate with the cutting edge of the blade toward you and the fork beside it—tines up.

D. Break the slice of bread in half and then break the half to form two pieces. Spread only one-quarter of a slice of bread at a time and break the remaining half of bread when you are ready to eat it. Always keep the buttered roll or bread on your plate, never on the tablecloth.

E. *Spoons* are used for foods that you cannot eat with a fork. You use a teaspoon for stirring sugar or cream into a beverage and for tasting beverages. The used teaspoon is placed on the saucer; it never remains in the cup.

F. *Soup spoons* are larger spoons than teaspoons and are used for eating soup. When eating soup, dip the spoon away from you, fill it about half full, and sip the side of the spoon.

G. You use a *napkin* to protect your clothes, to blot your mouth, and wipe your fingers when soiled at the table.

Bibliography

Gardner, John N. A Jewler, A. Jerome. *College Is Only The Beginning*, Belmont, California, Wadsworth Publishing Company, 1989.

The College Board. *Academic Preparation For College*, New York, 1983.

Shepherd, James F. *College Study Skills*, Boston, Houghton-Mifflin Company, 1990.

Post, Emily. *Etiquette*, New York, Funk and Wagnalls Company, 1951.

Vanderbilt, Amy. *Complete Book of Etiquette: A Guide to Contemporary Living*, New York, Doubleday and Company, Inc., 1978.

Managing Social Relationships

Strategies and Informal Information on Managing Social Relationships

People are social creatures. Our relationships are important to us. We share our feelings and experiences with friends. Our families often provide us with an abiding love and a sense of security. Our love relationships enhance our feelings of self-esteem and, perhaps, help us meet our sensual needs. We also need to relate effectively to our professors. Social support helps us manage stress.

When we enter college, especially a residential college, our social worlds may meet with upheaval. We may leave friends and family behind—including boyfriends and girlfriends. Relationships and sources of support that we had taken for granted may be many miles—and expensive telephone calls—away. Even rapid answers to letters may address problems that we were thinking about last week. Residential students need to form new friendships and, perhaps, new dating relationships at college.

Commuting students, too, face social challenges. For them, as for residential students, college is made less stressful by congenial relationships with classmates and professors. Commuters usually want to develop closer relationships with students in elective courses and major fields because they share common interests. Commuters, like residential students, are likely to develop romantic relationships with other students. Even returning students find it valuable to develop relationships with other returning students: other returning students, after all, are best able to understand what they are going through.

In this unit, we first discuss friendship—what it is and what we want from it. We consider the Greek-letter organizations—fraternities and sororities—and see what kinds of roles they play in helping us meet our social needs. Then we turn our attention to love, sweet love. We take on the task that has eluded poets for centuries—defining love, that is. We also talk about a social problem that affects thousands of students all over the country, even on populous campuses—loneliness. We'll see why students are lonely and, if you're one of them, what you can do about it. Finally, we consider ways of handling social conflicts that are likely to arise with professors, other students, family members, and lovers. We also focus on conflicts that are bred by prejudice, particularly by sexism and racism.

FRIENDSHIP

From childhood, friends play essential roles in our lives. During our teenage years, it is important to be able to share our feelings with our friends. We want to tell friends "everything," without having to worry whether they will spread stories about us. Our college friendships, as in the song, are often "perfect blendships." Our friends tend to be like us in race, values, and social class. The tendency to team up with people who are like them prevents many students from enjoying the cultural and ethnic diversity they might otherwise find.

Sought After Qualities in Friends

Quality	Percentage of Respondents Endorsing the Quality
1. Ability to keep confidences	89
2. Loyalty	88
3. Warmth and affection	82
4. Supportiveness	75
5. Honesty and frankness	73
6. Humor	72
7. Willingness to set aside time for me	62
8. Independence	61
9. Converstational skills	59
10. Intelligence	58
11. Social conscience	49

QUALITIES OF GOOD FRIENDS

Knowing what people want in their friends can help *you* be a good friend. Consider the results of a *Psychology Today* survey of its readers, most of whom were college graduates. They reported that keeping confidences and loyalty were the most important qualities in a friend (table).

Warmth, humor, willingness to make time for one's friends, honesty, independence, and intelligence also count.

Many physically intimate love relationships are found wanting because they lack the kinds of intimacy found in good friendships— loyalty and the ability to keep confidences. Let us now consider the pluses and minuses of fraternities and sororities, where many college students find groups of "built-in" friends.

FRATERNITIES AND SORORITIES: "THE GREEKS VERSUS THE GEEKS"?

"The Greeks versus the Geeks" is an advertising slogan from a Revenge of the Nerds sequel. On some campuses, sad to say, there is so much pressure to join fraternities and sororities that nonjoiners are looked upon with scorn or suspicion. The assumption seems to be that everyone who can become a brother or a sister does so. Students who do not are seen as rejects. Fraternities and sororities have a lower profile on many campuses, and some colleges do not allow them at all. These societies often take on more prominence at residential colleges. At residential colleges, fraternities and sororities may provide housing and surrogate parents as well as social diversion.

Let us consider some of the advantages and disadvantages of Greek-letter societies. With this knowledge you may be able to make a more informed decision about whether they are right for you.

ADVANTAGES AND DISADVANTAGES OF FRATERNITIES AND SORORITIES

Fraternities and sororities confer advantages such as the following:

1. They offer handy sources of social support.

2. They offer a crowd of people with whom to do and share things.

3. They confer prestige upon brothers and sisters. On many campuses, members of Greek organizations feel superior to nonmembers.

4. They offer the beginnings of a lifelong network that may be of use in obtaining jobs and climbing the corporate ladder.

5. They channel social life into house and college occasions. Rather than wondering what you're going to be doing on a weekend, especially a "big" weekend, you're welcome at the house's parties and functions. If you don't have a date, a brother or sister may fix you up with someone from a brother fraternity or sister sorority, where the members tend to share interests and values. Houses also arrange mixers with brother fraternities or sister sororities. In other words, they do much social screening for members.

6. Joiners become part of a tradition. Fraternities and sororities have histories and aims that affect members in the same way the nation, one's religious group, and the college at large affect the individual.

7. Fraternities and sororities frequently provide high-quality living arrangements. They are often housed in splendid buildings, sometimes in converted mansions.

8. They provide social inducement to play on university and intramural athletic teams. Athletics are valued by many houses, and as a member of a fraternity or sorority, you may also be on the society's intramural teams.

9. They encourage participation in the planning of social occasions and the management of house business. These chores develop administrative and interpersonal skills that can be of help later on.

10. Many houses encourage studying. Some value academics more than others do, but most recognize that the primary goal of college is to receive an education and inspire members to do so.

11. Upperclass members often provide valuable information about the strengths and weaknesses of various courses and professors.

12. Many fraternities and sororities have superb (legitimately compiled) test files. Members who have taken courses place copies of their exams in the file, and old exams often contain recycled questions. Some professors reuse examinations in their entirety.

Fraternities and sororities thus confer many benefits. But there are drawbacks, and what is of value to one person may be a hindrance to another. It depends on who you are and who you want to be.

Fraternities and sororities have these drawbacks or disadvantages:

1. Fraternities and sororities have expectations for behavior, called norms, that pressure members to conform. Students may try to join societies that reflect their own values, but there is never a perfect fit. When "rushing"—that is, visiting fraternities and sororities so that the houses and students can decide who and where to pledge—*be yourself*. Express your own ideas and values—not what you think the brothers or sisters of the house want to hear. It is a mistake to join a house whose members are very different from you. A moment of glory—being invited to pledge for a prestigious society—may yield to years of mutual discomfort.

2. Members who seek friends among nonmembers may face disapproval. This is the flip side of the advantage of finding an instant cadre of "friends." As we grow, we often reappraise our values and seek different qualities in friends. The society that boosted our self-esteem as first-year students may weigh us down as juniors or seniors.

3. There may be pressure to date the "right kind" of people. This is the flip side of the advantage that fraternities and sororities often provide "built-in" pools of potential dates. A member of a Christian fraternity, Carlos, was dating a Jewish girl, Fran, and he heard a number of comments about it.

4. Exclusivity is also reflected in pressure to socialize with members of your own house and a number of similar "acceptable" houses. Peer pressure may thus prevent you from socializing with groups of people you will find in the "real world" once you graduate—people from diverse racial, ethnic, and socioeconomic groups. You may enter college with an open mind and pledge a house with blinders on.

5. For some, the living arrangements offered by the fraternity or sorority are not satisfactory. Some students prefer an apartment with one or two roommates to the hustle and bustle of the fraternity or sorority house. In many cases, however, members are required to live in the fraternity or sorority house, at least for a year.

6. The "opportunity" to play on intramural teams may provide pressure that you don't want. Are you athletic? If not, do you want to join a group that prizes athletics? If you are only somewhat athletic, do you prefer to compete against others, which is the "Greek" way, or do you prefer self-developing solitary jogs, bike rides, and swims?

7. The "opportunity" to plan and manage house functions can translate into pressure to assume administrative burdens. Many would prefer to spend their spare time in other ways.

8. Although fraternities and sororities may promote academics on certain levels, there may also be subtle—and, in some cases, explicit—pressures not to study. At athletically oriented houses, being overly cerebral may be seen as nerdish. Then, of course, the profusion of social activities, house responsibilities, and demands of pledging may eat into valuable study time. We have seen many students flunk out of college because they could not limit their involvements with their societies. It does little good to pledge a prestigious house if the demands of pledging cause you to flunk out of college. As a pledge, it is one thing to wear silly clothes to class; it is another to be so busy memorizing the names and addresses of the grandparents of house members that there's no time to study!

9. Then there are the perils of hazing. Over the years, hazing practices have ranged from the silly and annoying to the painful and dangerous. There have been times and places when pledges have been required to eat live goldfish. This may seem yucky (to use a sophisticated term), but goldfish are usually nutritious. However, hazing can also involve running naked in winter or overdosing on alcohol. Now and then, a pledge dies from an alcohol overdose. Now and then, fraternity members go to jail because of it. Hazing practices are usually not so noxious, but they are intended to be demanding hurdles—both to test pledges' sincerity and to build their loyalty to the house. (The thinking goes like this: if pledges tell themselves they went through hell to join, they'll believe that their fraternities and sororities must be very, very special.) You have to decide for yourself just what you'll go through—just where you'll draw the line.

Should *you* pledge a fraternity or a sorority? We wish we could answer this for you, but we can't. We hope that we have given you a number of factors to weigh in making your decision. We will say this: If you're into athletics and a social whirl and don't particularly value solitary, contemplative hours, a fraternity or sorority may be right for you. If you would rather socialize with one or two intimate friends and are not "into" belonging to prestigious groups, a fraternity or sorority could be a senseless diversion for you. On many campuses, fraternity or sorority membership is synonymous with social acceptance and success. Students on such campuses may not be certain that these societies are for them, yet they may want to pledge for fear of social rejection.

We noted that many fraternity and sorority members find their love relationships among the members of sister and brother organizations. Let's now consider the topic of love, which makes the world go round on campus for many students.

LOVE

From the dawn of civilization, philosophers and poets have sought to capture love in words. Our poets have portrayed love as ethereal and heavenly. But passionate love—romantic love—is also lusty brimming with sexual desire. For many students, love rules campus life. And for many, love is indeed "blind." That is, we tend not to perceive the flaws in our lovers and, now and then, we do rather silly things for love.

Social scientists as well as poets speak of love. Romantic love involves feelings of passion and intimacy. Passion embraces feelings of fascination, as shown by preoccupation with the person you love; sexual craving; and the desire for an exclusive, special relationship with her or him. Intimacy embraces caring—championing the interests of the person you love and sacrificing your own interests, if necessary. College undergraduates see helping one's lover as being more central to the concept of love than seeking to meet one's own needs with one's lover. ("Ask not what your lover can do for you" is the motto. "Ask what you can do for your lover.")

LONELINESS

Being lonely differs from being alone. Being alone can mean pleasurable solitude—a chance to study, to listen to one's favorite music, or to reflect on the world and one's place in the world. Loneliness is painful isolation, however. Many college students are lonely, even when they live on swarming campuses. Students who are lonely may know as many people as those who are not lonely, but their relationships are relatively superficial.

They are unlikely to share confidences with their acquaintances. Loneliness usually peaks in adolescence, when most of us are supplanting close ties to parents with peer relationships.

CAUSES OF LONELINESS

Lonely students have many of these earmarks:

1. They lack social skills. They are unresponsive to the feelings of others. They do not know how to make friends or how to handle conflicts.

2. They fear social rejection.

3. They lack interest in other people.

4. They lack empathy and understanding.

5. They criticize themselves sharply because of their social difficulties and expect to fail in their dealings with others.

6. They fail to engage in self-disclosure with possible friends.

7. They are cynical about human nature. They expect the worst from people.

8. They expect too much too soon. For example, they misconstrue other people as aloof and antagonistic rather than naturally cautious in the early stages of relationships.

9. They are generally pessimistic.

10. By and large, they assume that what happens to them is out of their own hands.

HOW TO HANDLE LONELINESS

Psychologists have learned that we can do many things to develop social relationships and combat loneliness:

1. Challenge your feelings of pessimism. Adopt the attitude that things happen when you make them happen. This is true of social relationships as it is of getting good grades.

2. Challenge your cynicism about human nature. Yes, lots of people are selfish and not worth knowing. If you assume that all people are like that, however, you may doom yourself to a lifetime of loneliness. Your mission—if you choose to accept it—is to find people who possess the qualities that you value.

3. Challenge the idea that failure in social relationships is awful and a valid reason for giving up on them. Sure, social rejection can be painful, but unless you happen to be Harrison Ford or Kim Basinger, you're not going to appeal to the majority of people. We must all learn to live with some rejection. But keep looking for the people who possess the qualities you value and who will find things of equal value in you.

4. Follow the nearby suggestions for date seeking. Sit down at a table with people in the cafeteria, not off in a corner by yourself. Smile and say "Hi" to people who intrigue you. Practice opening lines for different occasions—and a few follow-up lines. Try them out in the mirror. (Stop being so hard on yourself!)

PREJUDICE

College is a microcosm of society at large, and prejudice is found on campus as well as off campus. Nearly 20 percent of minority students who attend predominantly white college will encounter verbal harassment, assaults, or vandalism motivated by racial prejudice. President Vartan Gregorian of Brown University noted that at college

> *. . . many students confront their own attitudes about race for the first time.*
> *Because there is still de facto segregation in our country some of our freshmen*
> *are unprepared for the diverse population they encounter in our colleges and*
> *universities.*

Prejudices may be expressed straightforwardly as slurs and insults or more subtly through discrimination. In a recent year, for example, graffiti and leaflets on campuses said things like "Keep white supremacy alive" and "Kill homos." Campuses like Brown and Tufts consider such expressions to violate college codes that prohibit racial, sexual, and ethnic harassment. Melissa Russo, a political science major at Tufts University, notes that Tufts has responded to harassment of minority students by creating three levels of "allowable speech." She also notes that these prohibitions conflict with Constitutional guarantees of free expression:

> *Varying degrees of expression are permissible on campus, depending upon*
> *the ability of others to avoid "offensive" speech.*

> *In public areas and campus publications, freedom of speech is protected; even*
> *controversial T-shirts [such as those listing 15 reasons why beer is better than*
> *women at Tufts] can be sold or quoted. In other spaces, such as classrooms,*
> *dining halls and libraries, derogatory or demeaning speech can be restricted.*
> *The prohibition does not cover material relevant to class discussions.*

> *In dormitories, Tufts has deemed the right of free speech to be subordinate to*
> *that of privacy. It argues that students should be free from [offensive speech]*
> *in their own homes.*

Discrimination is the denial of privileges on the basis of group membership. In the world at large, discrimination usually takes the form of denial of access to jobs, housing, and club membership. On campus, discrimination may take the form of exclusion from fraternities and sororities, or of poor grades. Our prejudices may also affect whom we sit next to in the cafeteria and the library, and whom we confide in or ask out.

Two common forms of prejudice are sexism and racism.

SEXISM

Sexism has historically been directed against women. Women in modern U.S. society tend to be stereotyped as gentle, helpful, kind, and patient, which are positive traits, but also as dependent and submissive, which are not. Men are more likely to be stereotyped as independent, competitive, and tough—traits that aid them in the business world. Women are more often seen as warm but emotional, and as fit to take care of the kids and cook the meals. Men are traditionally expected to head the family and put bread on the table. Some people still believe that women are unsuited to the business world and that they should be educated in traditional areas such as homemaking and child rearing.

These stereotypes have exacted an enormous price, especially on women. It is only in the twentieth century that girls have been considered suitable for education. Even the Swiss-French philosopher Jean-Jacques Rousseau, who spearheaded an open approach to education, considered girls irrational and disposed to child rearing and homemaking—not to business and technology.

Women and men today are seen as about equal in overall intellectual ability, but men are still expected to outperform women in math, science, and spatially related tasks. Women are more likely to have "math anxiety," and it becomes progressively harder to persuade high school and college women to take math courses, even when their ability is superior.

Stereotyping also impairs our psychological well-being and our interpersonal relationships. For example, women who accept the traditional view are also apt to think that women should be seen but not heard. They are thus unlikely to express their needs and wants. Men who subscribe to traditional stereotypes are not apt to feel very comfortable caring for children. Traditional men are less likely to ask for help—including medical help—when they need it. And they are less apt to be compassionate and to express feelings of love—frustrating the women who care for them.

RACISM

In racism, one race or ethnic group holds negative attitudes toward another. Racism stains our perceptions. Social scientists have shown people photographs of people of different races in which one individual is holding a knife. Interestingly, many white viewers erroneously report that an African American was holding the knife when the aggressor was actually white. On the other hand, many African Americans are more likely to assume that whites are aggressors.

Members of ethnic minorities often encounter racism on campus. Fraternities and sororities may exclude them not necessarily because they are African, Asian, or Hispanic Americans but because the Greek-letter organizations recruit people who are similar in attitudes and behavior. When people look different, we may assume that their beliefs and behavior patterns are different as well—even when they are not. Ethnic minorities also complain that many white students assume that they are equal-opportunity students—that they were admitted to fill minority quotas despite academic deficiencies. We have even seen cases in which white professors told us they felt "threatened" by minority students requesting that grades be raised. However, when they described the behavior of the minority students, it was apparently identical to that of whites requesting higher grades. White students were less likely to be perceived as menacing, however.

SOURCES OF PREJUDICE

Prejudice has many sources:

1. *Attitudinal differences.* We tend to like people whose attitudes coincide with ours. Our opinions about other people are affected by their attitudes as well as by their race. People from other religious and racial groups are often reared in environments that differ from our own. They are thus likely to harbor different values and attitudes. We may assume that people of different religions and races do not share our attitudes, however, even when they agree with us.

2. *Social conflict and economic competition.* Many religious and racial groups have been at odds for many centuries. Social and economic conflict tend to breed negative attitudes. For example, many students in the white majority, whose families are going into debt to finance their education, resent minority students who have received equal opportunity scholarships and grants. From their perspective, tax money that their parents can ill afford is being used to finance the competition. Minority students, on the other hand, perceive majority resistance as part of a continuing effort to oppress them.

3. *Scapegoating.* Some social scientists argue that religious and racial minorities serve as convenient scapegoats when things go wrong. There is a tendency to blame the troubles of the country on African Americans, Hispanic Americans, Asian Americans, Jewish Americans and other cultural and ethnic minorities.

4. *Learning from parents.* We acquire many attitudes and opinions from other people, especially parents. Children like to imitate their parents and parents often reward children for doing so. Prejudices are thus apt to be transmitted from generation to generation.

5. *Stereotyping.* Even when we do not think of ourselves as being prejudiced, we may be susceptible to stereotypes, which are fixed conventional ideas about groups of people.

Stereotypes of Cultural and Ethnic Groups in the Unites States

African Americans

Physically powerful and
  well-coordinated

Unclean

Unintelligent and superstitious

Musically talented

Excelent as lovers

Lazy

Emotional and aggressive

Flashy (gaudy clothes and big cars)

Chinese Americans

Deceitful

Inscrutable

Wise

Cruel

Polite, quiet, and deferential

Possessing strong family ties

Law-abiding

Hispanic Americans

Macho

Unwilling to learn English

Disinterested in education

Not concerned about being on welfare

Lazy

Hot-tempered and violent

Irish Americans

Sexually repressed

Heavy drinkers

Overly religious

Political and nationalistic

Outgoing, witty, and literary

Hot-tempered ("fighting Irish")

Italian Americans

Overly interested in food

Ignorant, suspicious of education

Clannish

Great singers

Great shoemakers and barbers

Hot-tempered and violent

Connected to the Mafia

Talk with their hands

Cowardly in Battle

Japanese Americans

Ambitious, hardworking,
  and competitive

Intelligent, well-educated

Obedient, servile women

Sneaky

Poor lovers

Possessing strong family ties

Great imitators, not originators

Law-abiding

Jewish Americans

Cheap, shrewd in business

Clannish

Control banks, Wall Street,
  and the media

Wealthy and showy

Big-nosed

Pushy

Smothering mother

Polish Americans

Unintelligent and
  uneducated

Overly religious

Dirty

Racist, bigoted

Boorish, uncultured

"White Anglo-Saxon Protestants " ("WASPs")

Hardworking,ambitious,
  thrifty

Honorable

Wealthy, powerful

Insensitive, emotionally cold

Polite, well-mannered,
  genteel

Snobbish

Guilt-ridden do-gooders

Becoming Culturally Literate in a Multicultural Society

Overview

Cultural literacy is a command of that general body of knowledge that a person needs to succeed in the world today. It is not merely confined to "culture" narrowly understood as an acquaintance with the arts, nor is it confined to one social class. It provides the only one sure avenue of opportunity for successful communication. In order to speak effectively to people, we must have a reliable sense of what they do or do not know. For in communicating, whether in speaking, reading, or writing, it is essential to know the other person's unspoken systems of association. Hence, knowledge of that common body must exist in order to establish this sense of communication.

The importance of such widely shared information can best be appreciated if you understand how the idea of cultural literacy relates to the achievement of your educational goals. Only by accumulating shared symbols and the shared information can we learn to communicate effectively with one another in our local, national, and international community.

The following is a short self-score pre-test that will give you some insight on your present status in cultural literacy.

Pre-Test

1. The artist who created "The Last Supper" was:
   a. Raphael
   b. Da Vinci
   c. Titian
   d. Rembrandt

2. John Steinbeck, the American author, wrote many popular novels. One of his most famous was:
   a. *The Great Gatsby*
   b. *Last of the Mohicans*
   c. *Moby Dick*
   d. *Grapes of Wrath*

3. Galileo, an Italian astronomer, discovered that the Milky Way is made up of stars. Galileo is also known for having invented the:
   a. observatory
   b. microscope
   c. telescope
   d. chart of constellation

4. The "Nutcracker Suite" was composed by:
   a. Mendelson
   b. Handel
   c. Tchaikovsky
   d. Dvorak

5. The theory of architect Frank Lloyd Wright was that:
   a. form should follow function
   b. art existed only for the sake of art
   c. a building should not be artistically dependent upon its surroundings
   d. the present should reflect the past

6. *Leaves of Grass* is a collection of poems written by:
   a. Carl Sandburg
   b. Walt Whitman
   c. Ralph Waldo Emerson
   d. Robert Frost

7. Two United States Presidents who were assassinated while in office were:
   a. Taylor and Harrison
   b. Garfield and Hayes
   c. Garfield and Fillmore
   d. McKinley and Garfield

8. The famous speech that included the phrase, "Fourscore and seven years ago" was made by:
   a. Winston Churchill
   b. George Washington
   c. William Shakespeare
   d. Abraham Lincoln

9. Which states border the Great Lakes?
   a. Texas, Louisiana, and Florida
   b. Minnesota, Michigan, and New York
   c. California, Washington, and Arizona
   d. North Dakota, South Dakota, and Alabama

10. The Roman Emperor who, it is said, fiddled while Rome burned was:
   a. Caesar
   b. Cicero
   c. Nero
   d. Octavian

EXERCISE:

Humanities

1. Which of the following represents 15th–century art?
    a. the "Parthenon"
    b. the "Night Watch"
    c. the "Last Supper"
    d. portrait of "Whistler's Mother"

2. A painter who is famous for the portrayal of Mexican natives is:
    a. El Greco
    b. Diego Rivera
    c. Francesco Zurbaran
    d. Francesco Di Goya

3. The picture "Blue Boy" was painted by:
    a. Matisse
    b. Goya
    c. Gainsborough
    d. Manet

4. The composer known as "The King of Symphony Writers" is:
    a. Dvorak
    b. Beethoven
    c. Haydn
    d. Handel

5. Which of the following terms describes a choir that sings without accompaniment?
    a. a capella
    b. concertant
    c. bel canto
    d. philharmonic

6. If you were listening to Handel's "Messiah," you would be hearing a:
    a. symphony
    b. piano solo
    c. choral work
    d. trumpet solo

7. The painter whose portrait of himself shows "rust"–colored hair, restless blue eyes, and a strangely shaped skull is:
    a. Picasso
    b. Gaugin
    c. Van Gogh
    d. Renoir

8. A painter of decorative, barbaric, Tahitian landscape was
   a. Edgar Degas
   b. Pierre Renoir
   c. Vincent Van Gogh
   d. Paul Gaugin

9. Which of these musical compositions is not in the classical style?
   a. "Surprise Symphony" by Haydn
   b. "Gavotte" by Mozart
   c. "Pascaglia in C minor" by Bach
   d. "Tales of the Vienna Woods" by Strauss

10. Braque, a contemporary French painter, is best known for his:
    a. representational drawings
    b. landscape
    c. mother and child themes
    d. still-life paintings

PRACTICE EXERCISE:

Literature

Below are twenty questions that will test your literary expertise. For each, you will find four choices. Check the one you believe is the correct answer.

1. Of the following poems, the one not written by Alfred Lord Tennyson is:
   a. "The Charge of the Light Brigade"
   b. "Idylls of the King"
   c. "In memorian"
   d. "Dover Beach"

2. The author of the *Count of Monte Cristo* was:
   a. Victor Hugo
   b. Emile Zola
   c. Anatole France
   d. Alexander Dumas

3. Sydney Carter is the protagonist of Charles Dickens'
   a. *Tale of Two Cities*
   b. *Oliver Twist*
   c. *Bleak House*
   d. *Great Expectations*

4. F. Scott Fitzgerald's first novel was:
   a. *This Side of Paradise*
   b. *The Great Gatsby*
   c. *Tender is the Night*
   d. *The Beautiful and the Damned*

5. "The Wasteland" is a celebrated long poem by:
   a. Ezra Pound
   b. W. B. Yeats
   c. Robert Lowell Jr.
   d. T. S. Eliot

6. The protagonist of Victor Hugo's *Les Miserables* was named:
   a. Maurice Richard
   b. George Feydean
   c. Inspector Javert
   d. Jean Valjean

7. The author of *Catch-22* is
   a. Joseph Heller
   b. Thomas Pynchon
   c. James Baldwin
   d. John Gardner

8. "John Brown's Body," by Stephen Vincent Benet, is a:
   a. Biography
   b. Poem
   c. Novel
   d. Short Story

9. The man who wrote *Of Time and the River* was:
   a. Thomas Wolfe
   b. Ernest Hemingway
   c. Heraclitus
   d. F. Scott Fitzgerald

10. Gustave Flaubert wrote:
    a. *Pere Goriot*
    b. *Madame Bovary*
    c. *La Malade Imaginaire*
    d. *Nana*

11. The first American to win the Nobel Prize for Literature was:
    a. Henry James
    b. Sinclair Lewis
    c. Nathaniel Hawthorne
    d. Theodore Dreiser

12. In Shakespeare's "Julius Caesar," the one who has the lean and hungry look is:
    a. Brutus
    b. Antony
    c. Cassius
    d. Cinna

13. The author of Dracula was:
    a. Mary Shelley
    b. Boris Karloff
    c. Bram Stoker
    d. H. G. Wells

14. The county which is the setting for most of William Faulkner's writing is:
    a. Okefenokee
    b. Tyler
    c. Yoknapatawpha
    d. Chattohoochee

15. The real name of Lewis Carrol, author of *Alice in Wonderland,* was:
    a. Charles Dodgson
    b. Agatha Christie
    c. Sebastian Melmoth
    d. Booth Tarkington

16. The playwright of "Oedipus Rex" was:
    a. Aeschylus
    b. Euripides
    c. Aristophanes
    d. Sophocles

17. The Bronte sister who wrote *Wuthering Heights* was:
    a. Charlotte
    b. Emily
    c. Anne
    d. Jane

18. Sherwood Anderson's "Winesburg" is set in the state of:
    a. Nebraska
    b. New Hampshire
    c. Michigan
    d. Ohio

19. In John Steinbeck's *Of Mice and Men*, the simple-minded giant is named:
    a. George
    b. Curley
    c. Lennie
    d. Crooks

20. The boy in Marjorie Kinnan Rawling's *The Yearling* is named:
    a. Jeff
    b. John-Boy
    c. Jody
    d. Jeremy

EVALUATION

1. Thomas Gainsborough created a very famous painting titled:
   a. "Blue Boy"
   b. "Whistler's Mother"
   c. "The Harriest"
   d. "American Gothic"

2. Playwright George Bernard Shaw wrote:
   a. "Cleopatra"
   b. "Pygmalion"
   c. "My Fair Lady"
   d. "Death of a Salesman"

3. According to the religion of Islam:
   a. Muhammad is God
   b. Jesus did not exist
   c. the Islam faith began with the angel Gabriel
   d. Jews must not be allowed in

4. Three of the original thirteen American colonies were:
   a. Massachusetts, Delaware, and North Carolina
   b. Washington, Maine, and Rhode Island
   c. Vermont, Massachusetts, and New York
   d. West Virginia, Virginia, and Pennsylvania

5. If the President and Vice-President of the United States died while in office, the next acting president would be:
   a. Speaker of the House
   b. Commander, Joint Chiefs
   c. Secretary of State
   d. Senate Majority Leader

6. The composer who went on to create musical masterpieces even after losing his hearing was:
   a. Stravinsky
   b. Chopin
   c. Beethoven
   d. Mozart

7. Johnny Appleseed planted apple seeds throughout the Ohio Valley. Johnny's real name was:
   a. Taylor H. Johnson
   b. Johny Hardy
   c. John Chapman
   d. George Edwards

8. Oliver Twist's mentor in thievery is:
    a. Edwin Drood
    b. Mr. Micawber
    c. Pip
    d. Fagin

9. The pilgrim of John Bunyan's *Pilgrim's Progress* is named:
    a. Adam
    b. Virgil
    c. Christian
    d. Everyman

10. The fair Desdemona is the victim of Iago's perfidy in:
    a. *Macbeth*
    b. *King Lear*
    c. *Othello*
    d. *Hamlet*

11. Fyodor Dostoevsky's character Raskolnikov appears in the novel:
    a. *Crime and Punishment*
    b. *The Brothers Karamozov*
    c. *The Possessed*
    d. *The Idiot*

12. Johann Gutenberg is regarded as the inventor of:
    a. rocketry
    b. the telegraph
    c. moveable type
    d. the first radio

13. Stonehenge is an ancient monument:
    a. built by Egyptian slaves
    b. of unknown origin in England
    c. used in Irish religious ceremonies
    d. erected by Scottish pagans

14. Sinclair Lewis wrote two best selling novels. They were:
    a. *Miracle of The Bells* and *Elmer Gantry*
    b. *Main Street* and *The Good Earth*
    c. *Elmer Gantry* and *Main Street*
    d. *Miracle of the Bells* and *The Good Earth*

15. Emerald City is the home of:
    a. Queen Elizabeth
    b. the Dalai Lama
    c. the Wizard of Oz
    d. Wonder Woman

16. God Bless America" was written by:
    a. Duke Ellington
    b. Irving Berlin
    c. Aaron Copeland
    d. George Gershwin

17. *The Invisible Man* was written by H. G. Wells. *Invisible Man* is the work of:
    a. Ray Bradbury
    b. John Updike
    c. Ralph Ellison
    d. Gore Vidal

18. Lawrence Durrell's Alexandria Quartet consists of *Justine, Balthazar, Mountoline*, and:
    a. *Deirdre*
    b. *Delphine*
    c. *Chita*
    d. *Clea*

19. The heroine of Thackeray's *Vanity Fair* is:
    a. Elizabeth Bennet
    b. Becky Sharp
    c. Jo March
    d. Scarlett O'Hara

20. Italian composers often make use of the flexible type of soprano voice called:
    a. robusto
    b. lyric
    c. coloratura
    d. dramatic

21. Which of these compositions is an oratorio?
    a. Handel's "Messiah"
    b. Schubert's "Ave Maria"
    c. Wagner's "Pilgrim's Chorus"
    d. Brahm's "Lullaby"

22. There is only one good, that is knowledge, and there is only one evil, that is ignorance" was said by:
    a. Aristophanes
    b. Socrates
    c. Aristotle
    d. Sophocles

23. The Emancipation Proclamation freed the slaves in:
    a. all states resisting the union
    b. all the southern states
    c. the organized territories
    d. all states of the union

24. "To thine own self be true" is the philosophy uttered by:
   a. Jacques
   b. King Lear
   c. Macbeth
   d. Polonius

25. Which of the following types of architecture makes extensive use of the flying buttress?
   a. Egyptian
   b. Gothic
   c. Greek
   d. Romanesque

RESOURCE GUIDE

Cultural literacy does not occur overnight, nor does it happen in one semester. It requires constant reading, listening and associating with persons who are culturally literate. In addition, you should strive to keep abreast of what is happening locally, nationally and internationally. In an attempt to assist you in your endeavors to become culturally literate we have prepared this resource section for you. It consists of suggested readings, persons you should know about and certain significant dates and concepts. When you feel that you have made significant use of this section, we suggest that you attempt to answer the questions in the Evaluation Exercise.

Answers

Pre-Test		Practice Exercise: Humanities	
1.	b	1.	c
2.	d	2.	b
3.	c	3.	c
4.	c	4.	b
5.	a	5.	a
6.	b	6.	c
7.	d	7.	c
8.	d	8.	d
9.	b	9.	d
10.	c	10.	d

Practice Exercise: Literature

1.	d	11.	b
2.	d	12.	c
3.	a	13.	b
4.	a	14.	c
5.	d	15.	a
6.	d	16.	d
7.	a	17.	b
8.	b	18.	d
9.	a	19.	c
10.	b	20.	c

ANNOTATED GREAT BOOKS/ READING LIST

FORTY BOOKS THAT EVERY COLLEGE STUDENT SHOULD READ

1. Homer's *Iliad* and *Odyssey*. Every student should have contact with either or both of these works because of their positions in Western Civilization.

2. Virgil's *Aeneid*. This does for Rome what the Homer works do for Greece. The Rolfe Humphries translation is highly recommended.

3. Marcus Aurelius' *Meditations*. Not an exciting book, it is a monument of Stoic philosophy. Every college student should know what Stoicism means.

4. *Confessions of St. Augustine*. This book is hard to understand in the later chapters but is absolutely fun to read in the beginning—about how a man goes from sin to sainthood. You will see yourself in this book.

5. At least a half dozen of the most popular of Shakespeare's plays: *Hamlet*, *Romeo and Juliet*, *Macbeth*, *King Lear*, *Othello*, and possibly *Julius Caesar*.

6. At least a half dozen of 19th and 20th century plays: Ibsen's *A Doll's House*, Albee's *Who's Afraid of Virginia Woolfe*, George Bernard Shaw's *Pygmalion*, Lorraine Hansberry's *A Raisin in the Sun*, etc., Walker's *The River Niger*.

7. Karl Marx's *The Communist Manifesto*. This is too important a book for a college student not to have encountered.

8. At least a half dozen of the famous Greek plays: *Oedipus the King*, *Antigone*, *Lysistrata*, *Medea*, the *Oresteia*.

9. Niccolo Machiavelli's *The Prince*. This is a short but important book on political expediency.

10. Flaubert's *Madame Bovary*. One of the best novels ever written, it uses precise language. The Modern Library College Edition is recommended.

11. Henry Fielding's *Tom Jones*. For the same reason as listed in item 10 above, it is an excellent model for the use of the English language. Long but well written.

12. Nathaniel Hawthorne's *The Scarlet Letter*. A part of early America, this is one of the best novels written by an American.

13. Feodor Dostoevski's *The Brothers Karamazov* or *Crime and Punishment* or both. Many people have trouble deciding which of these is the best novel that has ever been written. Students can relate more easily to *Crime and Punishment*.

14. Stendahl's *The Red and the Black*. This was President Kennedy's favorite novel. It tells how a young man can rise by dint of his intelligence.

15. Ayn Rand's *The Fountainhead*. Rand is Russian by birth and the influence of Dostoevski on her work is unmistakable. Her thesis is that man's ego is the fountainhead of progress. This should be read.

16. Ralph Ellison's *The Invisible Man*. One of the best novels written by an American black, the author's style and the panoramic view of life in the United States, both North and South, make this must reading.

17. Richard Wright's *Native Son*. This is the first novel by an American black to gain international attention. It is sociological, revealing, and should be read.

18. Alex Haley's *Roots*. While it is a unique blend of fiction and fact, it should be read for its place in history.

19. John A. Williams's *The Man Who Cried I Am*. This is Williams' answer to Ellison's *Invisible Man*. Williams contends that black people do have existence and proclaims this in rather graphic language. Must reading.

20. W. E. B. Du Bois's *The Souls of Black Folks*. This is a collection of essays on the plight of black people in this country. Written around 1903, it is still excellent reading.

21. Booker T. Washington's *Up From Slavery*. This is not an extremely well-written book but should be read if for no other reason that to see the text of his famous "Compromise" speech of 1895.

22. *The Autobiography of Malcolm X*. Excellent biography—though assisted by Alex Haley, Haley never gets in the way of the story.

23. James Weldon Johnson's *Along the Way*. Though a biography, it gives insight into the whole era of the 20's and the Harlem Renaissance.

24. Toni Morrison's *Song of Solomon*. This is not an easy book to read but she is one of the best female black writers working today.

25. Frank Yerby's *The Foxes of Harrow*. This is his first novel and the one many consider his best. He did research for this novel while serving on the faculty of the Lab School at Southern University. He has had numerous consecutive best-sellers.

26. Frank Yerby's *Judas My Brother*. This novel will shake one's faith in the Jesus story—but controversial novels should be read as well.

27. William Styron's *The Confessions of Nat Turner*. This is a novel by a white writer about a black hero. It is well-written but controversial and should be read and perhaps refuted.

28. Harold Cruse's *The Crisis on the Negro Intellectual*. This presents a slated point of view by an important book in the development of black intellectual thought.

29. Alvin Toffler's *The Third Wave*. This is a contemporary book but it helps you to understand why we are in the computer age and where it is going.

30. E. Franklin Frazier's *Black Bourgeoisie*. This is an important sociological study of the "new" Negro who emerged in the thirties and forties.

31. James Baldwin's *Go Tell It On The Mountain*. His first and best novel, this tells of a young man coming of spiritual age in Harlem.

32. James Baldwin's *The Fire Next Time*. This is his best collection of essays—which is what some critics feel he does best.

33. Cervantes' *Don Quixote*. An abridged version of this is recommended. This book should be read for its place in literary history.

34. Plato's *The Republic*. Every college student should encounter this book. Someone has said that all philosophy is a footnote on Plato.

35. Ernest Gaines's *The Autobiography of Miss Jane Pittman*. This is not autobiography but fiction. Gaines is a very good Louisiana writer.

36. Frantz Fanon's *Black Skin, White Masks*. This was an important book in the sixties. Fanon is a psychologist trying to make sense of his blackness.

37. Chaim Potok's *The Chosen*. This is an excellent fictional insight into the Jewish experience in America. Potok also wrote a novel entitled *The Promise,* which is equally well-written.

38. James Joyce's *Ulysses*. This is a difficult novel to read but it is a milestone in the stream-of-consciousness style of writing.

39. Robert Penn Warren's *All the King's Men*. This is the best novel on politics and the South. It has a good idea—the web theory—that everything is connected to everything else.

40. Any one of Martin Luther King's books. *Stride Toward Freedom* is probably the best for understanding his philosophy.

DO YOU HAVE RENAISSANCE REACH?

Below are names that a well-educated person might reasonably be expected to know. Each person has achieved eminence in his or her particular field.

Sappho	George Bernard Shaw
Virgil	Isaac Newton
Aristophanes	William Allen White
Arnold Toynbee	Robert Frost
Eugene V. Debs	Vincent Van Gogh
Michael Faraday	Peter Tchaikowsky
Thomas Gainsborough	Thales
Thomas Aquinas	John Audubon
Aldous Huxley	Thorstein Veblen
Charles Gounod	John Locke
Robert Bouyle	Joseph Lister
William James	Jean Sibelius
Feodor Dostoevski	Toulouse Lautrec
William Harvey	Margaret Mead
Johann Goethe	Diego Martinez
John Keynes	Grant Wood
Rene Descarates	Frank Lloyd Wright
Stephen Crane	Ferede Grofe
Jacques Offenbach	Thomas Hardy
Albert Einstein	Thomas Mann

SOME LANDMARK WRITERS IN THE DEVELOPMENT OF PHILOSOPHIC THOUGHT

Plato (427–347 B.C.) — *The Dialogues (The Republic)*

Aristotle (348–322 B.C.) — *The Nicomachean Ethics, The Organon*

Lucretius (96?–55 B.C.) — *On the Nature of Things*

Aurelius Antonius, Marcus (121–180) — *Meditations*

Plotinus (205?–270) — *Ethical Treatises, Emneads*

St. Augustine (354–430) — *The City of God*

Aquinas, St. Thomas (1225–1274) — *Summa Thoelogica, Summa Contra Gentiles*

Machiavelli, Niccolo (1469–1527) — *Discourses, The Prince*

Bacon, Francis (1561–1626) — *Novum Organum*
The Advancement of Learning

Hobbes, Thomas (1588–1679) — *Leviathan*

Descartes, Rene (1596–1650) — *Discourse on Method*

Spinoza, Benedict (1632–1677) — *Ethics*

Locke, John (1632–1677) — *Essay Concerning the Human Understanding*

Leibniz, Gottfried Von (1646–1716) — *The Monadology*

Berkeley, George (1685–1716) — *The New Theory of Vision, A Treatise Concerning the Principles of Human Knowledge*

Hume, David (1711–1776) — *Enquiry Concerning Human Understanding*
A Treatise of Human Nature

Kant, Immanuel (1724–1804) — *Critique of the Pure Reason*

Fichte, Johann (1762–1814) — *Critique of All Revelation*

Hegel, George (1770–1831) — *Phenomenology of the Mind*
The Science of Logic

Schelling, Friedrich von (1774–1854) — *System of Transcendental Idealism*

Schopenhauer, Arthur (1788–1860) — *Pessimism, The World as Well and Idea*

Comte, Auguste (1798–1857) — *Course of Positive Philosophy*

Mill, John Stuart (1806–1873) — *Utilitarianism*
System of Logic

Kierkegaard, Soren (1813–1855) — *Philosophical Fragments*
Sickness Unto Death

Spencer, Herbert (1820–1903) — *First Principles*
Synthetic Philosophy

Pierce, Charles S. (1839–1914)	*The Destiny of Man*
Fiske, John (1842–1901)	*Outlines of Cosmic Philosophy*
James, William (1842–1910)	*Pragmatism*
Neitzsche, Freidrich (1844–1900)	*Thus Spake Zarathustra*
Royce, Josiah (1855–1916)	*The World and the Individual*
Bergson, Henri (1859–1941)	*Creative Evolution, Creative Mind*
Dewey, John (1859–1952)	*Human Nature and Conduct, Logic*
Whitehead, Alfred North (1861–1947)	*Science and the Modern World* *Process and Reality*
Santayana, George (1863–1952)	*Realms of Being* *Skepticism and Animal Faith*
Croce, Benedetto (1866–1952)	*Philosophy of the Spirit*
Russell, Bertrand (1872–)	*Problems of Philosophy* *Introduction to Mathematical Philosophy*
Volzybski, Alfred (1879–1950)	*Science and Sanity*
Sartre, Jean Paul (1905–)	*Existentialism*

REFERENCES

Arnold-Baker, Charles, *Everyman's Dictionary of Dates* compiled by C. Arnold-Baker and Anthony Dent. London: JM Dent; New York: EP Dutton, 1954.

Canby, Courtlandt, *The Encyclopedia of Historic Places*, New York: NY, 1984.

Duckles, Vincent Harris, *Music Reference and Research Materials*, an annotated bibliography compiled by Vincent Duckles, 3rd ed. New York: Free Press, 1974.

Ehresmann, Donald L., *Fine Arts*, a bibliographic guide to basic reference works, histories and handbooks, Littleton, CO: Libraries Unlimited, 1975.

Feibleman, James, *Aesthetics: A Study of the Fine Arts in Theory and Practice*, New York: Duell Sloan and Pearce, 1949.

Gilden, Eric, *The Dictionary of Composers and Their Music, Every Listener's Companion*: arranged chrono logically and alphabetically. New York: Paddington Press distributed by Grosset & Dunlap.

Lucas, Edna Louise, *The Harvard List of Books on Art*, Cambridge: Harvard University Press, 1952.

Taylor, Thomas Griffith, *Geography in the Twentieth Century*, A Study of Growths Freeds, Techniques Arms and Trends, New York: Philosophical Library, 1957.

Van Cleef, Eugene, *Our Modern World*, a textbook in global geography, Boston: Allyn and Bacon, 1949.

Wold, Milo Arlington, *An Introduction to Music and Art in the Western World*, Dubuque, Iowa: WC Brown Co., 1955.

1066
1492
1776
1861–1865
1914–1918
1939–1944
1984 (title)

Aaron, Hank
Abandon hope, all ye who enter here.
abbreviation
Aberdeen
abolitionism
abominable snowman
abortion
Absence makes the heart grow fonder.
absolute monarch
absenteeism
absolute zero
abstract art
abstract expressionism
academic freedom
a capella
accelerator, particle
accounting
acculturation
AC/DC
Achilles
Achilles' heel
acid
acid rain
acquittal
acronym
acrophobia
Acropolis
Actions speak louder than words.
act of God
actuary

acupuncture
A.D.
ad absurdum
adagio
Adam and Eve
Adams, John
Adams, John Quincy
adaptation
Addams, Jane
Addis Ababa
Adeste Fideles (song)
ad hoc
ad hominem
adieu
ad infinitum
adios
Adirondack Mountains
adjective
Adonis
adrenal gland
adrenaline (fight or flight)
adultery
adverb
AEC (Atomic Energy Commission)
Aegean, the
Aeneas
Aeneid, The (title)
aerobic
Aeschylus
Aesop's fables
aesthetics
affirmative action
affluent society
Afghanistan
afficionado
AFL-CIO
Africa
Agamemnon

Age cannot wither her, nor custom stale Her infinite variety.
aggression
agnosticism
agreement
agribusiness
Ahab, Captain
AIDS
air pollution
Air Quality Index
Akron, OH
Alabama
á la carte
Aladdin's lamp
Alamo
Alaska
Alaskan pipeline
Alas, poor Yorick . . .
Alabama
Albany, NY
albatross around one's neck
Albuquerque, NM
alchemy
Alcott, Louisa May
Aleutian Islands
Alexander the great
Alexandria, Egypt
al fresco
algae
Alger, Horatio
Algeria
Algiers
alias
Alice in Wonderlannd (title)
Alien and Sedition acts
alienation
Ali, Muhammad
alkaline
Allah

All animals are equal, but some animals are more equal than others.
Allegheny Mountains
allegory
allegro
Allen, Woody
allergy
Alliance for Progress
alliteration
alloy
All roads lead to Rome.
All's fair in love and war.
All's well that ends well.
All that glitters is not gold.
all the news that's fit to print
All the world's a stage.
all things to all men
allusion
All work and no play makes Jack a dull boy.
alma mater
alpha and omega
alpha radiation
Alps, the
alter ego
alternative current (AC)
alternator
alto
altruism
Alzheimer's disease
a.m.
Amazing Grace (song)
Amazonian
Amazon (myth)
Amazon River
America
American Gothic (image)
American Legion

IV.
Looking Ahead Concepts

Improving Money and Personal Economic Skills

Computer Literatacy

Looking Ahead Concepts

Unit Concepts

Emerging expectations of college students and enlightened members of our society are multifaceted:

      (1) Knowledge of Current issues

      (2) Money management and Personal Economic Skills

      (3) Computer Literacy

These areas assist us in making adequate career decisions.

A revolution in communication and information technology is making the computer a basic tool for acquiring knowledge, organizing systems, and keeping abreast of current issues.

Money management and personal economic skills are essential to everyone. Items related to personal finances:

      (1) Figuring your paycheck and deductions

      (2) Personal banking needs and procedures

      (3) Paying bills and financial obligations

      (4) Understanding basic economic ideas

Our society generally considers it only natural that each member become self-sufficient and enter the labor force.

From childhood on the individual is often asked, "What do you what to do?". We are aware that is necessary to focus on at least an occupational field, if not a specific job area within it. Work is the means of meeting needs in other areas of living. It is a central activity of human existence and we need to explore means of making useful career decisions.

The implementation of current issues in college or university curriculums serves as a unique mode of enhancement of cognitive skills. It is vital that students read a newspaper regularly.

Newspapers and magazines should be available in area Resource Center of individual college reading rooms. This may encourage many to even purchase the newspapers.

Periodically, inclusive of odd-numbered weeks, students will engage in reading exercises which only require ten minutes to complete. The majority of these exercises come from relevant newspaper clippings and are designed to promote reading accountability, reading improvement and reading for research.

A sample exercise relating to use of the newspaper in education is a part of this module.

Article analysis are utilized to facilitate the process of enhancement:

The format:

1. Reference
2. Purpose of the article
3. Main point to be made
4. Author's point-of-view
5. Synopsis of the article
6. Intent of the Author (Communicating with reader or public)
7. Implications
8. Educational goals or objectives
9. Knowledge or change of perceptions
10. Knowledge of other articles

Managing Money and Personal Economic Skills

Overview

Regardless of how you choose to live, you will need to master some basic personal economic skills. College expenses are basic and considered a financial investment that generally results in about 40 percent more lifetime earnings than high school graduates.

Objectives

This module is included to give:

1. A brief introduction to features of a paycheck and income tax.

2. An understanding of personal banking experiences and producers.

3. Purchasing goods and services and paying bills. (Including college costs)

4. Basic information relating to insuring yourself and your possessions.

5. Borrowing and using credit.

A major purpose of this module is to help students find ways of keeping the rhythm of money management in balance. For most to society, richer or poorer, we must manage, or mismanage money the rest of our lines.

College costs consists basically of tuition and fees, room and board (inclusive of apartments), books and supplies, transportation and personal expenses. It is generally projected that college graduates earn more in a lifetime than high school graduates—and those who complete professional school earn still more.

Financial resources for college students include:

(1) Parental assistance

(2) Student savings from summer part-time employment

(3) Other savings

(4) Guaranteed (Stafford) Student Loans

(5) College scholarships or grants

(6) Federal based—Pell Grant Program

(7) State grants or scholarships

(8) College work-study program

(9) Other sources

A great percent of college students work part-time during an academic year and have some orientation to paychecks and related deductions related to income taxes; fringe benefits like life insurance or medical resources. Examples of other personal economic skills are included in this module for your consideration and study. Personal budgets can serve as a financial instrument to help with your overall concern for money management.

A very useful guide to Personal Economic Skills has been developed by The Career Skills Assessment Program of The College Board.

TRUTH OR FICTION?

In. out. In. out. Do you think we're talking about breathing? We could be, but we meant to refer to another of life's basic rhythms—the flow and ebb of money. For many students, and for many graduates, the pattern is more like out, out, in, out, in, out, out, out. The purpose of this chapter is to help you find ways of keeping that rhythm in balance—that is, to manage money. More is at stake here than getting through college. For richer or poorer, you're going to be managing, or mismanaging, money for the rest of your life. So it may be helpful to work on developing some good money-management habits now.

First we talk about the costs of college. Then we'll cover the basics of money management, including budgeting. Then we'll go over some sources of financial aid. You're here, so you've obviously made financial arrangements for the current academic term or year. Needs can change, however, so the sources of aid we discuss may be of help to you in the future.

WHAT COLLEGE COSTS

One of the axioms of life is that what goes up must come down. This principle has little bearing on college expenses, however. They seem to move in one direction only: up. The cost of college consists of tuition and fees, room and board, books and supplies, transportation, and personal expenses. To add it up right, you also have to figure in what you could have earned if you had been working full time instead of being in school.

So is college worth it? Sure. By attending college, you become an educated person and feel better about yourself. College graduates also earn 33 to 40 percent more in their lifetimes than high school graduates. For graduates who go on to professional schools, the earning differentials are still greater.

That doesn't mean that college is easy to afford. For most of us, college is the second largest financial investment we'll ever make—right behind buying a house. For parents who try to support more than one child in college, the costs can be absolutely staggering.

Potential Resources for College Students

Resources	Percentage of Students Having Resource	Percentage of Costs Attained from Each Resource
Parental assistance	72	40
Savings from summer employment	51	11
Part-time employment	31	5
Other savings	26	6
Guaranteed (Stafford) Student Loan	25	10
College grant or scholarship	17	7
Pell Grant Program*	16	4
State grant or scholarship	13	3
College work-study program	9	2
Other Sources	—	12

A federal, needs-based student aid program

WHERE THE MONEY COMES FROM

If college is so expensive, how do students manage? Most students manage by piecing together the money they need from a variety of sources, as shown in the table.

Although parents contribute to the expenses of the great majority of college students, parents do not fully cover most of their children's costs.

The only other financial resources that reach double digits for the average student are summer employment (11 percent) and Guaranteed Student Loans (10 percent). Half (51 percent) of students work during the summer, but summer earnings account for little more than 10 percent of the costs of college. One student in four (26 percent) uses other savings, but these meet only 6 percent of the costs. One student in four also has a Guaranteed Student Loan, but, as noted, this resource provides only 10 percent of the needed finances. Four out of ten students work either part time (31 percent) or in work-study programs (9 percent) during the academic years, but their earnings make only small inroads against their costs.

One reason for the relatively small impact of part-time wages is the number of hours worked. As noted in the table below, about half (49 percent) of the full-time undergraduates who hold jobs put in 15 hours or less per week. For many students, squeezing in more hours would make a huge dent in the time available for studying and just plain living. There's no point in working part time if doing so kills your grade point average. A second reason for the small impact of part-time wages is the hourly wage itself. Most students who work part time provide unskilled labor, and they may make little more than the minimum wage.

Status of Student	10 hours or less	11–15 hours	16–20 hours	21–35 hours	36 hours or more
Full-time undergraduate	29	20	22	21	8
Part-time undergraduate	2	4	10	14	70

In sum, students draw on many resources to attend college. At least for the majority of students, no single resource does it all. And millions of students would not be able to attend college without receiving some kind of financial aid.

Now that we've seen how students bring in money to finance their educations, let's see what we can do to exercise control over its outflow. But first make note of some of your feelings about college costs.

HOW TO MAKE A BUDGET

The first step in managing spending is to make a budget. A budget is a plan or schedule for adjusting your expenses so that they fit your income.

In Chapter 3, we showed you how making a schedule of your time helps you find out what you're doing with your time and suggests ways of finding better uses for your time. A budget is a schedule for money, it helps you understand where your money is coming from and where its going. By raising your awareness of the ins and outs of your money, you can become a better money manager.

We suggest using three kinds of charts to track money:

1. A yearly budget to help you keep the big picture in mind

2. A monthly budget that allots money for specific kinds of expenses

3. A record of actual expenses.

YEARLY BUDGET

Your yearly budget provides your big picture—your overall estimate of your income and expenses for a year of college. You'll derive your monthly budget from the information included here. Much of the information you'll fill in here is exact, such as your tuition, your scholarships, and, if you're living on campus, the cost of room and board Some information is estimated, such as what you'll bring in from your part-time job and the amounts you'll spend for personal expenses and entertainment. You'll find an extra budget worksheet at the end of the chapter. Make as many copies as you need.

What Comes In: Income

From family	_____
Summer employment	_____
Part-time job	_____
College work-study program	_____
Perkins Loan	_____
Guaranteed Student Loan	_____
Pell Grant	_____
State grant or scholarship	_____
College grant or scholarship	_____
Savings	_____

Other sources:

1._____   _____
2._____   _____
3._____   _____

                    Total Income   _____

What Goes Out: Expenses

Tuition   _____
Fees (Registration fees, check catalog)   _____
Fees (Lab fees, tutoring, late registration)   _____
Books and Supplies (Estimate from catalog)   _____
Housing   _____
Utilities (if not included as part of housing)   _____
Furniture   _____
Food
    Meal ticket   _____
    Other meals not on ticket   _____
    Snacks   _____
Clothing   _____
Athletic equipment (other than clothing)   _____
Personal expenses (laundry, toothpaste, sanitary supplies)   _____
Medical
    Heath insurance fee   _____
    Medicines   _____
    Other   _____
Transportation   _____
Auto insurance   _____
Auto maintenance & repairs   _____
Entertainment
    Fraternity/sorority dues   _____
    Electronic (CDs, tapes, stereo, TV, etc.)   _____
    Eating out   _____
    Dating   _____
Telephone   _____
Other expenses:

1._____   _____
2._____   _____
3._____   _____
Emergency fund (at least $100)   _____

                    Total Expenses   _____

After filling in the worksheet, subtract your total expenses from your total income. You should wind up with a plus sign—that is, you should have something left over. If you wind up with a minus sign, you're not alone .You and the federal government are both running deficits. The federal government has a slight advantage, however; it can print money. You can't. If you're running a deficit, you have some choices:

1. You can try to increase your anticipated income.

2. You can try to cut your anticipated spending.

3. You can run out before the end of the year.

4. You can pretend that the problem doesn't exist and try not to think about it. Like Scarlet O'Hara in *Gone with the Wind,* you can think about "tomorrow."

We hope that you will reject the third and fourth options. You're likely to just dig yourself in deeper.* If you cannot think of a way to increase your income, try to cut down. Tracking your expenses and following some of the tips in the section on self-control should cut the job down to size.

Assuming that you at least break even, it's time to work on the monthly budget.

MONTHLY BUDGET

A monthly budget is particularly useful for students who live off campus. Rents and mortgage payments are made on a monthly basis. The bills for fuel, electricity, the telephone, and the charge cards come in each month.

You can arrive at a monthly budget by doing the following steps.

STEP	EXAMPLE
1. Write down your total anticipated income for the year. In your estimate, include the savings from the previous summer's work: don't borrow against the following summer.	Your total anticipated income (including Parental help, summer work, part-time work, and financial aid) is $21,150.00.

2. Deduct all one-shot expenses. These include tuition and fees (registration fees), insurance premiums (unless you pay them out monthly), textbooks (which are purchased at the beginning of the term), on-campus housing fees (unless these are paid out monthly), transportation (if you go back and forth between campus and home only once a term), and meal tickets.	Deduct the following:
	  Tuition and fees:_____ $12,400.00
	Insurance:_____ 300.00
	Textbooks:_____ 350.00
	Room and board
	  (meal ticket 19 meals per week)_ 4,500.00
	  Transportation_____ 900.00

3. Total the one-shot expenses.	Total:_____$18,450.00
4.Subtract the total expenses in item 3 from your total estimated income.	$21,150.00-18,450.00=_____$2,700.00

---

* Yes, this should be "more deeply," not "deeper." We're using the colloquialism for emphasis.

5. Take the amount that's left and divide it by the number of months you will be at school. The result is the amount of money you have to spend each month for everything else—from meals not covered on the meal plan to clothes to entertainment.

$2,700.00/9=_____$300.00

6. Allot a reasonable amount of money for each remaining category of expense.

Snacks:_____$30.00
Eight meals off campus:_____32.00
Clothing:_____45.00
Personal expenses:_____60.00
Auto maintenance:_____120.00
Entertainment:_____60.00
Telephone:_____25.00

7. Create a category for putting away monthly savings no matter how small. This category will encourage you to remain within your spending limits.

Savings:_____10.00

8. Total your estimated monthly expenses. If they don't fit your monthly allowance, do some pruning.

Your estimated total outflow, including savings, is $382.00—or $82.00 over budget! What are you going to downscale or give up?

9. Be reasonably flexible. It will take you a while to learn what electricity, the phone, snacks, and dating cost you. But, remain within your total monthly allotment. If you go over budget in one category, make it up by spending less in another category. If you don't, you'll be running a deficit. You might as well be in Congress.

You run for Congress. (Just kidding—wait until after you graduate.)

EXPENSE RECORD

The budget is useful in theory. An expense record allows you to determine whether or not you are sticking to the budget. An expense record includes the following elements:

- Date on which an expense was made

- What the expense was for

- The amount

Many different kinds of charts can be used for recording expenses. The trick is to use a chart that tells you what you need to know—fast. Here's a simple chart of expenses. As we said, this record is simple. You begin at the beginning of the month and record through the end of the month. Then you add it all up. It'll do the job of telling you how much you spent, but it won't telegraph *where* the money went very well.

Simple Expense Record, Month of _____

Date	Item	Amount	Date	Item	Amount	Date	Item	Amount

The next chart, which is more detailed, does a better job of showing you where your money goes. David filled in six categories of expenses, from housing to transportation, and left one column for items that didn't fit anywhere else ("Other").

Setting up a detailed chart takes a bit of work. Set up your categories in a way that makes the most sense for you. If you're living on campus, for example, you may choose not to include housing, since housing belongs to the one-shot expense category. Not including housing gives you another column to play with on the grid. It may take some trial and error for you to fill in the categories on the grid so that it works well for you.

With a detailed chart, you waste some space and some paper. Of the several columns that allow you to list items, you'll be using only one for each expense. The trade-off is that with a detailed chart, you can readily see where your money goes.

We've put a few sheets of the detailed kind of chart at the end of the chapter. Fill them out in a way that makes the most sense for you. Duplicate as many copies as you need.

Now let's turn to some practical financial issues, like checking accounts and credit cards.

Detailed expense Record, Month of _____

Date	Housing & Utilities	Food— meals. snacks	Books & Supplies	Personal Supplies	Entertain- ment	Transpor- tation	Other	Running Total

Money-Management Issues:
From Checking Accounts to Insurance

Should you open a checking account at school? Dare you have a credit card? Should you get a telephone? A car? What about insurance? These are some of the practical money matters that affect college students.

Checking Accounts

Checking accounts have pluses and minuses for students. First, the pluses. Checking accounts are convenient. They help students establish a credit profile. They also provide a written record of expenses, which aids in money managemen. Many students open checking accounts at banks near their schools because some local merchants balk at taking out-of-town checks and because they can deposit their paychecks in them. On the other hand, if students are going to make their lives in their home towns, it may make sense to establish accounts there. It's also easier for parents to make deposits at home.

Now, the negatives. Checking fees can be expensive. There is usually a monthly fee and a fee per check. Sometimes these fees are waived if you maintain a minimum balance. It is easier to buy big-ticket items by check so money can slip through your fingers more readily if you have an account.

If you are going to have a checking account, comparison shop for fees and interest. Often you do much better in a savings account. In either case, arrange for a cash card so that you have access to emergency funds 24 hours a day, if possible.

Credit Cards

Students do get credit. Visa and Mastercard offer cards with credit limits of about $600.00. Even prestigious American Express will issue credit cards to students with some verifiable income (even if only an allowance from parents) and no negative credit history. Between 1988 and 1990 alone, the number of undergraduates who owned credit cards grew by 37 percent. About 70 percent of the nations nearly six million undergraduates carry at least one card. The issue is whether or not it is *wise* for students to have credit cards.

It is advantageous to have a credit card if you want to prepay airline reservations or rent a car. (Your parents can put these charges on their cards, however. Moreover, many stores use a credit card as identification for accepting a check. Credit card companies also issue monthly statements that help you keep track of purchases.

The main danger is that you can have the feeling that you're spending "plastic," not money. You may be tempted to buy big-ticket items now rather than wait until you've saved enough. It is easy to dip into next year's finances if you ignore the devastating effects of compound interest. That tiny-sounding 1 1/2 percent a month interest charge is actually 18 percent a year. After a month goes by you're also paying interest on interest! You can avert this particular problem by using the American Express card which requires full payment upon billing.

Consider the comments of two University of Maine students:

A lot of students hare financial problems, and they look at Visa as a loan. They can cover their tuition with it and pay the bill with their summer job.

(A student who owes $2,400 on his Discover and Visa cards:) I am very in debt. I told myself I'd be rational with the cards, but then you start to think of it as a layaway. You get what you want and pay for it later. . . If credit

cards were more restrictive, required a minimum income and educated students about what the responsibilities are, kids wouldn't get into so much trouble.

You'll soon learn whether or not you can trust yourself in using credit cards. If you have any doubts, shred the monsters.

Telephones

Many college-age people seem to have telephones permanently attached to their ears. Is it a good idea for students to have phones in their rooms or apartments, or is a telephonectomy in order?

When students attend college away from home, homesickness and friends at other schools can lead to sky-high long-distance bills. If you live on campus and use the dorm phones, your long-distance bills will be curbed by the need to keep those quarters flowing (unless you're charging the call or calling collect). Having other people stamping their feet nearby while they're waiting to use the phone is also an excellent money-management device! We're not so concerned with the amount of time you spend on the phone in local calls. If you weren't doing that, you'd probably be using the same amount of time to socialize. But, the trick is to control those incoming calls so that they don't bite into the time you set aside for studying.

If you live off campus, we strongly recommend a phone. You can get sick and find it easier to phone the health center (or home) than to drag yourself out. You also want to be able to put in a call to the police or fire departments when problems arise. In addition, you make it easier for people to get in touch with you when they are in need.

Do you need a car? Do you really need a car? Why or why not?

> *Yes, I really need a car.*
> *I need a car to get to and from school and work. Waiting for the bus in the winter time is no fun. If I had a car I would be able to sleep longer on Sunday and Tuesday nights, having had to work 3 to 11 and attend classes on Monday and Wednesday mornings.*

Cars

Cars play an almost mystical role in American life. Many people equate automobiles with their sense of personal freedom. In some locations, cars are a necessity, especially for commuting students. Many Californians, in fact, find that it is nearly impossible to survive without a car. If a car is optional in your situation, however, seriously examine whether the "freedom" you desire will be affordable and whether it will make it more difficult for you to practice the self-discipline required to succeed in college. Cars are distractions. It can be too easy to hop into the car and go for a ride when you find yourself annoyed by a reading assignment or a paper that has to get written. Because cars are so diverting, some colleges restrict first-year students from having them on campus.

Commuters aren't the only people who need cars. If you're going to be driving to campus from a rural apartment or house, or if you're going to be going long distances at odd hours for a part-time job, you may need a car. Cars are also helpful for getting groceries from stores into apartments. But if you live on campus or in town near the campus, you can probably get around mostly on foot or by bicycle. Colleges with spread-out campuses frequently run shuttle buses from dorms to classrooms. Some colleges even run free shuttles between campus and town. Cars also have a way of creating more problems than they solve. For example, cars need parking spaces— which can be at a premium. Although faculty and staff may be able to park near classrooms and other campus facilities, students are frequently consigned to lots in Outer Mongolia.

If you are going to have a car, two of the most costly expenses will be for the car itself and for insurance. When choosing the car, weigh the relative merits of buying new or fancy "wheels" as opposed to a reliable used car that will get you from place to place. Many students go into major debt over their automobile purchases. They wind up holding jobs just to make their monthly payments. Jobs, of course, take time away from the books. If a job is enabling you to make tuition payments and meet your living expenses, it is probably laudable and necessary. If, however, a job serves the sole purpose of enabling you to make the payments on a sexy car, as opposed to a car that's just transportation, you may want to reconsider your priorities.

Now, a few words about insurance: High-risk pools do not have piranha fish: they have insurance agents! The merciless ripping away at your purse is about the same for the fish and the agents, however. College-age students, especially males, usually pay exorbitant insurance premiums.

Cars also require gasoline, tune-ups, oil changes, registration fees, and, all too often, costly repairs. And, depending on your school situation, you may also run into parking fees and parking tickets!

Note that your parents may be able to receive discounts on their automobile insurance if you have gone off to college. Their rates may be reduced as much as 10 to 33 percent! (Perhaps your parents will be able to funnel some of the savings into your education.) Also note that you may be able to get insurance discounts for good grades. The idea behind such discounts is that good students spend more time hitting the books than other cars. If your insurance company does not offer such discounts, or perhaps another one will.

Health Insurance

Adequate health insurance is a must. Without it, you're playing Russian roulette with your financial well-being as well as your physical health. Parents' employment-related health plans usually cover children until the age of 18 or 19, but they may be extended for college students, even through the ages of 23 to 25. Most colleges sponsor student-health programs. See how far the benefits extend. Find out whether health benefits are included in overall college fees. If not, find out whether you can pay an additional fee to use campus health facilities. Also see whether benefits extend to off-campus hospital stays, surgery, laboratory tests, and the like. Many colleges offer supplemental health insurance for hospital care and medical services not routinely available on campus. One day in a hospital—uncovered—usually costs more than a year's worth of supplemental insurance.

Most college students are young and healthy, but students get sick. Students get injured. Trying to save money by foregoing health insurance is a bad bet.

Renter's Insurance

What if there's a fire in your dorm room or apartment? What if someone walks off with your stereo and your personal computer? Are you covered? Many residential students are covered by their family's homeowner coverage. Homeowner insurance policies may cover students property that is stolen from a dormitory or an off-campus apartment—as long as the student is still a permanent resident of the family household. Students who live in apartments near campus year round normally do not qualify.

Student's coverage is usually limited to 10 percent of the coverage for home contents. Contents coverage is normally half the house coverage. If the house is covered for $180,000, the contents are probably covered for $90,000. Coverage for students property in a dormitory or an apartment near the school is then $9,000. A deductible amount is also subtracted from the value of the loss to determine the payout. So if the $500 stereo is stolen and the deductible is $250, the payout is $250.

When the homeowner policy does not cover students living away at college, this coverage is often available for additional premiums. Policies that cover movable items are called "floaters," and they can be bought to protect specific big-ticket items like computers and stereos. Students who are not permanent residents of the family household can take out their own renters' policies to cover personal properties medical payments, and liability.

Unfortunately, you can't take out insurance to protect yourself against a spending spree. For that, you need to practice some self-control. The following section has suggestions for how to handle the feeling that you've got to buy that special _____ (you fill it in) *now*.

How to Practice Self-Control in Spending

Does it seem that mysterious forces are at work to prevent you from living within your means? After all, how can you be expected to hold down spending when that sweater finally goes on sale? And it's not your fault that the pizza place raised its prices, is it? Or that tuition was raised again? And how can you go on living in your apartment without giving it a couple of coats of paint? And don't you want to see *Rocky 1*, and *Jaws 42*, in which the shark takes bites out of your wallet?

Yes, life is filled with temptations. So what is there to do? Actually, quite a lot. Here are some ideas.

Avoid Temptations

Are your legs in danger from money burning a hole in your pocket? One way to control spending is to avoid obvious sources of temptation. Students who go window shopping often wind up with more than windows. If you can't browse in the bookstore without picking up sweatshirts for all your relatives, stay out of the bookstore. If you can't walk through the mall without checking out all the clothing sales, don't walk through the mall.

A list of places that vacuum the money from your wallet may help you develop strategies for avoidance.

It also helps to make a list of items you need before you go shopping, and then to stick to it. Try to walk through stores as if you had blinders on. You'll see that you should avoid pretty packages at the supermarket, because fattening things come in them. Expensive things do, too. Shop owners put hot items on display up front in stores. In racks or on the counter near the cashier lurk small items intended to lure you into impulse buying. Beware!

A *Sale!* sign will only *mark down* your resistance, *discount* your intelligence, and lead to a *reduction* of your *special* savings. You'll wind up disgusted with yourself, into the *bargain*. *Fire Sale!* only means that your savings will be *burned up* twice as fast. The best sale is the one that doesn't take place.

Consider the line from Shakespeare's *Othello*: "Who steals my purse steals trash." It may have been spoken by someone who attended too many sales.

IN YOUR OWN WRITE

What are some of the places where you get (your budget) into trouble?

> *Whenever I go out with friends and they want to get something so eat or drink I always buy something. I spend quite a bit of money on the weekends either when I go to see my girlfriend or she comes home, which is all right. I always buy a Coke or a candy bar when I'm at school, too.*

What are some free or really cheap places you can go to or use?

There are many places in the Kansas City area for free or cheap entertainment. I have found going to the library—it has much literature or material re: free service, free entertainment, free medical service and sometimes places re: free money.

Another place I always try to go is to the park and zoo, and I pack lunches to cut on expenses.

The free concert is great, and Music in the Park, offered through the summer months, is good entertainment.

I always keep up with information re: free lectures and refreshments served afterward, especially at church and the neighborhood community centers.

I watch T.V. and notice the community billboard. I pay close attention to events that are taking place on the job.

I talk to friends, and sometimes I am invited to a ballgame or picnic from their company. I watch movies at home.

Place Yourself in Settings in Which There's Little to Spend On

Sound impossible? How about the library? You wanted to spend some time there, anyhow, and there's little to spend on in the library except for the vending and copying machines. What about the gym? You wanted to do something to get in shape, anyhow, and there's little to spend on at the gym except for those vending machines. All right, you may need some workout clothes for the gym, but you don't really have to buy the most fashionable sweats, do you?

Leave Your "Spending Equipment" at Home

Your impulse buying is curbed when you leave your checkbook in the drawer, shred your credit cards, and carry only a couple of dollars with you.

Make Spending Difficult

Is it too easy for you to pull out the checkbook from the drawer? Why not put the checkbooks, and the credit cards and the big bills in a locked box? Put the box on the top shelf in the back of the closet. Put the key in the drawer of the desk. When you feel the urge to make a big purchase, you've got to get out the key, move the chair, reach for the box, and so on. During that time you can be asking yourself, "Do I really want to be doing this?"

Count to Ten (Days)

You have probably heard the old saw that you should count to ten when you get angry. By doing so, you give yourself time to cool off and avoid doing something you'll regret. When you feel the urge to buy new outerwear, sports gear, or whatever, first count to ten—ten days, that is, for a really big-ticket item. Make yourself wait a day for every $10.00. If at the end of five days, you still believe that you really can't do without the $50 athletic equipment, perhaps you can't.

Do Something Else

When you feel like spending the cash in your pocket on something that you can live without, why not go to the bank and deposit it instead? You can't deposit and spend money at the same time. Yes, we know that you can write a check on the account after you've made the deposit, but you're putting your checkbook in that locked box on the top shelf, aren't you? So you'll have time to think it over.

Spark Motivation by Considering Your Reasons for Not Going over Your Budget

Write down a list of reasons for holding onto your money. Perhaps you don't want to have to take out a college loan. Or perhaps you are in serious danger of running out before the end of the term! When you are tempted to spend, read through the list first.

Reward Yourself for Not Spending Money

Reward yourself when you avoid spending, but not by buying yourself something! Instead, pick out one of the free (or at least inexpensive) enjoyable activities from the list of 101 turn-ons that you will find on the following pages, or put a dollar away toward a necessary big-ticket item.

IN YOUR OWN WRITE

What are some ridiculous but reasonable places where you can stash your checkbook, cash, and credit cards?
What are some of your reasons for not spending money and going over your budget?
What are some of your reasons for saving money?

> *To get an economical small car.*
> *To get my own apartment.*
> *For clothes.*
> *For tuition and books if I can't get financial aid.*
> *For a girlfriend.*
> *For a membership at Bally.*
> *For Christmas and birthday gifts for family and friends.*
> *For a color T.V. and V.C.R.*
> *To build up my bank account.*
> *To pay off credit cards.*

Save Money

We suggest that you set aside something every month, even if it's only a few pennies. In this way you will get into the habit of winding up with small surpluses instead of deficits. You can also save toward costly items such as a spring vacation and athletic equipment.

Review reasons for setting money aside on a regular basis.

How to Obtain (more) Financial Aid

Let us assume that you have established a reasonable budget. You may still discover that you need more money. Students' financial needs change for many reasons. For one thing, some items may cost more than anticipated. For another, your family situation may change. Your family's income might undergo a dramatic decline because of fitness or economic conditions. Or you may now be attending a two-year school and realize that you're going to need to make financial arrangements for completing four undergraduate years. Or you may be thirsting about graduate or professional school, but you have only enough resources to get your bachelor's degree.

Although you have apparently made financial arrangements for the current academic term or year, you may have a number of concerns about financing the remainder of your education. So the following sections review some of the basics about attaining financial aid.

Financial aid comes from many government and private sources, including self-help. Your college financial aid office can help put together a financial aid package that meets your needs.

Showing Need

To be eligible for most kinds of financial aid, you must show financial need. If you applied for financial aid when you were in high school, you probably filled out the Financial Aid Form (FAF), printed by the College Scholarship Service (Box CN 6341, Princeton, NJ 08541), or the Family Financial Statement (FFS), published by the ACT Student Assistance Program (2201 North Dodge Street, P.O. Box 1000, Iowa City, IA 52243).

You may have discovered that the College Scholarship Service and the ACT Student Assistance Program expect families to make serious sacrifices to send their children to college—the equivalent of taking out mortgages and sizable automobile loans. If, now that you are at college, you believe they have completely overestimated your family's ability to pay drop by the financial aid office and explain why.

Most students receive aid from a number of sources. A financial aid package usually includes:

1. *Grants and Scholarships.* These kinds of aid are gifts. You need not repay them or work to collect them. Grants are typically awarded because of need. Scholarships are usually awarded on the basis of academic achievement as well as need, although some scholarships are awarded for academic excellence alone.

2. *Educational Loans.* Educational loans are often subsidized or guaranteed by the federal or state government or by the college. They carry low interest rates and usually do not have to be repaid until you have graduated or left college or are taking less than a full-time load.

3. *Student Employment.* The federal college work-study program is an example of student employment or work aid. Students must usually work 10 to 15 hours a week to earn this kind of aid.

Lets go through the sources of these kinds of aid. Fortunately there are many of them.

Something for Everyone: Sources of Financial Aid for the Non-Hispanic White Majority and for Cultural and Ethnic Minorities

There are federal, state, college, and private sources of financial aid that are available to first-year and more advanced students as well as to high school seniors. We will try to describe these sources in sufficient detail to make you aware of them, but you can get complete descriptions of the programs and learn about your eligibility for them at your campus financial aid office.

FEDERAL SOURCES

In recent years federal aid programs have not kept pace with college costs. There has also been a shift of emphasis from grants and scholarships to loans. These changes reflect political conflict over the role of the federal government in education and efforts to cope with the increasing federal budget deficit. Still, a great deal of money is available. *The Student Guide,* a free government publication, fully describes the first five of the following programs. Check the list of bibliographic resources.

PELL GRANT PROGRAM. This is the largest need-based aid program. The amount awarded depends on the students need and the costs of his or her college.

SUPPLEMENTAL EDUCATIONAL OPPORTUNITY GRANT PROGRAM. This is a campus-based program. This means that the college determines who receives the grants, although the money comes from the federal government. It is also based on need.

COLLEGE WORK-STUDY PROGRAM. Work-study programs are campus-based, and eligibility is based on need. Students are paid at least the minimum wage and work 10 to 15 hours a week, on the average. Most jobs are on campus, and students often work in the dining halls or libraries. They may also work as office secretaries, groundskeepers, peer counselors, or assistants to faculty. Now and then, jobs are arranged off campus. Scout around campus and try requesting a job that is consistent with your academic or career interests.

PERKINS LOAN PROGRAM. Perkins loans are campus-based and available to graduate as well as undergraduate students. They carry low interest rates (currently 5 percent), and payment is deferred until nine months after graduation, although additional delays are available for military or some other kinds of service (e.g., the Peace Corps). Perkins loans are paid back over a ten-year period.

GUARANTEED STUDENT LOAN (GSL) PROGRAM. With the GSL—also known as the Stafford Student Loan—you borrow money from a private lender (for example, a bank, Credit union, or savings and loan association) or your college. In some states a public agency acts as a lender, too. Interest rates are lower than those for most commercial loans, but not as low as those in the Perkins Loan Program. Repayment is deferred until graduation. Further deferment is possible for military or similar service or for graduate school. Most states guarantee these loans, if your state doesn't, the federal government will: then they're called Federally Insured Student Loans.

You can borrow larger amounts through the GSL than the Perkins program, but, if possible, stick to the Perkins. You're charged an origination fee of 5 percent on the GSL. In other words, if you borrow $4,000 a year, you get only $3,800, but you have to pay back the full amount. In addition, your guaranty agency may lop off another 3 percent as an insurance premium. Ouch.

PARENT LOANS FOR UNDERGRADUATE STUDENTS (PLUS). This federally subsidized program makes loans to parents. The interest rate "floats" and is indexed to Treasury Bills, which means that they will be less costly than other loans most of the time.

Whereas payments on student loans are deferred until after graduation (or after the student drops out of school), payments on PLUS loans begin within 60 days after borrowing and must be repaid within ten years. Check with local banks to find out whether or not they participate in the program. Interest on PLUS loans and other college loans is not tax deductible.

Parents, therefore, may want to consider the alternatives of home-equity loans or refinancing their homes. Mortgage interest is deductible and the period of repayment may be more favorable.

SUPPLEMENTAL LOANS FOR STUDENTS (SLS). SLS loans are like PLUS loans, but they are taken out by the student rather than the parent. SLS loans are available to self-supporting undergraduates and to students in graduate and professional schools.

RESERVE OFFICERS- TRAINING CORPS (ROTC). ROTC scholarships are competitive and are available to high school seniors. To qualify you have to meet academic and physical standards and agree to enter the military as a commissioned officer upon graduation. You'll serve for a minimum of four years' active duty and two years' reserve duty.

For high school seniors, the payoff is solid: four-year ROTC scholarships typically cover tuition, fees, and books, *and* provide a stipend of $100 a month. At a private college or university, that is a package worth $40,000 to $80,000!

But here's the good news for students who weren't thinking about the ROTC during their senior years in high school! In some cases, you can join as a sophomore or even as a junior. Entry requirements and obligations differ from those for students on four-year scholarships. If you're thinking about going the ROTC route, contact the units at your college, or write:

> *Air Force ROTC Four-Year Scholarship Branch*
> *Maxwell Air Force Base*
> *Maxwell, AL 36112-5001*
>
> *Army ROTC Scholarship Program*
> *HQ-Cadet Command*
> *Building 56/ Scholarship Branch*
> *Fort Monroe, VA 23651*
>
> *Navy-Marine Corps NROTC Scholarship Program*
> *Chief of Naval Education and Training*
> *Code N-1/ 081*
> *Naval Air Station*
> *Pensacola, FL 32508-5100*
> *Telephone: 1-800-NAV-ROTC*

In addition to the ROTC, there are other financial aid programs available to students who pledge to fulfill a term of military service upon graduation. Funds are available under the new GI bill that pay for college courses while on active duty or allow service people to accumulate benefits for use after discharge. Check with the financial aid office.

State Sources

All states have grant or scholarship programs for legal residents. Most programs are based on need, but some awards are available purely because of academic excellence. Some states limit their awards to colleges and universities within the state. A few have reciprocal arrangements with nearby states.

Most state colleges and universities charge out-of-state residents higher tuition. Sometimes you can become eligible for lower tuition in your upper class years by assuming legal residency when you go off to college. Check with your college or university about residency requirements. Even if you pay extra tuition as an out-of-state student at a public institution, however, your tuition will probably remain significantly below what you would pay at a private college.

College Sources

College and university scholarships and grants are usually awarded to students who show a combination of need and academic promise. Some colleges have programs that value tuition or fees for minority students who show need. Once the college kicks in, you might find that it costs little or nothing more to attend a private college than a public institution. Private colleges usually offer more aid than public colleges—at least to students who show need. It may be easier for a college to offer you a "tuition remission"—that is, to let you sit in class for free—than to actually hand out cash. Ask about a tuition remission if you're in need and you've proved yourself academically. You maybe a better candidate for a tuition remission in your second, third, or fourth years than you were as a high school senior.

Occasionally, wealthy alumni leave endowments that make funds available to students entering their fields of interest, and not all of these are based on financial need. So check them out if you're changing your major or field. Your college catalog and financial aid office should have a list

Colleges also put students to work through offices other than the college work-study program. These jobs are intended to get things done on campus as well as to help students. So they are more likely to be based on your skills than on your need. Positions as resident advisers (RA's) and laboratory assistants usually fall into this category. So check out these positions once you have gotten some basic courses under your belt.

Almost any college will provide you with a short-term or emergency loan to bridge a gap in your finances.

COOPERATIVE EDUCATION

Cooperative education programs alternate terms of full-time employment with terms of full-time study. At Boston's Northeastern University, the largest of the "co-op" schools, undergraduates graduate in five rather than four years. Their undergraduate programs are almost completely paid for by their employment however.

Co-op programs offer more than a way of working your way through college. They offer valuable experience and meaningful job references. This is because colleges develop work sites in industry and government that teach students skills and provide them with experience in their chosen fields. As a result, students are much more marketable upon graduation. Students also have the opportunity to test whether or not their expectations about their fields fit the realities.

Cooperative education is offered by 1,000 college and universities and 50,000 companies. The 200,000 co-op students in the nation average $7,000 a year. Yes, you can transfer into a co-op program!

A free directory of colleges offering co-op education is available from:

National Commission for Cooperative Education
P.O. Box 775
Dept. RD
Boston, MA 02115

Private Sources

There's less money available from private sources than from the government or from one's college. On the other hand, these sources can spell the difference between staying or not staying in college. If you're in need, leave no stone unturned.

Many private sources have restrictive and detailed eligibility requirements. For example, you might have to be a New Jersey resident of Polish origin—and show that you're in dire financial straits. It's not unusual for private sources to make awards on the basis of

- academic performance
- religious affiliation
- racial or ethnic heritage
- proposed major field
- proposed career
- parents' employment
- parents' union membership
- parents' membership in a fraternal or civic organization
- your special abilities, interests, and hobbies, and need.

The financial aid office may keep track of some of these sources. Also check with your church or synagogue, local civic and fraternal groups, even veterans posts. A few here, a few there—it all adds up. Be on the alert.

The following "In-Your-Own-Write" worksheet may be of help.

QUESTIONNARIE

Questions to Consider Before you Commit to a Loan

Taking out a loan is a huge responsibility. In a sense, you're taking out a mortgage on your future. Before you commit yourself to any loan, government subsidized or commercial, it is a good idea to weigh the answers to the following questions:

1. What is the interest rate? (Financial advisers suggest that you comparison shop between loans by using the simple interest rate.) _____

2. When do you have to start to repay the loan? (Under what circumsatnces can repayment be deferred?) _____

3. How much will the monthly paymnents be? What is the term of the loan (that is, how long will you have to repay it?) _____

4. Are there hidden or extra charges for taking the loan? (Is there an orientation fee? How much? An insurance premium? How much?) _____

5. Can the lender vcancel the loan? Under what circumstances? _____

6. Do I have to be notified before the loan is terminated? _____

7. Can I cancel the loan before the end of the contracted period? How much notice do I have to give? Is there a prepayment penalty? What is it? _____

8. Is there balloon clause? (that is, do you have to make on big payment at the end? If so, you may need to refinance at that time, and for less favorable conditions.) _____

9. Can my wages be assigned or garnished in case of default? _____

10. Am I really comfortable with this loan? Can I pay it back without breaking my back? _____

IN YOUR OWN WRITE

Note here some local groups you may be able to contact in the search for additional scholarships and grant money.

Church and religious groups

1. _____

2. _____

3. _____

4. _____

5. _____

Civic and fraternal organizations

1. _____

2. _____

3. _____

4. _____

5. _____

The Exxon Credit Union will give out memberships for their members only. You can also apply at the college in the Financial Aid office for a Pell Grant. If you get a Pell Grant it is money given by the Federal government for tuition and books for students who show financial needs. Other scholarships you can apply for are Stella Pepper Journalism Scholarship for journalism majors, intended for the editor of the Lee Lantern. Also A Jean Shepherd Scholarship for students interested in history of the Bay area. Then there is Henry Lee Holocomb (4). Any Lee or Sterling graduate who is a member of Grace Methodist Church.

Other scholarships: Various organizations within the community offer scholarships to students attending Lee College. Students may apply through the Financial Aid office or contact their high school counselors for information and applications. They also have a Young Mothers Scholarship. This scholarship is for women who are Baytown residents with young children. The recipient is not required to be a full-time student. Tuition and fees are covered by this scholarship. They have a lot of scholarships out there. Here is one more, it is the Carmage Walls Scholarship. They prefer a major in business administration specializing in accounting.

BIBLIOGRAPHIC RESOURCES FOR FINANCIAL AID

Source	Comments
Annual Register of Grant Support. Wilamette, IL: National Register Publishing Company.	Contains over 3,000 financial-aid programs. Updated annually. Too expensive to buy. Check with your guidance counsel or library.
The College Blue Book: Scholarships, Fellowships, Grants, and Loans. New York: Macmillan.	Too expensive to buy. Covers undergraduate, graduate, and professional programs.
The Federal Student Aid Factsheet. Washington, DC: U.S. Department of Education.	Describes federally sponsored financial aid programs. Free. Order from Consumer Information Center, Dept. 506, Pueblo, CO 81009
Financial Aid to Education. New Haven, CT: Knights of Columbus.	Another freebie. Financial aid for children of members of Knights of Columbus.
Keeslar, O. *Financial Aids for Higher Education.* Dubuque, IA: Wm. C. Brown.	Expensive. Updated biennially. Focuses on students entering as college first-year students.
Lesko, M. *Getting Yours: The Complete Guide to Government Money.* New York: Penguin Books.	Affordable. Lists federal government programs— scholarship, grants, and fellowships (for graduate students).
Need a Lift? Indianapolis, IN: The American Legion.	Updated annually. $2, prepaid. Lists sources of aid, emphasizing opportunities for veterans, dependents, and children.
Renz, L. *Foundation Grants to Individuals.* New York: Foundation Center.	Expensive. Focuses on monies offered by U.S. foundations and companies.
Student Aid Annual. Moravia, NY: Chronicle Guidance Publications, Inc.	Moderately expensive. Lists government and private sources of financial aid for undergraduate and graduate students. Order #502-A.
The Student Guide: Five Federal Aid Programs. Washington, DC: U.S. Government Printing Office. Catalogue number 511T.	Still another freebie, updated annually. Write: Consumer Information Center, Pueblo, CO 81009

Source	Comments
Betterton, D.M. *How the Military Will Help You Pay for College*. Princeton, NJ: Peterson's Guides.	Inexpensive, comprehensive guide to programs offered to service personnel, students who enter college directly from high school, ROTC programs, the service academies, and more.
Davis, H.,& Kennedy, J.L. *The College Financial Aid Emergency Kit (1991-1992)*. Cardiff, CA: Sun Features, Inc.	Inexpensive pocket guide to sources of financial aid. Look for current annual edition.
Schlachter, G.A. & Weber, R.D. *Financial Aid for Veterans*, Military Personnel, and Their Dependents. San Carlos, CA: Reference Service Press.	Biennial. Moderately expensive guide to 1,100 sources of aid to students associated with the military.
Schlachter, G.A. *Directory of Financial Aids for Women*. San Carlos, CA: Reference Service Press.	Moderately expensive guide to more than 2,000 sources of aid.
Schlachter, G.A .& Weber, R.D. *Financial Aid for the Disabled and Their Families*. San Carlos, CA: Reference Service Press.	Moderately expensive guide to almost 1,000 sources of aid targeted for the disabled and their families.
Bureau of Indian Affairs Higher Education Grants and Scholarships. Washington, DC: Bureau of Indian Affairs.	Free. You must be at least one-fourth Native American (including Alaskan) to qualify for the sources of aid listed here.
Financial Aid for Minorities in Business and Law, etc. Garrett Park, MD: Garrett Park Press.	Inexpensive guide. Other volumes in series list sources of aid for minorities in allied health professions, education, engineering, mass communication and journalism, and science.
Frankel, N. *Grants Register*. New York: St. Martin's Press.	Expensive guide to financial aid for graduate study. Lists grants of interest to minorities.
Funding for U.S. Study: A Guide for Foreign Nationals. New York: Institute of International Education.	In 1990, nearly 3 percent of college students in the United States (or 400,000 students) were from foreign countries. This volume contains sources of aid targeted for foreign students.

Source	Comments
Higher Education Opportunities for Minorities and Women. Washington, DC: U.S. Government Printing Office.	Inexpensive guide to assistance for minority groups and women.
Johnson, W. *Directory of Special Programs for Minority Group Members: Career Information Services. Employment Skills Banks, Financial Aid Sources*. Barrett Park, MD: Garrett Park Press.	Moderately priced guide to programs that target minority group members.
Schlachter, G.A. *Directory of Financial Aids for Minorities*. San Carlos, CA: Reference Service Press.	Moderately expensive. Check with your guidance counselor, your college financial aid office, and your library. (Arrange for an interlibrary loan, if possible.)

BIBLIOGRAPHIC RESOURCES

The bibliographic sources (books and booklets) listed in Tables 4.3 and 4.4 provide additional information about where and how to find financial aid. They do not give you money. Instead, they tell you—in Willie Sutton's words—"where the money is."

Now that we have come to the end of our lists of financial resources let's turn to some of the things you can do whether or not cash is jingling in your pockets.

WHAT DO YOU DO NOW?

One Hundred Free (or almost free) Turn-ons

Working out, loving, reading, collecting, redecorating different people enjoy different things. Here is a list of 100 free, or nearly free, activities that you can schedule in your free time or use to reward yourself for meeting study goals. You can use the following list to help get in touch with what turns you on by rating the activities according to the scale given below.

As you go through the list, some favorite, inexpensive activities that are not mentioned here are bound to pop into mind. There is some space at the end of the list for you to write them in.

3 = Fantastic!

2 = Very pleasant

I = Pleasant

0 = Yuck (not pleasant)

_____1. Being in the country

_____2. Wearing old clothes

_____3. Wearing new clothes

_____4. Talking about sports

_____5. Meeting someone new

_____6. Writing a letter-to-the-editor about a pet peeve

_____7. Playing baseball, softball, football, or basketball

_____8. Going to an on-campus aerobics class

_____9. Starting a game of tic-tac-toe with a stranger

_____10. Being at the beach

_____11. Doing artwork (painting, sculpture, drawing, moviemaking. etc)

_____12. Rock climbing or mountaineering

_____13. Reading the Scriptures

_____14. Rearranging or redecorating your room

_____15. Playing video games (one owned by you or a friend—the slots at video arcades devour quarters like peanuts)

_____16. Going to a free intramural or intercollegiate sports event

_____17. Shooting a few baskets

_____18. Weaving a few baskets

_____19. Reading stories, novels, poems, plays, magazines, newspapers

_____20. Going to a free lecture or talk

_____21. Creating or arranging songs or music

_____22. Boating (don't get a yacht: some campuses make small boats available for student rental at nominal charges)

_____23. Restoring or repairing furniture (doesn't your Salvation Army chipped-and-frail furniture need some loving attention?)

_____24. Watching television or listening to the radio

_____25. Camping

_____26. Working in politics

_____27. Working on machines (cars, bikes, radios, television sets)

_____28. Playing cards or board games (don't get addicted!)

_____29. Doing puzzles or math games

_____30. Having lunch with classmates or friends

_____31. Playing tennis (you really don't need the most expensive racket and balls)

_____32. Woodworking, carpentry (can you sell something you make?)

_____33. Writing stories, novels, poems, plays, articles (can you sell articles to student or local newspapers?)

_____34. Being with animals

_____35. Exploring (hiking away from known routes, spelunking, etc.)

_____36. Singing (if you're like your first author, you need to find a spot where you won't offend anyone)

_____37. Going to a party

_____38. Going to church functions

_____39. Playing a musical instrument

_____40. Snow skiing, ice skating

_____41. Acting (you don't have to pay to get in the play)

_____42. Being in the city, downtown

_____43. Taking a long, hot bath (unless you pay for your own hot water)

_____44. Playing pool or billiards (available at the student center?)

_____45. Using a microcomputer

_____46. Watching wild animals (not your roommates)

_____47. Gardening, landscaping

_____48. Sitting with your eyes closed for five minutes

_____49. Dancing

_____50. Sitting or lying in the sun

_____51. Just sitting and thinking

_____52. Going to a fair or zoo

_____53. Talking (arguing?) about philosophy or religion

_____54. Giving a friend a massage or back rub

_____55. Getting a massage or a back rub

_____56. Dating, courting

_____57. Having friends come to visit

_____58. Going out to visit friends

_____59. Giving gifts of no monetary value

_____60. Listening to sounds of nature (not your roommates)

_____ 61. Photography (will the photography club equipment save you money ? Can you sell photos to school or local newspapers?)

_____62. Checking through your stamp, coin, or rock collection

_____63. Skipping stones across the surface of the lake

_____64. Eating good (nutritious and tasty, not costly) meals

_____65. Working on your health (changing your diet, having a checkup at the student health center)

_____66. Fishing (can you reel in an inexpensive meal?)

_____67. Looking at the stars or the moon

_____68. Horseback riding

_____69. Protesting social, political, or environmental conditions

_____70. Going to the movies (on campus? in the library?)

_____71. Cooking meals

_____72. Washing your hair

_____73. Putting on some cologne or perfume (don't buy some especially for this occasion!)

_____74. Getting up early in the morning (really—watch the sun rise)

_____75. Keeping a diary and making entries

_____76. Meditating

_____77. Practicing yoga

_____78. Doing heavy outdoor work

_____79. Being in a body-awareness, encounter, or "rap" group

_____80. Swimming

_____81. Running, jogging

_____82. Walking barefoot

_____83. Playing frisbee or catch

_____84. Doing housework or laundry, cleaning things (honest, for some people it makes a nice break)

_____85. Listening to music

_____86. Knitting, crocheting

_____87. Being with someone you love

_____88. Going to the library (yes, we're serious!)

_____89. Preparing a new or special dish (not one with expensive ingredients)

_____90. Watching people

_____91. Bicycling

_____92. Writing letters, cards, or notes

_____93. Talking about politics or public affairs

_____94. Watching attractive women or men

_____95. Caring for houseplants (root a cutting for a friend)

_____96. Having coffee, tea, or Coke, etc. with friends

_____97. Beachcombing

_____98. Going to thrift shops, garage sales, etc.

_____ 99. Surfing, diving

_____100. Attending the opera, ballet, or a play (special student rates?)

_____101._____

_____102._____

_____103._____

_____104._____

_____105._____

How nice to end the chapter with a list of turn-ons!

TRUTH OR FICTION? REVISITED

- Actually, parents cover only 40 percent of the costs of the average college student.
- The majority of students do not work part time during the school year. Slightly more than half work during the summers, however.
- Unemployed students can obtain credit cards as long as they have a verifiable income and no negative credit history.
- Good grades do earn many students discounts on their automobile insurance. Apparently the grades attest to their sense of responsibility. (Remember to check with the insurance company!)
- Interest on college loans is not tax deductible.
- In some cases, you can join the Reserve Officers Training Corps (ROTC) as a sophomore or a junior.
- Some schools do arrange for you to work your way through college by alternating terms of full-time work with terms of full-time academic study. This practice is referred to as cooperative education.
- Sure, many wonderful things in life are free, or at least relatively low in cost. Participate in some of them and your life may be immeasurably enriched.

SUMMING UP

1. How do students generally finance their college educations? Do your own financial arrangements fit the typical picture?

2. How is a budget akin to a time schedule? What are the steps in making out a budget?

3. Do you keep an expense record? Why or why not?

4. What are the pros and cons of your keeping a checking account? Of using credit cards?

5. Do you have a telephone? Should you?

6. Do you need a car? What financial sacrifices does having a car entail?

7. Do you have adequate health coverage? How can you find out? What does adequate coverage cost?

8. What temptations make it difficult for you to remain within your budget?

9. What are some ways in which you can fight the temptation to squander money?

10. Do you think that you will need more financial aid as you further your education? What sources of aid are available to you?

BUDGET WORKSHEET—YEARLY VERSION

What Comes In: Income

From family   _____
Summer employment   _____
Part-time job   _____
College work-study program   _____
Perkins Loan   _____
Guaranteed Student Loan   _____
Pell Grant   _____
State grant or scholarship   _____
College grant or scholarship   _____
Savings   _____
Other sources:

1._____   _____
2._____   _____
3._____   _____

Total Income   _____

What Goes Out: Expenses

Tuition _____

Fees (Registration fees, check catalog) _____

Fees (Lab fees, tutoring, late registration) _____

Books and Supplies (Estimate from catalog) _____

Housing _____

Utilities (if not included as part of housing) _____

Furniture _____

Food

    Meal ticket _____

    Other meals not on ticket _____

    Snacks _____

Clothing _____

Athletic equipment (other then clothing) _____

Personal expenses (laundry, toothpaste, sanitary supplies) _____

Medical

        Heath insurance fee _____

        Medicines _____

        Other _____

Transportation _____

Auto insurance _____

Auto maintenance & repairs _____

Entertainment

        Fraternity/sorority dues _____

        Electronic (CDs, tapes, stereo, TV, etc.) _____

        Eating out _____

        Dating _____

Telephone _____

Other expenses:

1._____ _____

2._____ _____

3._____ _____

Emergency fund (at least $100) _____

Total Expenses _____

-Total Income: _____

-Total Expenses: _____

Surplus / Deficit: _____

Date	Expense Record, Month of _____							Running Total

Date	Expense Record, Month of _____								Running Total

Computer Literacy

Overview

A revolution in communications and information technology is making the computer a basic tool for acquiring knowledge, organizing systems, and solving problems. As such, it is having a profound impact on learning. Competency in its use is emerging as a basic skill complementary to other competencies such as reading, writing, mathematics, and reasoning. The computer also provides access to bodies of knowledge in each of the academic disciplines.

Applications of the computer to the study of writing, literature, art, music, and dance have highlighted its potential as a creative tool in the college curriculum. Leaning to use a computer could be crucial to your success in college and later in the job market.

Colleges are bringing computers into the classroom and are providing courses on computer applications. If you can use the computer successfully for these applications you will be "computer literate." Computer literacy is a working understanding of the different ways in which computers can be used for word processing and for accessing information.

A tremendous advantage of using a computer is that you will continue to want to learn. Learning simple applications encourages you to move on to more complex ones. As this occurs, you will find that you can teach yourself to a greater degree than you may have ever considered possible. As you progress through a college and move into your job or career, you will find that using the computer encourages and rewards self-motivation.

The ways in which we learn are changing at an increasingly fast pace. You will undoubtedly find yourself being challenged to learn on the computer in the next few years. And, because you will continue to learn in conventional ways, you will be in a position to take advantage of both worlds, adapting the choices you have to your personal learning style and preferences. Thus learning can continue to be an invigorating and personally rewarding experience.

Objectives

Once you have completed this unit of study on computer literacy, you will be able to:

- identify the common functions performed by certain computer programs;
- articulate basic technical terminology relevant to computer usage;
- understand the components of a computer system (hardware and software) and how they work and interact; and
- use the computer for instructional purposes by using computer-assisted instructional software in the library, laboratories, and other facilities on the Southern University campus.

List of Common Functions Performed by Word-Processing and Spreadsheet Programs

Create	Names a file and enters the document into it
Edit	Inserts and deletes information in document already created.
Format	Arranges page margins, line spacing, tabs and other features.
File Management	Stores and retrieves the document
Print	Transfers document to printed copy.
Spell Checker	Scans manuscript, highlights misspelled words, and allows you to correct them.
Electronic Thesaurus	Lists synonyms and antonyms.
Style Checkers	Look for awkward or grammatically incorrect phrases and sentences and punctuation errors.

BASIC TECHNICAL COMPUTER TERMINOLOGY

1. *Program*

   Internal commands that the computer reads everytime it performs a task.

2. *Software*

   Instructions written onto a disk or tape, that direct the computer to perform a particular operation.

3. *Computer*

   Any electronic device that can accept (or input), process, store, display, and print information.

4. *Terminal*

   A keyboard and a screen.

5. *Printer*

   The device that gives you a printed version of your work.

6. *Hard Copy*

   Printed version of your work.

7. *Data*

   Information.

8. *Output*

   To print out.

9. *Laser Printer*

   Produces professionally printed correspondence and documents.

10. *Dot Matrix Printer*

    Uses a series of pins that strike the printer ribbon to produce characters composed of small dots.

11. *Word-Processing*

    Typing text into the computer.

12. *Spreadsheet*

    Horizontal rows and vertical columns that intersect so that data can be inserted at the cells.

13. *Database*

    The place where information is stored.
    - a. Database File/Stores largest amount of information.
    - b. Database Records/Stored in database files.
    - c. Database Fields/Information stored in the records.
    - d. Database Characters/Individual numbers, letters and symbols which are inserted into the fields.

14. *Computer–Aided Learning*

    General categories of software designed for improvement in specific subject areas.

General Categories of Computer-Aided Learning

1. *Drill and Practice Software (Programmed Instruction)*

   Requires only simple word-processing skills. It resembles flash cards on the screen. A problem, accompanying question, and possible answers are simultaneously displayed on the screen. You are allowed to choose the correct answer and receive immediate feedback about your response. Questions are usually matching or multiple choice.

2. *Tutorial Software*

   All necessary instructions appear on the screen. No other supplemental instructions are required. Information in different fields of study can be presented and adapted to a number of formats. Tutorial programs have even been written to teach students how to use the computer!

3. *Problem-Solving Software*

   Software using the procedural model typically asks you to recognize a problem, formulate a hypothesis or possible solution, gather information, test potential solutions, and arrive at probable solutions.

4. *Simulation Software*

   This program uses data to model a real-life event. The software allows you to vary certain conditions so that you can test various hypotheses and predict different outcomes. It allows for immediate feedback and teaches and reinforces principles about complex phenomena that might otherwise exist only as abstractions.

5. *Educational Games*

   A game format is used to teach strategies, logical skills, and concept skills. An educational game can lower your anxiety about using the computer in the first place, or it can sharpen your skills and relax you during a particularly intense studying session.

PRACTICE EXERCISES

Directions: The following exercise consists of several questions that you should be able to answer after internalizing the content of your overview. Hopefully, some of your misgivings or questions about computers have been resolved. Put on your computer thinking caps and see how computer literate you are!

1. Why is it important that you learn to use a computer?

2. What are the primary ways that computer application is relevant to your field of study and impending career? (Don't be complacent! Find out how you may be affected in your field.)

3. Have you learned what your computer needs will be this semester? (If you haven't, please get started!)

4. What are the specific benefits of learning to use word-processing software?

5. What do you know about spreadsheet and database management programs?

6. Where can you use computers on the Southern University campus? (This may take some footwork, but it will certainly be to your advantage.)

7. What are the common functions performed by word-processing and spreadsheet programs?

8. Have you learned all of the basic technical computer terminology you were introduced to in this unit of study?

9. Can you articulate the general categories of computer-aided learning?

10. Have you actively participated in a computer laboratory setting on the Southern University campus? (A "yes" answer is an indicator that you are now ready to make the transition to more complex computer application. You are also ready to pass the evaluation for this unit. GOOD LUCK!)

EVALUATION

A. MULTIPLE CHOICE

Directions: Choose the word or phrase that completes each of the following sentences most accurately.

1. Using a word-processing program is likely to increase your
    a. productivity
    b. labor
    c. activity
    d. logic

2. Hard copy refers to
    a. mainframe
    b. printout
    c. disk
    d. field

3. Probably the biggest advantage to becoming computer literate is that you
    a. understand programming languages
    b. know complex terminology
    c. can take advantage of new ways of learning
    d. know which computer to buy for yourself

4. Large amounts of information are stored in database's
    a. characters
    b. files
    c. fields
    d. records

5. Individual numbers, letters, and symbols that are inserted into fields are
    a. records
    b. characters
    c. fields
    d. files

6. Information stored in database records is called
    a. fields
    b. files
    c. characters
    d. records

7. The internal commands that the computer reads everytime it performs a task is known as the
    a. data
    b. laser printer
    c. computer
    d. program

8. Inserting and deleting information in an already created document is
   a. printing
   b. creating
   c. editing
   d. formating

9. A file management system
   a. names a file
   b. stores and retrieves documents
   c. transfers documents to printed copy
   d. enters document into terminal

10. The arranging of page margins, line spacing, and tabs is known as
   a. formating
   b. editing
   c. creating
   d. manipulating

B. TRUE-FALSE

Directions: Shade in "A" if a statement is true; if it is false, shade in "B."

1. You can learn to use simple computer software by mastering six or seven basic steps.
2. Files, fields, and characters are used in database management programs.
3. Spreadsheet software is useful for performing off-campus bibliography searches.
4. Learning to use one kind of computer software makes it difficult to learn to use a different kind.
5. I need to learn to use a computer only if I am going to major in a technical field.

C. MATCHING

Directions: Shade in the alphabet of the correct response that matches the terms in the left-hand column.

1. Terminal		a.	instructions written on disk or tape
2. Computer Applications		b.	provides sources for research
3. Computer Software		c.	a keyboard and a screen
4. Work Processing		d.	word processing, database management, and spreadsheets
5. Bibliographic Search		e.	allows for document revision

Guide to Personal Economics Skills

Now that you've completed the Personal Economics Skills exercises, read this booklet.

Regardless of how you choose to live, you will need to master basic personal economics skills. This **Guide** is intended to give a brief introduction to the seven areas of personal finance and economics covered in the Personal Economics Skills exercises: figuring your paycheck and income tax, understanding personal banking procedures, purchasing goods and services and paying bills, insuring yourself and your possessions, borrowing and using credit, understanding investment procedures, and understanding basic economic ideas. The booklet may answer some questions you have, and it will refer you to further sources of information.

Remember that you can add to your understanding and information in specific areas by reading and by talking to people who are specialists. You may never be an expert in any of these fields yourself, and you certainly cannot be an expert in all. But you can go to experts for information or advice when you need it.

Whether you follow the advice of those you seek out as advisers is up to you. Listen carefully, try to sort out bias from fact, and apply what is said to your situation. By exploring, you can find out what your choices are. Then you will be in a position to decide for yourself what you want to do.

You may read the seven sections in this **Guide** in the order in which they are presented, or you may skip around, reading first the sections that interest you most or about which you have the most questions.

At the end of the **Guide,** you'll find an explanation of the preferred response for each question in the Personal Economics Skills exercise booklet. You may want to read the explanation, especially if you selected another response.

1. Figuring Your Paycheck and Income Tax

If you've always been paid in cash, your first paycheck may surprise you. It may also bewilder you. The amount you receive may be less than you had expected. Where did the rest go, and what is the meaning of all those letters and numbers on the stub?

Don't worry. You haven't been paid less than you were promised. Employers are required to make certain deductions from your gross (total) pay, and you may have agreed to other deductions. The amount of your check is what's left, your net (take-home) pay.

What are these deductions? FIT, FWH, or Fed W/H is federal income tax withheld. FICA (Federal Insurance Contributions Act) is social security tax. These two appear on nearly all pay stubs. State and municipal taxes may also have been withheld, depending on where you live and work. Your pay stub will show the amounts of each of these deductions for the current paycheck and for the calendar year to date (YTD). Take a look at the sample paycheck stub on this page to see how these deductions might appear.

Your pay stub will also show deductions for fringe benefit programs that you signed up for, like life insurance or medical insurance. It may also show how many hours you worked at your regular rate and how many hours of overtime, or how much of your pay was salary and how much was commission.

If there is a deduction you don't understand or an abbreviation that puzzles you, ask about it. Your employer or, if you work for a large company, someone in the personnel office, can explain it to you.

Save your pay stubs. They may be the only record you have of certain payments, like those for medical insurance. You'll find you can use the information when you prepare your income tax forms.

When do you start reporting income for federal income taxes and how do you get tax forms? Sometime before January 31 your employer must send you copies of a "Wage and Tax Statement" (Form W-2), which states your total salary for the previous year and the total amount of income and social security taxes withheld. The United States Treasury Department will send you a booklet of tax forms and instructions. If you do not receive these, you can get them from a district Internal Revenue Service (IRS) office or from some post offices and libraries.

These instructions include guidelines for reporting income or requesting a refund of taxes withheld. You can also find this information in **Your Federal Income Tax,** a free booklet available from your local IRS offices. These booklets also explain the differences between Form 1040 (regular

◄ Ask your employer's personnel department if you have questions about your paycheck or deductions.

> The clearest introduction to federal income taxes, including instructions for filling out the forms and examples, is **Understanding Taxes,** Publication 21 of the United States Department of the Treasury, Internal Revenue Service. Order it by letter or by phone from the Understanding Taxes Coordinator at the IRS district office in your area.

Figure 1. What Your Pay Stub Might Look Like

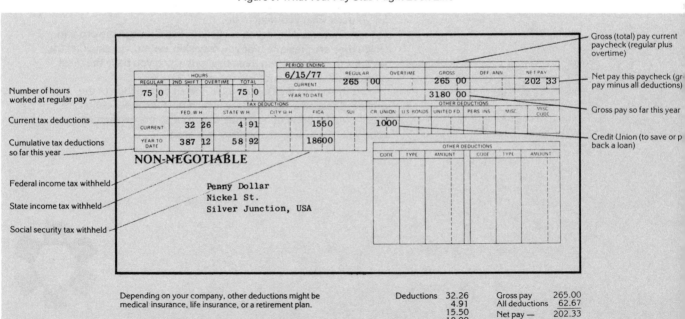

or "long" form) and Form 1040A ("short" form) and who can use them.

How much tax will you pay? That depends on how much you earn. The lowest rate is 14 percent of taxable income. To find taxable income, start with your total (gross) income and then subtract the amount allowed for exemptions for yourself and your dependents and for deductions.

What are deductions? They are expenses like state and local taxes, contributions to charitable organizations, interest on loans, and certain medical expenses that you can subtract from your gross income. In other words, they are a part of your income on which you are not taxed.

You can take the "standard" deduction—that is, the amount allowed by the IRS as deductions for your income level—or you can "itemize" deductions (list them separately). You should use whichever method gives you the least tax to pay.

Once you've found your taxable income, use the tax tables that come with the tax forms to find out how much you should pay. Compare this amount with the amount withheld during the year to see if you've overpaid or underpaid. Send in your return by April 15.

> **Don't be afraid to ask IRS for help!**

If you need help in preparing your tax return, you may be able to get it from your district IRS office. Companies and individuals listed under "Tax Return Preparation" in the Yellow Pages will help you for a fee.

2. Understanding Personal Banking Procedures

Banks offer you many services. You'll probably use banks for checking and savings accounts and for loans. Loans are discussed later in the **Guide.** Here we'll concentrate on checking and savings accounts.

Books on money management usually have a section on banking. For a separate, clear summary of the topic, see **Banking Services and You,** a booklet prepared by the American Bankers Association. If it is not available from your bank, write to American Bankers Association, 1120 Connecticut Avenue, N.W., Washington DC 20036.

Paying by check is safer and more convenient than paying with cash. Cancelled checks are proof of payment and, together with check stubs, they are a record of where your money has gone. You'll find the record useful in planning a budget and in preparing income tax forms. The bank will explain the different types of checking accounts it offers.

Most banks send a monthly statement of your account and instructions for checking your records against theirs. By doing this you make sure you have a record of all the checks you've written and all the deposits you've made. You can also be sure that no one is forging checks in your name. If there is a difference between your record and the bank's, you should notify the bank. (Even banks can make an occasional error!)

> **Compare the checking account policies at several banks before selecting one that best meets your needs.**

Savings accounts are for saving for whatever goal you choose: an emergency fund in case of illness or unemployment, next summer's vacation, a new car, college costs, a down payment on a house.

You can have a savings account at a savings bank or at a commercial bank. Interest rates are higher at the savings bank. Depending on how much money you can deposit and for how long, you can earn up to a federally set maximum interest of 7½ percent per year.

Several factors influence how much interest your money earns and therefore how fast it grows. The rate of interest has the largest effect. The higher the interest, the faster the money grows (see Figure 2).

> **Is your money earning as much as it can?**

Figure 2. How Much Your Money Can Earn

This sum	with annual interest of:	at end of one year will become
$500	5%	$525.00
	5¼%	526.25
	5½%	527.50
	5¾%	528.75
	6%	530.00
	6¼%	531.25
	6½%	532.50
	6¾%	533.75
	7%	535.00

How often the interest is compounded (calculated and added to the principal) has the next greatest effect. The more frequently the interest is compounded, the more interest the money will earn in a year.

Finally, the method the bank uses to calculate the interest will affect the amount of interest. The most favorable method (for you) is the day-of-deposit-to-day-of-withdrawal method, which provides that money earns interest for the number of days it is on deposit. The least favorable method (for you) is the low-balance method, which provides that interest is calculated on the lowest balance in your account for the interest period.

► **Remember! The interest rate is more important than the frequency of compounding.**

When you hear that an account earning 5¼ percent interest has an "effective annual yield" of 5.47 percent, that means that the bank's method of calculating the interest and the frequency with which that 5¼ percent interest is compounded bring you the same amount of interest in a year as you would get from interest of 5.47 percent added once a year.

Banks offer several kinds of savings accounts.

Passbook (or statement) accounts earn the lowest interest (5 to 5¼ percent). You can deposit and withdraw at any time. Time deposit accounts and certificates of deposit earn interest up to 7½ percent. Both require a minimum deposit and a commitment to leave the money for a longer period of time (2 to 6 years is common).

At most banks you can also get a loan, rent a safe deposit box, arrange for a regular transfer of funds from your checking account to your savings account, get financial advice, buy traveler's checks, and even get a loan simply by overdrawing your account (write checks for more money than you have in the account). Watch out for this, though; the interest on these loans is high, and banks usually make the loan in $100 units, even if you overdraw by only a few dollars.

Banks add new services all the time. Before you open an account, shop around, asking each bank what services it offers to its customers and what fees it charges for the services. Then choose the bank that suits you best because of its services as well as the convenience of its location and the hours it is open.

◄ **Compare the services offered by different banks before choosing one.**

3. Purchasing Goods and Services and Paying Bills

No one is born knowing how to shop wisely. It's something you learn gradually. Did you ever buy a "lemon"? Can you remember a time when you had just bought something, maybe an article of clothing, only to find the same thing, or nearly the same thing, for sale at a lower price at another store? From experiences like these you've probably learned to do a little comparison shopping, checking prices at more than one store and examining the quality of a product before putting your money down.

> **The Consumer Survival Book: How to Fight Inflation** by Marvin L. Bittinger has hundreds of tips for saving money on nearly everything you can think of buying. Published by Barron's Educational Series, Inc., Woodbury, NY 11797, $2.25.

How much time does comparison shopping take? Only a few seconds when you're at the grocery store, for example, and comparing the cost of three different brands of catsup or three different-sized boxes of breakfast cereal.

◄ **Use the "unit price" on grocery labels to compare costs for equal quantities.**

For a large purchase, a stereo, for example, or a car, you may spend hours or even days shopping. Some of that time you may be inspecting products, asking questions of salespeople, checking with friends who own stereos or cars, and reading articles in magazines that specialize in stereo equipment or automobiles. You may want to put in a bit more time reading some of the consumer periodicals that rate such items.

◄ **Most libraries have the magazines and periodicals you will need.**

Articles in the consumer magazines answer questions like: What is the suggested retail price? Can I get it at a discount? What is its overall quality? What features does it have? How well does it perform? Was it designed with the user's safety in mind? How well does it hold up over time?

What else should you know to shop wisely? You should be aware of the terms of guarantees or warranties (they mean

> Three periodicals for consumers that contain unbiased, independent ratings of products, based on inspection and testing of the products, are **Consumer Reports,** published by Consumers Union, Mount Vernon, NY 10550; **Consumers Digest,** published by Consumers Digest, Inc., Chicago, IL 60659; and **Consumers' Research,** published by Consumers' Research, Inc., Washington, NJ 07882.

about the same). Read them carefully **before you buy** and ask the salesclerk to explain anything you don't understand. Does the manufacturer promise to replace the entire item if a part is defective, or only to repair it? To pay for the parts and the labor, or only the parts? How long does the guarantee last? What will the store do for you? Will it replace a defective item? Or take it back and deal with the manufacturer for you? Or will the store leave it all up to you? You may decide to spend a little more money and buy from the store that will save you time and inconvenience by handling defective merchandise for you.

You should also know how to be sure you are dealing with an honest seller. Suppose you've found what looks like a good buy, but you're not familiar with the store. You can call your local Better Business Bureau, which can give you information that will help you decide whether the store is reliable.

Both people and computers make mistakes, so it's wise to keep copies of sales slips and check them against the statement the store sends you. Then you can notify the seller and get mistakes corrected.

Pay promptly. Late payment often means having to pay a finance charge. Frequent late payments or failure to pay may give you a poor credit rating that will make it difficult for you to get a loan or to open a charge account at another store.

If you're having trouble paying your bills, let your creditors know why, and try to tell them when you think you will be able to pay. If they don't hear from you, they're likely to think the worst, and they may eventually take you to court.

As a buyer, you can make sure you get what you pay for in a number of ways. Suppose you buy

> Additional sources of information and advice for consumers: The Better Business Bureau (see the telephone directory) has a series of free booklets (for example, **Facts on Car Repair, Facts on Shopping for Food, Tips on Tape Recorders and Players, Tips on Tires,** and **Tips on Sales Contracts**). Household Finance Corporation's Money Management Institute publishes the **Money Management Library,** 12 booklets (for example, **Your Shopping Dollar, Your Automobile Dollar**) available for 35 cents each or $3.50 for a set. Call your local HFC office or order directly from Household Finance Corporation, Prudential Plaza, Chicago, IL 60601.

that stereo. You can make a down payment and pay the rest after you have received the set and made sure it works properly.

If the seller insists on payment in full and after you get the set home you discover it's defective or it's not the set you ordered, you can quickly call the bank and stop payment on your check.

During the last decade, a movement has been growing to protect the rights of individual consumers, especially in their dealings with large corporations. Many organizations, from private citizens to government agencies, are involved. These groups work toward seeing that producers keep up the

> For a good guide to the numerous organizations in the consumer rights movement, including government agencies, see Joseph Rosenbloom's **Consumer Complaint Guide 1977** published by Macmillan Information, Macmillan Publishing Co., 866 Third Avenue, New York, NY 10022, at $4.95.

quality of their products, pay attention to product safety, and deliver what they promise. They also work toward making companies more responsive to consumer complaints. Learn the steps for pursuing a complaint. Make use of nearby resources, like "action line" run by your local newspaper, television, or radio station; the Better Business Bureau; or local

> For some suggestions on the best way to pursue a complaint, see John Dorfman's **A Consumer's Arsenal.** $3.95 from Praeger Publishers, 111 Fourth Avenue, New York, NY 10003.

or state consumer protection agencies (look under your city or state name in the telephone directory).

Try your library for information on government publications in the area of consumer rights, especially those from the Office of Consumer Affairs and the Federal Trade Commission. Some of these publications inform you of agencies involved in consumer affairs, or of laws recently passed or being considered that affect consumers. Others give practical tips on everything from buying household and personal products to comparing the cost of renting versus buying a home.

4. Insuring Yourself and Your Possessions

Everyone welcomes the unexpected when it's good news, like a visit from a friend you haven't seen in ages. When the unexpected is bad news like sickness, however, it's unwelcome.

Insurance doesn't prevent sickness, accidents, fires, or death. It doesn't lessen your chances of experiencing any of these misfortunes either. But it can pay the high costs of these kinds of events: replacing a wrecked car, rebuilding a house damaged by fire, paying doctors and hospitals for a serious illness, providing a continuing income for a family if the breadwinner is disabled or dies. If you have insurance, you know that if the unwanted happens, at least it won't put you deeply in debt.

How does insurance work? When you buy insurance, you share with others the risk or chance of some misfortune that may never happen to you but will happen to some people sometimes. Take automobile insurance, for example. All automobile drivers are exposed to the risk of accidents whenever they get behind the wheel, but in any given year, only some drivers will have accidents. These few will receive money from the insurance fund to pay for their accidents.

The greater the number of people paying into the fund (sharing the risk), the less each will have to pay. The smaller the risk they are taking, the less each person needs to pay. (Insuring a house costs less than insuring a car, because the chances of damage to a home are less than the chances of an automobile accident.)

Insurance agents and brokers sell insurance policies. Since there are many insurance companies and many policies with varying costs, you will have to shop around to find the one that best fits your needs. Compare coverage (how much will be paid for what events) and rates (how much it will cost you). If you can pay the whole premium (price) on a policy once a year, you pay less than if you divide it and pay twice or four times a year.

How much insurance should you get? That de-

▶
Do some comparison shopping when you buy insurance.

pends on many factors, including your personal values, and differs from one kind of insurance to another. Automobile, property, medical, and life insurance are the kinds of insurance most people need.

Many states require **automobile insurance** by law. All 50 states have laws under which you, the driver, must pay for damage you cause in an accident. If you don't pay, your driver's license will be suspended or taken away.

Automobile insurance pays mainly for damage to people (personal injury) and to property (the car or fence you ran into), but some kinds of policies pay for damage caused by theft, vandalism, fire, and the like.

It is common for automobile insurance policies to have a "deductible" provision. If it's $100 deductible, for example, you pay the first $100 of the costs, and the insurance company pays the rest, or whatever portion of the rest the policy states.

◀
Are you planning to buy a car? Have you taken into account the cost of your automobile insurance as well as the monthly installment payments on your car? Check your budget again.

> Write to the Insurance Information Institute, 110 William Street, New York, NY 10038 for its booklet **A Family Guide to Property and Liability Insurance** for more information on automobile and homeowner's insurance.

Your insurance rate, how much you pay for a given amount of coverage, depends on your age, where and how much you drive, whether you've been involved in any accidents, and what kind of car you drive. Coverage costs more when you are under 25, if you drive in congested areas, if you drive long distances to work or as part of your work, if you've been in an accident, and if you drive an expensive car.

Suppose you had to repair or replace the house you owned if it were badly damaged or destroyed. The costs would be so great that you'd find it difficult and maybe even impossible to manage them. You can't afford not to have **insurance on a house.** In fact, the bank that lends you the money for your home mortgage may insist that you have a homeowner's policy in order to get the loan.

Just like automobile insurance and homeowner's insurance, **medical insurance** protects you against events that may never happen to you. Unlike automobile and homeowner's insurance, however, medical insurance is usually voluntary. It's entirely up to you to decide whether you have it or not.

Your employer may have group medical insurance for all employees, or you can have an individual contract. Group contracts, paid for through payroll deductions, cost less per person than individual contracts.

Medical insurance can cover regular medical expenses such as visits to the doctor's office, the dentist's, and the eye doctor's. Most medical insurance plans, however, concentrate on the most expensive parts of medical care: the costs of having surgery and of staying in the hospital.

In addition, many companies offer "major medical" insurance against long-term or chronic medical problems or for added coverage on short-term illness.

Medicaid and Medicare are government health programs. Medicaid, which pays some hospital and doctor bills for low-income individuals and families, is provided by state governments with federal assistance. To find out about the benefits and whether you qualify, contact the Welfare Department in your community. Medicare, which pays some hospital and doctor bills for people over 65, is a federal program, administered through the Social Security Administration. Inquire about benefits at your local social security office.

What would you do if an accident left you disabled—unable to do your job—temporarily or permanently? Here's where **workers' compensation and disability insurance** come in.

Individual states offer workers' compensation. Employers pay for this insurance. You may or may not be covered, depending on your job.

You can buy disability insurance either separately or as part of a life insurance policy. Or your company may provide disability insurance as one of its fringe benefits. You and your dependents may be eligible for disability benefits through social security. If you have a limited income and very small assets, you might also qualify for a supplemental security income disability payment, also handled by the Social Security Administration. Ask your local office.

> Any local office of the Social Security Administration (listed under United States Government in the telephone directory) can send you its booklet **If You Become Disabled,** which explains who is eligible for disability payments through social security.

Like medical insurance, **life insurance** is usually voluntary. You decide whether you want it and if so how much and what kind you want. Its primary purpose is to provide an income for your family when you die.

It follows from this that a single person with no dependents has less need of life insurance than a married person with a nonemployed spouse. Similarly, a person with grown children has less need than one whose children are young.

There are three basic kinds of life insurance policies: term, whole life, and endowment.

Term insurance covers you for a specified term (period of time), say 5, 10, 20 years. If you die before the term is up, the insurance company pays the "face value" (the amount of money named on the front or face of the policy) to your "beneficiary" (the person you have named to get the money if you die). The policy ends when the term is up.

Whole life (straight life or permanent) insurance, covers you as long as you live and pay the premiums. Unlike term insurance, whole life insurance has "cash value"—you can cash in the policy and get some of your money back (you lose the insurance protection, of course). The cash value increases as you pay into the policy. You can also stop paying or pay less and still keep some coverage.

Whole life insurance costs more than term insurance when you are young, but less than term insurance when you are older. However, if you decide in favor of whole life insurance, it will be cheaper (cost less per year) to buy it when you're still young (age 20 or 25, for example) than to wait until you're older (age 40, for example). The reason is that if you buy whole life insurance when you're young, you spread the total cost of it over a longer period of years.

Endowment insurance is a kind of savings plan with insurance protection. The premiums are higher than those for either term or whole life insurance. At the end of a specified period of time (perhaps 20 years) you receive the face value of the policy. If you die before the time ends, your beneficiary receives the face value. Like whole life insurance, endowment insurance has cash value.

Most companies also offer various combinations of the three kinds.

How much you pay for your insurance depends on how old you are when you buy the policy, whether you are male or female (rates for women are lower since they live longer), whether you are in good health, and whether you work in a hazardous occupation.

Critics of the life insurance industry charge that most insurance, especially whole life and endowment, is a poor bargain for the buyer. They suggest that you can work out a plan to protect your family at less cost by combining term insurance with other methods of saving and investing.

> The Institute of Life Insurance, 277 Park Avenue, New York, NY 10017, can send you several brief, clear booklets on life insurance. **Plain Talk About Your Life Insurance Policy** defines the terms you'll see in your policy; **The Life Insurance Answer Book** answers questions most frequently asked about life insurance; and **The Booklet You Have in Your Hand Is Not Designed to Sell You Life Insurance** covers in greater detail the material in this section.

If you buy life insurance, be ready to ask lots of questions. Each company and each policy are different. Good insurance agents are prepared to explain what they sell and to help you figure out precisely what you will be paying and what you get for your money. If you're not satisfied, try another agent.

> Two books that approach insurance from the consumer's point of view are **The Consumer's Guide to Life Insurance** by J. Tracy Oehlbeck, available for $1.75 from Pyramid Communications, Inc., 919 Third Avenue, New York, NY 10022; and **What's Wrong with Your Life Insurance** by Norman F. Dacey, available for $1.95 from Collier Books, Macmillan Publishing Co., Inc., 866 Third Avenue, New York, NY 10022.

Be prepared, too, to go over your needs every few years as your life changes, your income goes up or down, you gain or lose dependents, your company adds or subtracts benefits. Each of these events may make a difference to your insurance needs or to what you can afford.

◄ Recognize changing insurance needs.

Social security means retirement income to most people. Employers and employees each contribute a portion of the employee's wage each year to build a fund for retirement as early as age 62. The social security program also provides disability benefits, payments to blind people, to dependents and survivors of covered workers, and, under Medicare, the most recent addition, medical payments for people over 65. To qualify for social security benefits, a person must have paid social security taxes for a certain number of years (check with your local Social Security Administration office). To collect the benefits, you must apply for them at your local social security office.

5. Borrowing and Using Credit

How often do you say "Charge it please"? Many Americans charge nearly everything except their groceries. Every time you charge, that is, buy goods or services now and pay for them later, you are buying on credit. You and the seller have an agreement that you will pay for the goods or services you have received within a stated period of time.

Some credit buying, like the 30-day charge account, costs no more than paying cash so long as you pay the bill on time. Most credit buying, however, involves a fee, a service or finance charge, especially if payment takes longer than 30 days.

Being in debt used to be thought undesirable, but today borrowing is an acceptable way of acquiring things you want such as cars, furniture and appliances, house repairs and remodeling, and education. Most Americans are in debt to some extent at some time during their lives. What matters is to keep debts in a reasonable relationship to income and to pay them off regularly. Most books on family money management suggest guidelines for keeping debts in proportion to your income.

Some disadvantages to buying on credit are obvious: interest (or finance) charges increase the cost of a purchase over its cash price; the ease with which you can charge may lure you into buying more than you can really afford and into paying finance charges

you might avoid by waiting and paying cash; your future income may not be as much as you anticipated so that you cannot make payments; failure to pay leads to a poor credit rating and may even cause you to lose your purchase.

◄ **Establish a good credit rating.**

What is a credit rating? It's an estimate of your reliability as a payer of debts. Credit bureaus compile the information for your credit record. When you open a charge account or apply for a loan, your credit record will be checked before the account or loan is approved. The better your record for paying, the easier you'll find it to open charge accounts and get loans.

If you are refused credit, however, you have the right under the Fair Credit Reporting Act to find out why. Mistakes are sometimes made in credit bureau records through computer error, because your record has been confused with the record of another person of identical or similar name, or for some other reason. You can obtain a copy of your record from the credit bureau and insist that errors be investigated and inaccurate or out-of-date information corrected. You should also be aware that, under the Equal Credit Opportunity Act of 1975, you cannot be denied credit because of sex or marital status.

Charge accounts and credit cards are handiest for everyday purchases. If you pay before the date due, this credit costs you nothing, but if you spread your payments over several months, you'll pay 1 to 1½ percent a month (annual percentage rate of 12 to 18 percent).

Charge accounts are a great convenience; they are, however, an expensive way of financing large purchases. You might be able to get a lower annual interest rate on a loan from another source.

What are the common sources of loans?

The seller. A store or a car dealer, for example, may offer you an installment contract. After making a down payment you pay the remainder of the cost over a period of months. You also pay a finance charge (18 percent annually is standard) on the latter amount. The larger your down payment and the shorter the period of time in which you pay, the lower the amount of the finance charge.

◄ **Shop for loans as you would for other services. Rates from different lenders vary considerably.**

Although installment contracts are convenient, there are some drawbacks. The interest rates are high, and you don't own the item you're buying until you have paid the whole contract. Read the contract carefully to understand what could happen if you are late or miss a payment. According to some contracts the seller can repossess your purchase, you can be required to pay up the whole contract immediately or lose your purchase. You might even have to continue to pay after your purchase has been repossessed.

◄ **Understand what you are signing.**

Don't accept a contract with any blanks that could be filled in to your disadvantage after you've signed. Above all, remember that you don't have to finance the purchase with the installment contract offered by the store. You can probably arrange to get the money somewhere else, perhaps at one of the lenders described in the following paragraphs.

Banks. Banks usually charge between 11 and 18 percent interest for a signature, or unsecured, loan (one that requires only your signature) and a bit less for secured loans (one for which you have some security or collateral—property, insurance, or investments that could be sold to pay off the loan if you could not repay it otherwise). Since banks look for safe credit risks, they tend to be cautious in lending. If they are unsure of you as a credit risk, they may ask you to get a cosigner, someone who agrees to pay off the loan if you fail to do so. If you are asked to cosign a loan, remember that you are obligated to pay the loan if the borrower fails to pay.

Credit unions. Credit unions usually charge between 9 and 15 percent. They are also willing to lend smaller amounts than a bank will. You have to be a member of the credit union in order to borrow from it.

Consumer finance companies. They are licensed by the state in which they operate, charge 15 to 36 percent, and may be willing to lend to people the bank will not take a chance on.

Savings banks. If you have a savings account at a savings and loan association or mutual savings bank, you can borrow from your savings on a passbook loan, at 8 to 12 percent interest.

Insurance companies. If you have whole life insurance, you can borrow up to the amount of its cash value at rates of 5 to 8 percent. You reduce the amount of your coverage by the amount you've borrowed.

Pawnbrokers. Pawnbrokers exchange your possession for money. When you pay back, you'll retrieve your possession. Pawnbrokers' rates are very high (24 percent and up); and if you haven't claimed your possession by the end of the stated time, they can sell it.

Write to the National Foundation for Consumer Credit, Inc., Federal Bar Building West, 1819 H Street N.W., Washington, DC 20006, for the booklet **The Consumer and Truth in Lending,** which tells you exactly what information must appear on charge account statements and loan disclosure statements according to the Truth-in-Lending law.

As you comparison shop for loans you will be helped by the Consumer Credit Protection Act, which went into effect in 1969. It's also called the Truth-in-Lending law, and it requires lenders to inform you of exactly how much the total finance charge will be in dollars and what "true" or "effec-

tive" annual rate of interest that amount represents. This means the ratio of the finance charge to the average amount of credit. For example, if you borrowed $1,200 for a year at 6 percent and paid it back in one installment at the end of the year, you'd pay $1,200 plus $72 interest. The average amount of credit you had during the year was $1,200, since you had the money for the full year, and $72 is 6 percent of $1,200. If, on the other hand, you pay the loan back in monthly installments of $106 each, your total finance charge is still $72, but you have not had the use of all the money for the whole year. Each month you've had less. The average amount of credit you've had is about $600, so your "true" or "effective" annual rate of interest is close to 12 percent. Both total finance charge and annual percentage rate (APR) must now appear on the loan "disclosure" statement that you sign when you take the loan.

If you get carried away and find yourself too deeply in debt, you can go to a credit bureau. The people there may help you themselves, or they may refer you to a reliable credit counseling service that will help you work out a way to pay off your debts.

The National Foundation for Consumer Credit, Federal Bar Building West, 1819 H Street, N.W., Washington, DC 20006, can refer you to the Consumer Credit Counseling Service nearest you. Or your local Family Service Agency may direct you to good sources of help in handling debts.

In using credit, observe several common-sense rules: don't go beyond your debt limit; pay off one debt before beginning another; don't let payments for something last longer than the thing itself (for example it wouldn't make sense to be paying installments on a coat that had already worn out); don't borrow for something you don't really need or wouldn't buy if you had the cash; don't buy more expensive things on credit than you would buy with cash.

◄ Think before you say, "Charge it."

6. Understanding Investment Procedures

When you invest, you spend now with the expectation of earning benefits later. People speak of investing time and effort, for example, in planning a program or in developing a personal relationship, or of investing in an education. But investing most commonly refers to spending money in ways that will bring more money in the future. What ways can money be invested?

▶ How hard did your money work for you today?

Savings accounts. Savings accounts, sometimes called fixed-dollar investments, are a way of investing without risk. If you put in $200, you will never get back less than $200.

Investments like securities and real estate involve risk—the chance of losing as well as gaining. Put in $200 and you may get back $175 or $225. Some people never invest in securities because they're unwilling to take risks with their money. People who buy stocks and bonds do so because they want more than the interest their money could earn in a savings account.

Real Estate. Investing in real estate is not for the small investor since it involves large sums of money. Real estate is, however, a common investment and thousands of people who never own a stock or bond may own the houses they live in. If you buy a house, consider, as you would for any investment, the safety of your money and give particular thought to risk factors: Is this house in basically sound condition? Is it in a stable or improving neighborhood? Is it of a size and design that would appeal to future buyers so that you could resell it with reason-

Figure 3. Reports of Stock and Bond Trading

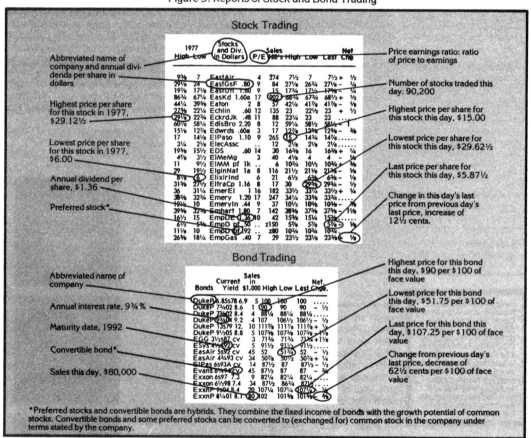

*Preferred stocks and convertible bonds are hybrids. They combine the fixed income of bonds with the growth potential of common stocks. Convertible bonds and some preferred stocks can be converted to (exchanged for) common stock in the company under terms stated by the company.

able speed if you wanted to, and at the price you wanted? Is the value of the house likely to grow at least as fast as other prices increase?

Securities: Stocks and Bonds. How do you know whether you should invest in stocks and bonds? As a general rule, you should not go into the stock market until you have an adequate amount of insurance, savings equal to about two months'

> See Sylvia Porter's **Money Book** for 10 guidelines on how to inform yourself before you get into the stock market (Avon Books, 959 Eighth Avenue, New York, NY 10019, paperback $5.95).

salary for emergencies, and some income left over after you have paid your current expenses. That leftover income is what is available for investing. It may be as small as $25 a month.

> **Journey Through a Stock Exchange** is an entertaining introduction to the stock market. You can get it from the American Stock Exchange, 86 Trinity Place, New York, NY 10006. The **Investors Information Kit,** six booklets on financial statements, stocks, bonds, and the like, including a glossary of investing terms, is available for $2 from New York Stock Exchange, Inc., Publication Section, 11 Wall Street, New York, NY 10005.

Before you buy anything, you should know what your goals are. Do you want income now, or do you want money in the future? Different investments satisfy different goals.

Learn how to read the stock market information in the newspaper. See Figure 3.

In all investing, you will be concerned with the safety of your money. Does the company manage its money well? How quickly and easily could you sell the investment and get your cash out? What percent of interest are you earning, or what rate of growth is the company experiencing? Send for the company's financial report to find information to help you judge these three things.

> See Sylvia Porter's **Money Book** for a two-page introduction to understanding annual reports. For greater detail, see **How To Read a Financial Report,** Merrill Lynch Pierce Fenner & Smith, Inc., One Liberty Plaza, 165 Broadway, New York, NY 10006.

In addition, most advisers would encourage you to diversify your investments, that is, to invest in more than one kind of security (stocks **and** bonds), or in more than one industry (automobile **and** fast foods), or in more than one company (Honey's Hots **and** Burger Bite). That way, a loss in one area is likely to be offset by a gain in another.

Choose a company to invest in only after you have read its financial report and followed its profit record and the price of its shares over a period of time.

▶ Many investments involve risk. How much risk are you willing to take?

How do you buy stocks and bonds? You buy through a stock broker. A broker will do as much or as little for you as you wish. Some investors want to do the research themselves and decide whether and when to buy and sell; others prefer to hand the responsibility to the broker.

You pay brokers a commission for their services on the basis of how much they do for you and the size of the transaction.

If you're interested in financial affairs and investing and want to learn more, start by reading the financial section of your newspaper, which probably includes some stock market quotations (prices) and articles about local and national business affairs.

> Further sources of information on financial affairs are **The Wall Street Journal,** a daily newspaper of financial news, weekly and monthly magazines like **Business Week, Barron's,** and **Forbes,** and the weekly program "Wall Street Week" on Public Broadcasting System television channels.

Bonds. Corporations, cities, states, and the federal government all sell bonds to raise money for purposes like constructing buildings or highways. When you buy a $1,000 bond, you are lending the company $1,000. The company agrees to pay you interest on the loan at a fixed rate each year from the time you buy it until it matures (the time at which the company promises to repay the $1,000, the face value of the bond).

Bonds are considered a safer investment than common stock since they pay a fixed interest plus a guaranteed face value if held until maturity. A disadvantage of bonds, especially for the small investor, is that they are sold in large units, usually $1,000 and up.

Both municipal bonds (those issued by cities and states) and United States Government bonds pay lower interest rates than most corporation bonds. But there is no federal tax on municipal bond interest. Government bonds have the advantage of being sold in small denominations ($18.75 will purchase a $25 Series E Savings Bond).

Stocks. When you buy shares of stock, you become a part owner of the company whose stock you buy.

Stocks are a much riskier investment than bonds. The company does not have to pay a dividend (a share of the profits), and the price of the stock fluctuates from day to day. If the company makes a profit, it may declare a dividend (a small sum per share) twice or four times a year. Up to $100 of dividend income per person may be exempt from federal income tax.

Dividends on common stocks fluctuate,

depending on profits and management policy. A company may choose **not** to pay a common stock dividend but instead to use the profits to expand the business, improve its product, or finance research.

Stocks can be a better protection against inflation than bonds because the price of the stock may increase over the years, while the face value of the bond remains the same. If the company is growing fast, the value of the stock may increase faster than other price increases, like food, clothes, housing. You do not pay taxes on the increased value (capital gains) of stock until you sell it. And then, if you've owned the stock for more than 12 months, as of January 1978, these gains are taxed at a lower rate than other kinds of income.

Securities: Mutual Funds. If you want to invest but you do not feel confident in making decisions about individual securities or you do not want to spend the time making those decisions, you can consider buying shares in a mutual fund. These funds pool the money from many individual shareholders to buy stocks and bonds. The managers of the mutual fund do the research, decide what and when to buy and sell. As a shareholder in the mutual fund, you share in whatever profits or losses the fund makes on its investments.

Some mutual funds are no-load funds; others are load funds. The difference is that you pay no sales commission on no-load shares.

7. Understanding Basic Economic Ideas

What is economics and what does it have to do with you, the consumer-worker-citizen? Here are a few basic economic ideas and some examples of how they may affect you.

Most people think of endless things they want—places to go, things to do, and objects to buy; and most people never have enough resources—time, energy, and money—to satisfy all these desires. Everyone, therefore, faces the problem of scarcity: not enough resources to satisfy all desires. The answer to the problem is to make choices.

For a good statement of several economic principles, each illustrated with specific examples, see **Introducing Economics,** a publication of the Federal Reserve Bank of Boston, available by writing to the Bank and Public Information Center, Federal Reserve Bank of Boston, Boston, MA 02106.

If you wanted to watch a football game, finish a book, and shop for the week's groceries and you had only three hours to spend, you'd either have to give up one or two of the three activities or spend less time on each one.

If you wanted to buy furniture, a television set, and a car in the same year and didn't have enough money for all three, you could buy one thing this year and the others next, or buy all three on credit, paying over a few years, or settle for cheaper products than you had hoped to have.

Nations, too, have limited resources to satisfy the unlimited wants of their citizens. What are a nation's resources? First, human resources—the people trained and available for the jobs that need to be filled; second, capital resources—money, factories, and equipment for producing goods; and third, natural resources—land, minerals, and water.

Every nation must choose what resources to use and how to use them. In making these choices, nations ask three questions: What goods and services shall we produce (houses, highways, space satellites)? How shall we produce these goods and services—by manual labor or by machines? Should each person be self-sufficient or should each person be a specialist? For whom shall we produce the goods and services, only for those who can pay or for everyone, regardless of their ability to pay?

Different economic systems answer these questions differently. The American economic system is basically a free enterprise (or capitalist) system. In such a system, individuals determine what and how and for whom resources are used. Individuals rather than government own the capital resources. Individuals are free to choose what jobs they do, and businesses decide what products they make.

Ours is not a planned economy, though it is not purely a free enterprise system either. Government enters the picture as a regulator of businesses to protect citizens from abuses, as a provider of goods and services that, as we believe, should be available to all people, and as an adjuster of the economy to prevent depression and control inflation.

> If you want to find out a little more about economics, see **The World Book Encyclopedia** entry "Economics." To find out still more, you might read **What is Economics** by Jim Eggert. $3.95 from William Kaufman, Inc., One First Street, Los Altos, CA 94022. Eggert's book explains basic economic principles simply and directly using examples from everyday life. It contains lots of informative cartoons.

Figure 4 is a diagram that shows how the public (workers and investors) and business and industry contribute to each other in the American economy.

Figure 4. Interrelationship of the Public and Business and Industry

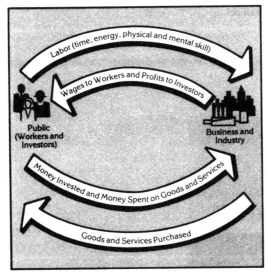

The arrows represent never-ending processes. Workers sell their labor to businesses and industry which pay them wages. Investors buy stocks and bonds, and businesses pay them dividends and interest from their profits. Businesses produce goods that people want, and people pay businesses for these goods.

What keeps everything moving? In part, it's the profit motive that keeps people working and companies producing. You need money to live, so you work; if you want more money, you may change jobs. Companies need to earn profits to pay stock and bond holders and to encourage further investment. Companies may try to increase profits by increasing productivity (producing more and spending less in the same amount of time) or by introducing new products.

When everything moves at a steady rate, the economy is stable. When things speed up (more products produced, higher employment, more products bought, higher profits) the economy is in a period of growth. When things slow down (fewer products produced, lower employment, fewer products bought, lower profits) the economy is in a recession. If recession becomes severe, it is called depression.

In a free enterprise system, competition tends to keep prices at a reasonable level. If John were the only hot dog seller at the football game (if he had a monopoly), he might be able to keep raising his prices. As long as people wanted to eat hot dogs at the game, they would pay what he asked. As soon as Beth arrives with her hot dog stand, however, John will find himself losing customers if his prices are higher than Beth's. If both agree to raise their prices together, they are price fixing. Government regulations attempt to protect consumers against the high prices that can result from either price fixing or monopolies.

Consumers express what they want (demand) by what they buy. Producers meet consumer demand by producing the goods (supply) consumers want. For example, as more consumers have had more leisure time in recent years, more of them have taken up sports. They express their demand for sports equipment and clothes by buying skis and skates, camping equipment, hunting jackets, and swim suits. Producers answer that demand by producing sports equipment and clothing.

Prices reflect the relationship between supply and demand. Prices rise when the demand for goods is greater than their supply. Thus, when an oil embargo drastically cut the amount of oil being imported, domestic oil producers were the sole source for gasoline. Gasoline prices rose while gasoline was in short supply and drivers continued to need fuel for their cars.

Prices fall when the supply of goods is greater than the demand for them. Suppose the demand for melons this week has been low. Not many customers have bought them, so on Friday the grocer still has a large supply of melons on hand. When the grocer lowers the price, more purchasers are attracted, and the melons are sold.

The "product" being bought and sold may be a person's services as well as gasoline or melons. When there are many jobs and few workers to fill them (demand for workers is greater than the supply of workers), salaries for those jobs may go up. When there are many workers and few jobs (supply of workers is greater than demand for them), salaries for those jobs may go down.

That a change in one process produces a change in another shows that individuals in our society are not self-sufficient. Instead, there is division of labor, each person becoming a specialist. When there is division of labor, if any group fails to do its job, all groups suffer. All are interdependent; that is, each one depends on the other for survival.

Twentieth-century America is a nation of specialists. Each of us depends on many other specialists in order to satisfy our wants. And our entire country is dependent on other countries for goods we import from them, as they depend on us for goods we export to them.

What are the consequences of specialization and division of labor? Dependence on others is the main consequence. A situation or action in one place may affect people at great distance who have no direct connection.

When there is an oil shortage, American consumers may find gasoline scarce; a coffee crop failure in Brazil will raise the price of coffee; an increase in wages for steel workers may eventually increase the prices for cars and household appliances.

Some of the consequences of specialization and division of labor are advantages: In medicine, specialization brings more knowledge in depth and more advanced and sophisticated treatment for people. In factories, specialization means increased productivity as workers need to master one task rather than many and no time is lost between tasks.

But some of the consequences of specialization and division of labor are disadvantages: confusion about which person to go to with a particular ailment, or uncertainty about which worker to hold responsible for a faulty product. There are other disadvantages such as workers' boredom from doing the same task repeatedly, alienation as it becomes harder for workers to see where their efforts fit into the whole picture, and absence of pride in the product being made, in contrast to the sense of achievement of individual craftsmen who see objects develop from start to finish in their own hands.

Research and inventions bring about new products and new ways of producing them. Some of the consequences of this technological change are increased productivity, temporary loss of jobs, the need for retraining workers, and eventual creation of new jobs.

These few pages are the barest beginning to an understanding of the American economy. There are so many events taking place at the same time, all of them affecting one another, that even economists disagree about the possible effects of actions being proposed or about what caused a change that has occurred. If you understand a few basic economic ideas, you will be better able to make decisions about your own financial affairs and also to see how different government policies and actions might affect you.

Now that you've read this **Guide,** you have been introduced to the main areas of money management that you are bound to meet during your lifetime. You can take it from here to get to know them better in order to make intelligent decisions for your financial well-being.

Item Explanations

Each numbered paragraph below explains the preferred response to an item in the Personal Economics Skills exercises. The geometric shapes around the item numbers refer to the seven skill areas named on the inside front cover of this **Guide.**

1 A checking account is the banking service that would best meet Janet's needs. Checks ordinarily cannot be written on deposits in a savings account, although some banks now offer special accounts that combine both checking and savings account features. Banks rent safe deposit boxes to individuals who want to store valuables in the bank vault. A trust is a legal device for transferring your assets to some person or organization, like a bank, to manage for you.

2 The student should file a United States Individual Income Tax Return form in order to get back any surplus of money withheld over taxes due. The federal government, not the employer, now has the money that was withheld. If students know that their gross income for a particular year will not exceed the IRS minimum required for filing a tax return ($2,450 in 1977), they can file Form W-4E, **Exemption from Withholding,** so that their employers will not withhold any income tax from their pay.

3 Mrs. Smith should call the billing department and ask for another bill. Checks should **never** be issued with the amount of payment left blank. If she waits for next month's bill, she may have to pay interest charges for late payment. If she sends a partial payment without enclosing the return section of the bill, she may confuse the store's billing department, and she will also be charged interest on the unpaid balance.

4 Both the Family Service Agency and the Consumer Credit Counseling Service offer debt counseling. You can find their addresses and telephone numbers in the Yellow Pages of the telephone directory. If you can't locate the nearest Family Service agency in your area, write the Family Service Association of America, 44 East 23rd Street, New York, N.Y. 10010. Get the address of the Consumer Credit Counseling Service nearest you from the National Foundation for Consumer Credit, 1819 H Street, N.W., Washington, D.C. 20006. Many banks offer informal debt counseling to customers.

5 Most financial advisers would agree that the first thing the Evans family should do is to notify their creditors of the change in their circumstances. Some creditors may defer payments or refinance the debt to reduce the amount owed each month. If neither of these options is possible, the Evans family might raise the money from a debt consolidation loan or a second mortgage. Filing for bankruptcy usually occurs when someone with much larger debts than the Evans's has been unable to pay for a long time.

6 After the words "Pay to the order of," Mr. Carlsen should indicate the organization that is to receive the amount of money specified on the check, in this case, the name of the lumber company. The name of the bank is already printed on the check. Mr. Carlsen's signature goes on the line at the lower right. The amount of money to be paid appears in numbers following the $ sign and is spelled out in words on the line below it.

7 The middle line ending with the word "dollars" should always be filled out like this: "one hundred twenty and $\frac{68}{100}$ _____." The amount in words should be written as far to the left on the check as possible so that no one can insert a word in front of it and thereby increase the amount of the check. For the same reason, a line should also be inserted between the end of the written amount and the word "dollars" printed on the check.

8 Because a company's profits are used both for stock dividends and for improving production capability, an increase in profits is quite likely to lead to payment of higher dividends or to purchase of new equipment. Increased profits will probably result in **higher** rather than lower taxes. Also, higher profits are not a basis for thinking that the company president will work fewer hours.

9 Competition among companies usually results in lower prices to consumers. When a company is the only producer of a particular product that has no close substitute, it has a monopoly. A company with a monopoly can set prices without regard to customer reactions, since it cannot be undersold by a competitor. The federal government, therefore, often opposes mergers of companies that produce similar products, because the reduced competition that will result may cause prices to increase.

10 Erik should compare the costs of similar insurance policies from several different insurance companies because rates differ significantly from one company to another. He could also investigate insurance that might be available through a local savings bank on an "over-the-counter" basis. After he has selected a policy, he will arrange to have a physical examination, name beneficiaries, and decide whether to pay premiums quarterly or annually.

11 Although car dealers do try to make car purchases convenient for purchasers, the **most** likely reason was that the dealer will also make a profit on the financing arrangement. Some car dealers have their own loan department and may offer attractive loan rates for purchasers who make reasonable down payments. However, it is good advice to shop around for a car loan. Another lender may offer a lower rate than the dealer.

12 The French Club divided up the work, demonstrating the economic principle of **division of labor.** The committees also performed specialized tasks (illustrating **specialization**), and depended on each other to get the various jobs done (**interdependence**).

13 The fixed charge for having telephone service is listed on the bill as "Service and Equipment," which cost $7.91. Other charges are $5.10 for long-distance calls and telegrams and $0.78 for federal tax. The total cost of telephone service to Kay Smith for one month is $13.79.

14 Kay Smith should call the telephone company's business office to explain about the call she didn't make and ask that the telephone company drop the charge for that call. If she deducts the amount of the Ewing call from her payment without explaining why, the charge will reappear on her next month's bill. Calling the Ewing number would result in yet another charge. Obtaining an unlisted number would neither remove the present charge nor prevent further wrong charges.

15 "Double indemnity" is an important optional benefit that may be included in a life insurance policy. The option doubles the face value of an insurance policy if the insured person dies accidentally. Because the incidence of accidental death in the United States is relatively high, this option is a valuable one. The double indemnity option adds relatively little cost to the basic insurance premium. A glossary of life insurance terms may be found in many books on financial planning.

16 To find out how much more the racing bicycle would cost if purchased on the installment plan rather than with cash, first find the total installment price by **multiplying** the price per month times the number of payments ($22 × 18 = $396). Then **subtract** the cash price ($340) to find the difference ($396 − $340 = $56). The bicycle would cost $56 more if purchased on the installment plan.

17 To find out the sales representative's total earnings for the month, first **multiply** her total sales of $6,000 times her commission rate of 5 percent ($6,000 × .05 = $300). Then **add** her commission of $300 to her $400 monthly salary ($400 + $300 = $700).

18 Shares of stock in Company XYZ would be most appropriate for the investor who can take a risk on "growth" stocks that he or she hopes to resell when they have increased in value. Such stocks would not be a wise choice for a person who needed dividend income. They would be equally unwise for someone who could not afford loss of investment or for someone with limited savings since there is a risk that the company's stock may not increase in value.

19 Among the benefits John can expect to receive are partial reimbursement for income loss caused by his injury and coverage of medical costs. Mortgage payments would not be covered. See also explanation 32.

20 The total amount Bill Walker would have to pay in addition to the down payment is $379.50. That total is listed as item 8 on the form, called the "deferred payment price."

21 By paying cash for the television set instead of buying it on the installment plan, Bill would save the "total finance charge" of $66.00, listed as item 7.C. on the form. The 2 percent city tax and the installation charge would still be paid.

22 To find the highest price at which International Harvester stock was sold on the day reported, locate the abbreviated name of the corporation (IntHarv) in the third column from the left. Then read across that line of information to the right until you come to the column headed "High." That column lists the highest price paid for this security during the day's trading session, in this case, 28¾. The "High" and "Low" columns to the left of the abbreviated company name indicate the highest and lowest prices per share paid for this stock during the year.

23 The most likely disadvantage would be difficulty in getting satisfaction if the appliance turns out to be defective. You would have to seek repairs from the manufacturer or from an independent appliance repair firm. The sale price of the item would not affect its durability. The warranty is the manufacturer's promise to the purchaser and applies even if the seller goes out of business. It is unlikely that the store would require payment via credit card.

24 Practically everything an employee receives from an employer or for services rendered directly to customers is taxable income. All tip income is classified by the Internal Revenue Service as taxable income. Ann should report her tip income on her United States Individual Income Tax Return form.

25 Paul should **first** call the bank and ask it to stop payment on the stolen check. Once this is done, the bank will not cash the check, even if it is presented by the utility company. Paul should then notify the utility company and issue another check to replace the one that was stolen. Under no condition should he wait until his next bank statement arrives to see if the check has been cashed.

26 To find out Andy's net income, first total his expenses for the month. Adding the list of expenses in the table produces a sum of $494.85. Subtracting Andy's total expenses of $494.85 from his gross income of $1,130 leaves a net income of $635.15.

27 The difference between gross pay and net pay shown on the earnings statement is the total of all deductions. It is not at all unusual to have about one-third of your paycheck withheld for a variety of deductions.

28 Only the federal income tax and social security deductions are required by law. The credit union and dental insurance deductions are typical of deductions made for voluntary programs available through an employer.

29 The demand for charcoal would most likely increase. As people buy more steak for barbecues, they will also need charcoal for the barbecue fire. Items that buyers tend to buy together like steak and barbecue charcoal are called complements. A drop in the price of one causes buyers to buy more of both.

30 Tables such as the one used in the question are found in magazines that provide information and advice for investors. This one, from **Forbes** magazine, enables the reader to compare the performance of several computer manufacturers. An investor interested in rapid-growth companies could use the right-hand portion of the table headed "Growth." By checking the rankings of the several companies, the investor would find out that Digital Equipment Corporation was ranked first in both sales and earnings per share over the past five years.

31 To determine Mrs. Johnson's base pay, multiply her hourly rate of $4 times 40 hours ($4 × 40 = $160). Add 10 hours overtime at 1½ times her regular $4 hourly rate or $6 ($6 × 10 = $60). Base pay ($160) + overtime ($60) = total pay ($220).

32 Workers' compensation covers job-related accidents, illnesses, and injuries. Typically, it provides payment of a portion of lost wages, reimbursement of medical, surgical and hospital expenses, and payments to survivors of workers killed in on-the-job accidents. It does **not** provide unemployment benefits for laid-off or dismissed workers.

33 The first paragraph of the guarantee states that "This guarantee excludes broken glass bowls . . . ." Therefore, if the Sanchez family wants to repair the percolator, they should purchase a replacement bowl.

34 The first paragraph states that "This guarantee . . . only applies if the appliance is . . . not used commercially." Using the percolator in a small luncheonette would be classified as a commercial use. Therefore, the guarantee would no longer be in effect.

35 To find out the amount of income tax due on Jerry's earnings, read down the income column until you find the income range in which Jerry's income of $2,430 falls. That range is "at least 2,425 but less than 2,450." Then read across that line until you find the column heading that describes Jerry's status. Jerry is unmarried and lives with his parents. Therefore, column A (Single, not head of household) best describes Jerry's status. The tax indicated in that column is $12.

36 If the extra revenue obtained from selling one extra unit is greater than the cost of producing and selling that unit and if a market exists for that product, profit can be increased by expanding output. Restricting exports and reducing advertising would lower sales and reduce demand, neither of which will increase profits.

37 Supply and demand usually tend to become equal or "reach equilibrium," at which point prices become more stable. In a high-demand situation with increasing prices, prices fall eventually because additional manufacturers begin making the product and current producers increase their production capability. Retailers offer discount prices when they are oversupplied and demand for a product is low.

38 A Federal Trade Commission rule gives Donna the right to cancel the contract within three days after signing the purchase contract. The seller cannot keep any of Donna's down payment if she cancels. Her down payment must be returned within 10 days after the seller is notified of the cancellation.

39 Negative consequences of a worker's specialization include a sense of isolation and frustration from being unable to complete the product by oneself. It is probably unrelated to commuting time.

40 To find out the social security benefits Mr. Brown is entitled to, first compare his status with the several disability classifications listed at the left of the table. Being unmarried, Mr. Brown is classified as a "disabled worker." Because his annual earnings averaged $8,000 before his accident, look at the column headed $8,000. Look down that column to the entry opposite "disabled worker" to find that he is entitled to monthly benefits of $427.80.

41 In our economy, people earn most of their incomes from selling resources to business firms. The most common resource is the use of a worker's time and efforts, usually referred to as labor. Options I, II, and III are examples of income payments made in exchange for services rendered. A couple giving $500 to their son because he needs the money is not an example of income payment in an economic sense.

42 The cash price Bob can expect to see on the contract would include the purchase price of the car ($4,200) **plus** the 6 percent sales tax ($4,200 × .06 = $252). Thus, the cash price on the contract would be $4,452.

43 Only statements II and V are true. Coupons are attached to bonds, not to stock certificates. The coupons represent the interest payments which are to be made on the bond. The bondholder clips the coupons as they come due and presents them for payment of interest. Bond prices fluctuate—sometimes up, sometimes down—just as they do for stocks, depending upon what buyers are willing to pay and what sellers are willing to accept for them. However, the face value of a bond (the amount the corporation must pay when the bond matures) does not vary. A corporation that is "publicly owned" is a corporation whose shares are sold to the public.

44 Add the monthly service charge and the cost of 10 checks to find Martha's cost per month at each bank. Bank A would cost her $3.50 a month. Bank B would cost her $3.00 a month. Bank C would cost $2.50 a month, and Bank D would cost approximately $2.27 per month. A checking account at Bank D would be least expensive to maintain over a one-year period.

45 When the demand for a given item like coffee remains constant and the supply falls significantly, an economic consequence will be a sharp increase in price. Shortages of certain products, like shoes, can be resolved over a relatively short period by manufacturers increasing their production. The supply of a product like coffee, however, is dependent on many factors, including weather, crop cycles, and acreage in current production. The only way coffee prices could be reduced until the supply increased would be through reduced demand. A lower demand could be achieved if consumers switched to other beverages and drank less coffee.

46 When you file a withholding certificate Form W-4 with your employer, you indicate how many exemptions you claim. The fewer exemptions claimed, the larger the amount withheld. If Jim changes his withholding exemptions from none to one, his take-home pay will increase. He will still owe the same total amount of taxes, however.

47 To find out how much Michael would save if he paid cash for the car instead of paying for it on the installment plan, first multiply $160 per month times 36 months ($160 × 36 = $5,760) and then add the $1,000 down payment ($5,760 + $1,000 = $6,760) to find the total cost of the installment purchase. Then subtract the cash price from the installment price ($6,760 − $5,600 = $1,160) to find the difference of $1,160.

48 The price of stock is determined by buyers and sellers. In other words, the person who wants to buy a particular stock and the person who wants to sell must agree on a price. A point in the price of stock is equal to $1. If Company A's stock sells for twice as much as Company B's, purchasers are willing to pay twice as much for Company A's stock as for Company B's.

49 In the statement illustrated in this question, the total amount owed is the "new balance" or $97.77. Obtain the new balance by subtracting payments and credits from the previous balance and then adding any finance charges owed.

50 See explanation 49 above. To maintain a good credit standing with the credit card company, the person must make at least one installment payment of $10. The finance charge will continue to be applied to the unpaid balance. Interest rates on charge accounts usually range from 12 to 18 percent annually, which is somewhat higher than rates charged by credit unions and most banks.

51 To find out how much interest Emily's savings account has earned in three months, you first must multiply $400, the amount in her account, by the interest rate of 5 percent ($400 × .05 = $20) for the annual amount. The interest earned in three months is one-fourth of the annual total or $5 ($20 × 1/4 = $5). Note that in the next three months Emily's account will earn interest on the original $400 plus the $5 interest added at the end of the first three months.

52 Find the cost per ounce by dividing total price by the number of ounces. Brand A contains 24 oz. for 72¢ or 3¢ per ounce. Brand B contains 1 lb. 10 oz. (26 oz.) at 78¢ or 3¢ per ounce. Brand C contains 1 lb. 8 oz. (24 oz.) at 72¢ or 3¢ per ounce. All three brands have the same cost per ounce.

53 This excerpt from a social security publication means that while Roberta is a full-time student under 23 years old and unmarried, she can receive half of the social security income her father would have received had he lived to retire at age 65.

54 As soon as Mr. Arnold realized that his credit cards were lost, he should have telephoned the companies that had issued the cards, obtained the name of the persons to whom he spoke, and followed up with written confirmation letters. The Truth-in-Lending law states that maximum liability in the case of unauthorized use of a stolen credit card is $50 for each card.

55 A result of division of labor in the manufacture of automobiles is that automobiles can be sold at lower prices than would be possible if only a few workers performed all the manufacturing tasks. Division of labor increases output per worker because each worker becomes more skilled in one specialized job instead of having to know how to do many jobs. Division of labor has also resulted in shorter working hours and production of greater numbers of automobiles.

56 All the types of income listed in the question must be reported on taxpayers' federal income tax returns. A prize won in a contest like a raffle or TV quiz program must be included at its fair market value. Total gambling winnings must be included in your income. However, if you itemize deductions, you may deduct gambling losses incurred during the year.

57 If she had collision insurance, Terry would be reimbursed for damage to her car if it were in a collision with another car or if she ran into an object like a wall or telephone pole. Coverage of medical treatment is provided through "medical payments" and "personal injury" portions of her automobile insurance policy. So-called "comprehensive" insurance covers losses from fire, theft, windstorms, and vandalism. "Liability" insurance would offer Terry protection in case she injured others while driving.

58 In general, "deductible" insurance is a form of coverage under which the policyholder agrees to pay a specified sum in each claim or accident toward the total amount of the insured loss. In Terry's case, she will have to pay the first $100 for repairs of collision damage, and the insurance company will pay the rest. The higher the "deductible" amount, the lower the insurance premium paid by the policyholder.

59 The only advantage among the options presented is that the premiums are lower than on insurance bought by an individual. Group health and life insurance are the most common type. Group insurance policies typically do not build cash value or provide for loans. They do not automatically cover every member of a family.

60 An advantage of a mutual fund is that risk is spread over a variety of stocks. They do not have Federal Deposit Insurance Corporation (FDIC) protection as savings accounts do. Nor do they yield dividends at a guaranteed rate. Shareholders may or may not have common professional interests.